Jython Essentials

Jython Essentials

Samuele Pedroni and Noel Rappin

Foreword by Jim Hugunin

O'REILLY®

Beijing · Cambridge · Farnham · Köln · Sebastopol · Tokyo

Jython Essentials
by Samuele Pedroni and Noel Rappin
Foreword by Jim Hugunin

Published by O'Reilly Media, Inc., 1005 Gravenstein Highway North,
Sebastopol, CA 95472.

O'Reilly Media, Inc. books may be purchased for educational, business, or sales promotional use. On-line editions are also available for most titles (*safari.oreilly.com*). For more information, contact our corporate/institutional sales department: (800) 998-9938 or *corporate@oreilly.com*.

Editor:	Laura Lewin
Production Editor:	Linley Dolby
Cover Designer:	Emma Colby
Interior Designer:	Melanie Wang

Printing History:

March 2002:	First Edition.

ISBN: 978-0-596-00247-3
[LSI]   [2010-09-30]

Table of Contents

Foreword

The purpose of a programming language is to let software developers express their intentions as simply and directly as possible.

The story of Jython begins one summer in Ashland, Oregon. I was juggling in a park behind a theater when I met Pavel Curtis, a scientist at Xerox PARC, who wanted to pass clubs. While we were juggling together, he told me about a wonderful new programming language called Python. Writing code in Python felt like writing the sort of natural, informal code that developers would use when they wanted to share ideas quickly. It was executable pseudocode.

In addition to telling me about Python, Pavel gave me some advice on what would make for an interesting computer science research project. He felt that the most interesting projects were those that dealt with groups of people working together rather than individuals working in isolation. Open source projects have proven the power of groups of people spread all over the world working together.

The story of Jython begins with the pain of finishing my master's thesis at MIT. In that thesis I fabricated, measured, and analyzed superconductor-semiconductor junctions as potential building blocks for a quantum computer. For analyzing the measurements and comparing them with theory (the Bogoliubov-deGennes equations), I used matlab extensively. Matlab is a wonderful language for a wide range numerical analyses; however, it is a terrible language in which to do anything else. In order to overcome its shortcomings, I eventually cobbled together a hodge-podge of C, Python, and matlab code to produce my final results.

I knew there had to be a better way. After finishing my thesis, I started to work on an extension to Python to support numeric analysis as naturally as matlab does, without sacrificing any of the power of Python as a rich, general-purpose programming language. This was the first project where I discovered the power of a collaborative open source community. The contributions of Jim Fulton, David Ascher, Paul DuBois, Konrad Hinsen, and many others made that project much more successful than it could ever have been as an isolated endeavor. It is still thriving now on sourceforge under the leadership of many of the original community members.

The story of Jython begins in the spring of 1997, while I was working on my Ph.D. at MIT. While doing some benchmark work comparing the performance of Numeric Python to a variety of other programming languages, I was amazed to discover that Java was as fast as C code for simple numeric benchmarks. Previously, I had been uninterested in Java because I saw it as an inferior replacement for Python. But I began to see the possibility that Java could be a replacement for the ugly and error-prone C code that I was writing for the performance-intensive parts of my systems.

After a week spent experimenting with Python on Java, I'd learned some exciting things. First, it was possible to translate Python programs into Java bytecodes by hand without any significant loss in performance. Second, the Java language had many similarities with Python and was a nice static counterpart to Python's dynamic nature. Finally, I learned about the wonderful java.reflect package that made it possible to load and use arbitrary Java libraries from Python without having to write any glue code. This meant that it should be possible to download an interesting new Java library from the Net, put it on my classpath, and immediately start using it from Python.

That single week's worth of experiments convinced me that there was a beautiful and elegant match to be made between Python and Java and I wanted to be the one to do it. So I took an extended hiatus from the Ph.D. program at MIT and started working full time to make Jython real. One week later, Al Vezza invited me to lunch and convinced me that CNRI was the best place to do this work. This gave me the wonderful opportunity to work closely with many of the key Python developers there, including Guido van Rossum himself. The initial feeling of the inevitability of the beautiful match between Python and Java never died. The project was consistently a pleasure to work on. This is a testament to the great people who designed and built both Python and Java.

Guido's sense of the aesthetics of language design is amazing. I've met many fine language designers who could build theoretically beautiful languages that no one would ever use, but Guido is one of those rare people who can build a language that is just slightly less theoretically beautiful but thereby is a joy to write programs in.

While I never had any direct contact with the developers of Java, they continued to make advances that improved Jython significantly. The addition of the collection API in Java 2 made the integration with Python's rich collection data types much more elegant. The amazing progress in virtual machine performance from the HotSpot team at Sun meant that every six months Jython's performance would get faster, while I wasn't spending any time on performance optimization at all.

My role in the Jython story ends early in 1999. Once again, it was a researcher at Xerox PARC who told me a story about a wonderful new programming language. This time it was Gregor Kiczales who was extolling the virtues of aspect-oriented programming and AspectJ. His story about capturing crosscutting concerns in modular aspects to solve the persistent problem of tangled source code resonated strongly with me. The fact that he was offering me a chance to move back out to California and to work a few miles away from the Stanford Court Jugglers was only a secondary motivation.

The story of Jython as a flourishing open source community really begins after I left to work on AspectJ. Barry Warsaw started the ball rolling by ensuring that Jython was released by CNRI under an officially approved Open Source™ license. Finn Bock stepped up immediately to take over the development leadership on the project. At first his leadership was informal as he developed and maintained the definitive set of patches, later he took over formal leadership as the project was moved to sourceforge. Finn was soon joined by Samuele Pedroni; together they have done an amazing job of both keeping Jython in sync with several major improvements made to the Python language and continuing to improve the core functionality.

Jython has always been a simple and easy-to-use integration of Python and Java. However, since the earliest days of the project, people have complained that the lack of high-quality documentation has been a gaping hole in the usability of Jython. This book finally fills that hole.

The purpose of a programming language is to let software developers express their intentions as simply and directly as possible.

The story of Jython begins for you with this book. Here you have all the pieces you need to go out and start using Jython to make your development easier and more productive than ever before.

—Jim Hugunin

Preface

Every one of us who works with technology knows the feeling of finding a tool that perfectly fits the need for which it was designed. Jython is one of those perfect fits, combining the ease of Python scripting with the ubiquity and power of the Java libraries and Java Virtual Machine. Each of the book's two authors had an "Aha!" experience discovering the power of Jython.

Samuele Pedroni's moment came when a friend got him involved in a project about machine learning and artificial life. They originally planned to implement the project in Java. Java's garbage collection and rich libraries meant that they could focus just on their ideas. The system needed to be portable, and had to allow for the distribution of the computational load over many machines, when necessary.

At the same time, Samuele was reading O'Reilly's *Learning Python* and discovered what was then called JPython. The first thing he did with JPython was embed it in a CORBA server to manage startup configuration on his artificial life project. Samuele discovered that mixing Java and JPython gave him and his friend even more freedom to express their ideas.

Over time, they wrote a constellation of tools for their simulations in Jython. In the meantime, Samuele got involved in JPython development while it was transitioning from Jim Hugunin's original JPython project to the "truly" open source Jython project.

Noel Rappin's case is similar. He was working on a short program and wanted the flexibility and development speed of a scripting language like Python. However, the interface tools available didn't provide exactly what the program needed (in particular, a nice, easy-to-use table display). The Java Swing toolkit had the needed functionality, but it came with the complexity overhead of Java and Swing as compared to, say, Python and wxWindows.

Well, you can probably see where this is going. He downloaded Jython and set about building a Swing interface to a Python program, and he was hooked almost immediately. The Swing interface was up and running in very little time, and the resulting code was amazingly clean compared to wxWindows, or Java and Swing.

For both authors, it quickly became clear that Jython was good for more than just small programs that need GUIs. The combination of Python as a development language and Java's tool environment offers valuable leverage against a wide variety of development problems.

Jython Essentials is your guide to using Jython effectively for your development needs. The book provides an overview of the Python language and explains how Jython manages interaction between Python and Java code. Examples of using common Java libraries, such as the Swing API, Java servlets, and XML tools, are also provided.

Audience Expectations

Because Jython is a hybrid language, Jython users might come to it from a variety of different paths. Although we tried to make this book accessible to anyone who wants to learn Jython, some simplifying assumptions have been made.

We've assumed that you know enough Java that we do not need to explain basic Java or object-oriented programming concepts such as classes, types, constructors, loops, and so on. While you by no means need to be a Java guru to use this book, many of our definitions of Jython use Java functionality or syntax as a reference. We've also assumed that you are at least aware of the Java tools, libraries, and APIs discussed. Again, exhaustive knowledge is unnecessary.

Preexisting knowledge of Python is a benefit, but not a requirement. We've tried to explain enough of the Python language for you to use Python successfully. If you already know Python, you are ahead of the game. Appendix D, *Jython and CPython Differences*, is a good starting point for exploring how Jython is different from standard Python. Those differences are elaborated in the initial chapters of this book (if you already know Python, most of the material in Chapters 2 through 5 will be familiar to you). To get the most out of Jython, you will probably want to learn more about the Java libraries using one of the references suggested in the "Further Reading" section of this Preface.

Organization

Jython Essentials has 13 chapters and 5 appendixes. Chapter 1 is an introduction to Jython, and contains an overview of the rest of the book. Chapters 2 through 5 comprise an overview of the Python language. Chapters 6 through 10 focus specifically on Jython concerns, such as interaction with existing Java code and creating Java executables. Chapters 11 through 13 offer a tour of Python and Java libraries and APIs of interest.

Chapter 1, *Introduction to Jython*
> Provides a quick overview of the goals and functionality of Jython and a road map to the rest of the book.

Chapter 2, *Jython Basics*
> Describes the Python language base types, such as integer, float, string, list, tuple, and dictionary, and of the built-in methods and operations of each type.

Chapter 3, *Jython Control Flow*
> Describes the statements used for flow control in Python, along with Python's use of whitespace as a block delimiter.

Chapter 4, *Modules and Functions*
> Describes the module as the basic unit of a Python program and explores the important Python concept of namespaces. Shows how to define, call, and use functions. Shows how to import existing Python and Java modules.

Chapter 5, *Object-Oriented Jython*
> Introduces Python's object-oriented syntax and semantics. Explains how to create classes, construct instances, and make your new classes behave like built-in types.

Chapter 6, *Using Java from Jython*
> Explains how to use existing Java code from Jython. This includes Java object construction, Java method calling, automatic conversion between Java and Python types, and special handling of collection classes.

Chapter 7, *Inheriting from Java*
> Explores tighter Java/Jython integration by explaining how to subclass Java classes in your Jython code. Issues include overriding methods and access to the parent class.

Chapter 8, *Reflection and JavaBeans*
> Discusses how Jython uses Java reflection to allow Java code to be accessed using common Python idioms. Jython's uses of reflection are also discussed, including the list of Python's reflection-enabling special variables and functions.

Chapter 9, *Using Swing*
Gives examples of how using Jython simplifies access to the Swing GUI toolkit.

Chapter 10, *Using Java Libraries*
Presents examples of using specific Java tools from within Jython. The libraries used are the JDBC database library, the servlet API, and various XML parsing tools.

Chapter 11, *Jython Standard Library*
Discusses several useful standard Jython modules, including modules for system access, regular expression matching, and unit testing.

Chapter 12, *Embedding Jython Inside Java*
Discusses how to enhance a Java program by embedding Jython within it, allowing the Jython interpreter to be called programmatically.

Chapter 13, *Compiling Jython*
Covers the *jythonc* tool for creating Java *.class* and *.jar* files. The files created with *jythonc* can be used by any tool expecting to run a compiled Java file.

Appendix A, Installing Jython
Explains how to acquire and install Jython.

Appendix B, *Jython Options and Registry*
Provides a complete list of command-line options for Jython and *jythonc*. Also includes information about the Jython registry.

Appendix C, *Jython Exceptions*
Provides a list of Jython's built-in exceptions.

Appendix D, *Jython and CPython Differences*
Presents the complete list of differences between Jython and the original C implementation of Python.

Appendix E, *Java-to-Python Quick Reference*
Presents some of the most significant syntactic differences between Java and Python in a tabular format.

Further Reading

This book touches on Java and Python tools, which are covered in more detail in other O'Reilly books. Much of the content of these books is directly relevant to Jython. In particular, the following books might be particularly useful for a Jython programmer:

Learning Java, by Pat Niemeyer and Jonathan Knudsen or *Learning Python*, by Mark Lutz and David Ascher. Choose one based, of course, on which language you feel the need to learn more about.

Java & XML, by Brett McLaughlin, has a description of a number of more advanced XML tools we could not cover in this book. *Python & XML*, by Christopher A. Jones and Fred L. Drake, Jr., does the same from the Python side.

Java in a Nutshell, by David Flanagan, provides a good overview of Java concepts. *Python in a Nutshell*, by Alex Martelli, has not been published as this is written.

Java Servlet Programming, by Jason Hunter with William Crawford, talks about servlet programming in more detail.

Java Swing, by Robert Eckstein, Marc Loy, and Dave Wood, and *Java Foundation Classes in a Nutshell*, by David Flanagan, are both definitive references to Swing. The Eckstein book goes into much more detail on Swing concepts, while the Flanagan book is more of a reference, and also covers Java 2D.

Python Standard Library, by Fredrik Lundh, is a complete overview of what comes with a standard Python distribution. Much of this is also applicable to Jython.

Programming Python, by Mark Lutz, is a thorough rundown of Python programming techniques. Again, not all of this will apply to Jython, but it's still a very useful book.

Conventions Used in This Book

Throughout this book, the use of the name "Python" refers to information common to both Jython and the original implementation of Python. Using the name "Jython" is a signal that the concept is applicable only to Jython. Descriptions of the original C-language implementation are noted as "CPython." For example, "Python uses indentation to determine block boundaries, Jython lets you subclass Java classes, and CPython compiles to *.pyc* files."

The following typographical conventions are used throughout this book:

Italic
> Used to indicate commands, URLs, filenames, file extensions, directory or folder names, and UNC pathnames, as well as new terms where they are defined.

Constant width
> Used for all code listings, and to designate anything that would appear literally in a Jython or Java program. This includes module names, method names, class names, function names, statements, and HTML tags.

Constant width bold

Used to indicate output from executed programs. Also used to mark lines in a code listing of special interest.

Constant width italic

Used for general placeholders that indicate that an item should be replaced by some actual value in your own program.

 This icon indicates a tip, suggestion, or general note.

 This icon indicates a warning or caution.

How to Contact Us

We have tested and verified all the information in this book to the best of our abilities, but you may find that features have changed or that we have let errors slip through the production of the book. Please let us know of any errors that you find, as well as suggestions for future editions, by writing to:

O'Reilly & Associates, Inc.
1005 Gravenstein Highway North
Sebastopol, CA 95472
(800) 998-9938 (in the United States or Canada)
(707) 829-0515 (international/local)
(707) 829-0104 (fax)

To ask technical questions or comment on the book, send email to:

bookquestions@oreilly.com

We have a web site for the book, where we'll list examples, errata, and any plans for future editions. You can access this page at:

http://www.oreilly.com/catalog/jythoness/

For more information about books, conferences, Resource Centers, and the O'Reilly Network, see the O'Reilly web site at:

http://www.oreilly.com/

Samuele Pedroni's Acknowledgments

For me, this book is a kind of portrait of Jython by a maintainer (me). I learned a lot digging a bit more into Jython for this book. I hope you will profit from my journey, too.

First, I would like to thank our editor, Laura Lewin, for asking me in the first place whether I would enjoy writing this book. Indeed I did.

To my coauthor, Noel Rappin, goes the credit for most of the concrete examples in this book. Thanks, Noel, for help with the writing, for all the contributions to the material, and for bearing my bit of pedantry and putting in the right dose of pragmatism.

My acknowledgments go to Guido van Rossum for inventing Python, to Jim Hugunin for the Java implementation of Python we still hack on, to Barry Warsaw for the work on JPython and for making a "truly" open source Jython possible, and to Finn Bock (the current primary maintainer) for his past work, for trusting me, and for keeping Jython real.

Thanks to everybody who has contributed to Jython and to everybody who actually uses it or will use it.

Thanks to the community supporting Python, to the *python-dev* people, and to Guido van Rossum again for supporting Jython, and for their more-witty-than-dry list.

Finally I would like to thank—in my peculiar abstract way—all the people who have been supportive and inspiring for me in the last years. With them, I share a part of my enthusiasm for this accomplished work.

This book is dedicated to its readers.

Noel Rappin's Acknowledgments

I've had a lot of fun working on this book, and I'd like to thank a few people for making it possible.

First, thanks to Samuele Pedroni for being so open to my participation in this project, and for staying up late so that we could collaborate despite being six time zones apart. Laura Lewin, this book's editor, has been great to work with, and she has displayed a wonderful sense of how the book should read, line by line—if you find the text clear and comprehensible, thank Laura. It has been great to work with both of you.

Without Mark Guzdial's encouragement and advice, I would never have been in a position to work on this book in the first place. The technical reviewers, Finn Bock, Paula Ferguson, Clint Howarth, Jim Hugunin, Tom Kincaid, Alex Martelli, and Brian Zimmer, were extremely helpful in catching errors that got by us, and in keeping the book on track.

From a technical perspective, thanks to all the people who spent time developing the software critical to this book. Thanks also to Jim Hugunin, Barry Warsaw, Finn Bock, and Samuele, and the other contributors for their wonderful work on Jython, and to Guido van Rossum, Tim Peters, and the entire CPython team for everything they've done to build this exemplary tool and for their support of Jython. I'd also like to mention Slava Pestov, who designed the jEdit text editor on which much of the code for this book was written, for a great tool for both Java and Python editing.

Personally, I want to thank Amy McCulloch, who was my inspiration as a writer. She'd be thrilled to see me published and bored to tears by the subject matter. I also want to thank my parents, Donna and Donnie, for their unflagging support; my wife, Erin, who is the best part of my life, who is always willing to help me, and whose enthusiasm and encouragement are so important to me. And, last but not least, my daughter, Emma, whose main contribution was falling asleep early enough so that Daddy could have time to write.

CHAPTER 1

Introduction to Jython

Botanists know that if you cross-pollinate two different strains of plants, you create a hybrid; a new plant that exhibits the strengths of both its parents. Jython is a programming hybrid. It is an implementation of the Python scripting language written in 100% pure Java that runs under any compliant Java Virtual Machine (JVM). Using Jython, you can write Python programs that interact with any Java code. The Jython interpreter supports a number of shortcuts, which make using Java libraries as easy as using your own Python code.

Jython, then, combines a scripting language of unparalleled ease of development with an operating environment for which many powerful tools have been written. The combination can be immensely valuable for programmers, enabling you to cut development time significantly while still retaining the ability to use existing Java tools, such as applets and servlets. Just as Python was originally conceived as glue to bind together other programs, Jython acts as glue to help you get the most out of Java-based tools. In particular, Jython excels at simplifying the use of complex Java programming libraries and APIs, such as the Swing graphical interface toolkit or the JDBC database connectivity API.

This chapter is your road map to the rest of the book. We'll start with an extended example of using Jython to interactively develop a small graphical interface. Then we'll discuss why Jython will make it easier for you to get things done. Finally, we'll walk through the rest of the chapters.

Jython Requirements

To run the examples in this chapter and in the rest of the book, you need to have both Jython and a JVM installed. You can get Jython at *http://www.jython.org*; see Appendix A for full details. Unless otherwise specified, all Jython examples will run under Jython Version 2.0 or higher, and a fully compliant JVM running Java Version 1.2 or higher. For the examples in this book, we used Sun Microsystem's Java Development Kit, Version 1.3, but other JVMs should work as well.

Welcome to Jython

Before we offer arguments for why you should be using Jython, let's first show you what Jython looks like. For your first look at Jython we're going to do a five-finger exercise from the Jython interactive prompt, which will show off many of Jython's features. The goal here is to give you a sense of how the integration of Jython and Java libraries works, and how easy it is to play with running code using Jython. In the interest of ease of display, we're going to be a little looser with good Jython style than we'll be in the longer examples later in the book—this is just a demonstration, but we hope you'll find it fun and productive. You may find it useful to type along with this exercise to really get the feel.

Starting Jython

Start by running Jython. You should see an interactive prompt.

```
Jython 2.1a3 on java1.3.0 (JIT: null)
Type "copyright", "credits" or "license" for more information.
>>>
```

From this prompt you can type any Jython code and see the result. We're going to type in some Swing GUI code, so the first thing we need to do is import Swing:

```
>>> import javax.swing as swing
>>>
```

Whether you are a Java or Python programmer already, that line probably looks a little odd to you. We have told Jython to import the Java package *javax.swing* and refer to it using the identifier swing. Unlike a Java import, we don't need to tell Jython which classes to import, and unlike an ordinary Python import, this is importing Java code that was not specifically written to interact with Jython.

 Throughout this book, we'll use the word "Python" for things that are common to both Jython and the original implementation of Python. Using the name "Jython" is usually a signal that the concept is applicable only to Jython. Information relevant only to the C-language implementation is referred to using the word "CPython." For example, "Python uses indentation to determine block boundaries, Jython lets you subclass Java classes, and CPython compiles to *.pyc* files."

Next, we can create a window object:

```
>>> win = swing.JFrame("Welcome to Jython")
>>>
```

Nothing has happened visibly, but we can confirm that the object has been created by typing the identifier name at the prompt.

```
>>> win
javax.swing.JFrame[frame0,0,0,0x0,invalid,hidden,layout=java.awt.
BorderLayout,resizable,title=Welcome to Jython,defaultCloseOperation=HIDE_
ON_CLOSE,rootPane=javax.swing.JRootPane[,0,0,0x0,invalid,layout=javax.swing.
JRootPane$RootLayout,alignmentX=null,alignmentY=null,border=,flags=1538,maxi
mumSize=,minimumSize=,preferredSize=],rootPaneCheckingEnabled=true]
```

(The output probably won't be bold on your machine, we're just doing that here for emphasis.) What we've done here is use the Python syntax for instance creation to trigger a call to a Java class constructor. Also notice what we did not have to do—namely, declare win as a variable or specify a type for it in any way. The second line uses the Python interpreter to trigger the Java toString( ) method on the win object.

Now, we didn't set the size of the window. The first line of code will do the actual set, and the second will get the value and print it to confirm.

```
>>> win.size = (200, 200)
>>> win.size
java.awt.Dimension[width=200,height=200]
```

If you are a Java programmer, that code probably looks a little too simple to be true, because size is a private field of the window. In fact, Jython is using introspection to infer that win.size on the left side of the assignment refers to the size property, and automatically triggers a Java call to win.setSize( ). On the right side of the assignment, Jython is performing a similar inference. Taking the sequence (200, 200), and knowing that size is of type Dimension, Jython converts the sequence to a Java Dimension object (by calling the appropriate Dimension constructor) before making the assignment. Similarly, the win.size standing alone in the second line triggers a call to the Java method win.getSize( ). So, Jython allows you to write code that retains Python's simplicity and type flexibility, but still allows the objects to behave like Java objects.

Let's get that window on the screen.

```
>>> win.show( )
>>>
```

Nothing happens on the command prompt, but a blank window with a "Welcome to Jython" title, and size 200 by 200 should show up on your monitor. If you accidentally close it, just type win.show( ) again. Being able to interact with concrete objects can be of immense help in debugging.

Adding Items to the Window

The window seems rather dull, so let's do something for it.

```
>>> field = swing.JTextField(preferredSize=(200,20))
>>> win.contentPane.add(field)
javax.swing.JTextField[,0,0,200x20,. . .
>>> win.pack()
```

We cut off the output for clarity. At the end of this sequence, the window should have a text field in it (and probably resize itself as well). This time, we put the preferred size setting in the call to the constructor. As you may know, JTextFields in Java don't take preferred size as an argument to the constructor. Again, Jython infers the correct property call when the object is constructed.

Type something in the text box. Then go back to the Jython prompt to type:

```
>>> field.text
'Neat!'
```

Of course, you'll get whatever you typed into the box, not what we typed. This shows off the fact that Jython is interacting with the Java objects in both directions—again, excellent for debugging.

Now, let's put some buttons in.

```
>>> names = ["Groucho", "Chico", "Harpo"]
>>>
```

First, a list of names is created by enclosing the names inside brackets. In Python, a list is similar to Java's ArrayList class, but with more functionality and tighter integration to the core language. This line shows one example of that integration—the ability to type new lists directly without calling functions or explicit constructors. In this example, names is set to a list containing three strings. The assignment returns no value—in Python, an assignment is a statement, not an expression. Python's list type is an example of the high-level basic types that make programming in Python so easy to manage.

The actual buttons are created from the list of names using a different Python method for creating a list called a *list comprehension*.

```
>>> buttons = [swing.JButton(each) for each in names]
>>>
```

The line of code can be read almost as it looks in English: "Perform the statement swing.JButton() once for each element in the list called names." That code creates a new JButton with each string in the list names as an argument. When evaluating a list comprehension, Python holds onto the values for each statement and returns them as a list. In this case, the variable buttons now contains a list of three JButton instances.

Now that we have a list of buttons, we can add them to the window with the use of a simple for loop.

```
>>> for eachButton in buttons:
...     eachButton.preferredSize = (100, 20)
...     win.contentPane.add(eachButton)
...
javax.swing.JButton[,0,0,0x0,invalid,layout. . .
```

In the interpreter, ... is used to indicate that the next line of code is part of a block—you don't actually type the dots. However, you must indent the last two lines by the same amount (at least one character) for Jython to read the block properly. The top line of this block contains a for statement. In Python, for statements work only for iterating over sequences. They are roughly the equivalent of a Java Iterator, however the loop in the Python case is executed automatically once for each element of the sequence without having to either explicitly ask the iterator for the next object or cast the object to any specific type. From the interpreter, a blank line indicates the end of a block (outside the interpreter, you'd just start the next line back at column one).

Inside the loop, the code sets the preferred size of each button and adds it to the window's content pane, again using the introspection shortcuts. Once all the buttons are added, we can pack the window again.

```
>>> win.pack( )
```

But now, the window is a mess—the buttons are placed on top of each other, and on top of the text field. We've forgotten to give the window a layout manager (which is the mechanism Swing uses to automatically place items within a window). No problem, we can just add it after we import the appropriate package.

```
>>> import java.awt as awt
>>> win.contentPane.layout = awt.FlowLayout( )
>>> win.pack( )
```

Adding Behavior

At this point, the window should look right, but it doesn't do anything. We want it to place some text in the text field depending on what button you push. First, we need to create the text we want used.

```
>>> quotes = {"Groucho": "Say the secret word", "Chico": "Viaduct?",
"Harpo": "HONK!"}
```

This line sets up a Python *dictionary*. A dictionary in Python is more or less equivalent to a Java HashMap: a collection of key/value pairs designed to be accessed in constant time no matter which element is accessed or how large the dictionary is. Again, the Python type is well integrated with the core language, allowing the creation in one line of what would take a series of put(key, value) calls in Java.

Once the text is in place, we can define a function that will perform the actual text replacement.

```
>>> def buttonPressed(event):
...     field.text = quotes[event.source.text]
...
>>>
```

This pair of lines defines a function to be called when a button is pressed. The event parameter in the first line will be the actual Java Event object created from the mouseclick. The line of code inside the function uses Jython shortcuts, looks up the quotes dictionary with the text of the source button, and sets the field with that value. The Java equivalent would be something like:

```
field.setText(quotes.get((javax.swing.JTextField) event.getSource()).
getText()))
```

We hope that we aren't losing credibility by suggesting that the Python example is a little bit easier to read.

Finally, we associate the function with the buttons.

```
>>> for eachButton in buttons:
...     eachButton.actionPerformed = buttonPressed
...
>>>
```

This for loop puts the buttonPressed function in the actionPerformed slot for each button. This is another Jython shortcut—as used in Java, buttons don't have an actionPerformed attribute. Instead, actionPerformed is the method defined inside an ActionListener interface. When you assign to actionPerformed Jython performs the appropriate call to the button's addActionListener( ) method, such that the function buttonPressed is triggered when the action is performed. Also notice that Jython allows us to use a function as the righthand side of an assignment statement, we're using the function as a value. At this point, the window should work, and look more or less like Figure 1-1.

Figure 1-1. The sample window

Of course, Jython does not have to be run interactively. The code that we used in the interactive shell session is shown as a standalone file in

Example 1-1. The code is equivalent to the preceding session, but we did clean it up some, removing duplicate calls to pack( ), putting import and definitions where they would more typically come in a Python module, adding code to exit Jython when the window closes, and refactoring button creation into a separate function. Example 1-1 is typical of a Jython script as it would actually be written.

Example 1-1. The sample standalone window

```
import java.lang as lang
import javax.swing as swing
import java.awt as awt

names = ["Groucho", "Chico", "Harpo"]
quotes = {"Groucho": "Say the secret word",
          "Chico": "Viaduct?", "Harpo": "HONK!"}

def buttonPressed(event):
    field.text = quotes[event.source.text]

def exit(event):
    lang.System.exit(0)

def createButton(name):
    return swing.JButton(name, preferredSize=(100,20),
            actionPerformed=buttonPressed)

win = swing.JFrame("Welcome to Jython", size=(200, 200),windowClosing=exit)
win.contentPane.layout = awt.FlowLayout( )

field = swing.JTextField(preferredSize=(200,20))
win.contentPane.add(field)

buttons = [createButton(each) for each in names]
for eachButton in buttons:
    win.contentPane.add(eachButton)
win.pack( )
win.show( )
```

Running this script from Jython (for example, by executing jython *filename* at an ordinary command prompt) will give you the same window and behavior as in Figure 1-1.

What's Jython Good For?

Having seen the interactive example, hopefully you are interested in learning more about Jython. But you may be wondering exactly what you might use it for. It can help to think of the JVM as a platform in its own right. Java has been the overwhelming choice of programming language for the JVM platform—a number of different languages other than Jython run under a JVM in one way or another, but for most people, so far, the JVM and Java programming have been effectively synonymous. Uses of Jython can be split into two areas: things you might want to do within a JVM for which Java is not a great choice, and things you might want to do where Java does seem like a strong choice.

In the first category are the kinds of programs at which scripting languages have traditionally excelled. Programs that are small utility tools, or one-time-only scripts, or rapid development prototypes, have all been in the purview of scripting languages such as Python. The Java language, for all its usability benefits over, say, C++, was not designed for that kind of rapid development or scripting work. Jython makes that kind of programming easier on a JVM, giving you scripting language flexibility where it did not exist previously. This also suggests a place for Jython as an adjunct to existing Java programs—performing cleanup and maintenance functions, for example.

Web programming is another area in the first category. Java has made tremendous strides as a server-side web application tool over the last few years, primarily because of the creation of really good industrial-strength server environments. Writing the actual web application in Java, however, is still a chore, especially when maximum response to changed requirements is needed. Outside the Java world, many (if not most) web applications are still written in dynamic scripting-style languages such as ColdFusion, Perl, or Python. It's no accident that template languages or other scripting languages written specifically for Java web applications have proliferated. Jython as a web language gives you a scripting language that is more powerful and established than other Java web tools such as WebMacro or Tea, yet still gives you full access to the Java servlet libraries.

Another area that Java doesn't really cover is the use of a scripting language by your Java program. The Jython interpreter can be embedded inside any Java program, allowing you full access to Jython for scripting inside the program. One use of this feature common in Python is to have your preference or properties file be a "live" Jython script, saving you the trouble of having to convert a properties or XML file to actual functionality.

We do not, however, want to give you the impression that Jython is good only for tasks that Java is weak at. In fact, we also think that you will find Jython useful even for the kinds of applet or GUI applications traditionally thought of as Java's strengths. We believe that if you decide to prototype your program in Jython, there is a very good chance that you will find that development of the Jython version is so smooth, you will keep the prototype rather than port it to Java.

The Benefits of Jython

We think that Jython is likely to improve your productivity for a great number of project types that are currently performed in Java. In this section, we'll start to explore the reasons why we believe this to be true. We'll also suggest some reasons why Jython might be a good addition to your toolkit even if you are already a CPython programmer.

For Java Programmers

If you are already programming in Java, you are probably wondering why you need another language to run under the JVM. Doesn't Java work just fine? Sure, Java is great. But, by using Jython instead of Java, you'll probably find that the number of lines of code in your program has dropped by as much as 50%. Many empirical studies of programming suggest that shorter programs have fewer bugs. In addition, programmer productivity tends to be about the same for any number of lines of code even if, as in Jython, each line of code tends to do more than it might in another language. In other words, an expert Jython programmer will likely produce programs faster, and with fewer bugs, than an expert Java programmer.

We don't mean to attack Java as a programming language. Java, like every programming language, is a tool, and it has its uses. However, it's hard to use Java for any length of time and not realize that it is an exceptionally verbose and often inflexible language. After you've written lines of code such as the following, which includes a typecast that is there only to keep the compiler happy:

```
MyClass instance = (MyClass)list.get(2);
```

it becomes easier to see the benefits of just writing:

```
instance = list[2]
```

The difference between the Java and Python code emphasizes one of the main sources of the productivity advantage of Jython—dynamic typing. In Python, you do not need to declare variables for use, nor do you need to tell the interpreter what the expected data type of a variable is. It is important to note that despite being dynamically typed, Python also has strong typing. This means that a line of code such as "1" + 1 is an error in Python (unlike many other scripting languages, which would quietly allow this).

If you have never programmed in a dynamic language, the idea of not declaring variables or types may make you a little nervous. After all, isn't the point of static typing to allow the compiler to catch errors before the program runs? It's certainly true that static typing can do that. Most programmers who switch to a dynamic language are surprised by how rarely those errors actually occur in practice, and how quickly they are usually found and fixed when they do occur.

In Python most type errors are caught immediately the first time you run the program—long before any users see it. Often type mistakes will result in errors the first time a module is loaded or the first time a function is called. Some basic unit testing makes it nearly impossible for a type check error to get by. When compared with the amount of effort spent in Java convincing the compiler that your program is legal, it seems that static typing may not be worth the effort. It's worth your time to try it and see if your experience is similar to ours.

In addition to dynamic typing, the Python scripting language used in Jython offers several other features that will improve your programming productivity:

Clean, easy-to-read syntax
Python was designed from the ground up to be as readable as possible—it's been described as "executable pseudocode." Python's use of indentation to denote block boundaries makes for consistent and clear code. Unlike some other scripting languages, Python syntax tends to be in words rather than typographical syntax—it's very unlikely you'll be writing lines of code that look like comic book curse words. As a result, when you have to come back to your code six months later, odds are you will still be able to understand it.

Interactive interpreter
Jython has a command-line interpreter where you can enter any Jython expression (including function definitions, class definitions, and module imports) and evaluate it interactively. The interactive session makes it easy to test and debug Jython code and also to explore existing Java libraries by trial and error.

Module-based organization
Unlike Java, where every line of code has to be inside a class definition, Jython separates the package organization from the class system. A Jython module can contain any valid statement, including class and function definitions as well as normal program code. The lack of insistence on structure is particularly nice in short scripts, but also helpful for distributing a number of related classes together.

High-level, built-in types
Jython's list of basic types includes a few that go beyond Java's basic data types. These include sequence types similar to Java collection classes and dictionaries similar to Java's map classes. Having these types built into

the language makes them easier to work with—you can enter an entire dictionary as a literal expression, for example. Jython also includes a built-in file type which is far easier to use than Java's I/O classes.

Simple object-oriented semantics

Classes, instances, and modules are all implemented using the same simple concept of a namespace or mapping between variable names and values. Syntax and behavior of all three are similar, and are only a short step from the behavior of any Python dictionary. This consistency makes the behavior of Python programs extremely easy to predict, with nearly no special cases or exceptions to be memorized.

Operator overloading

Python allows you to easily overload all operators and many built-in functions to work as desired on user-defined classes. This allows your classes to interoperate cleanly with built-in types, and can also result in clearer code.

Dynamic dispatch and polymorphism

Both Python and Java have *dynamic dispatch*, meaning that the class whose code is evaluated from a line such as instance.method( ) is determined at runtime based on the class to which that instance belongs. Unlike Java, Python does not test for the existence of method( ) in any particular class at compile time. This is a corollary of dynamic typing, and has many of the same strengths and weaknesses. However, the flexibility it gives you over Java is significant, removing the need for Java-style interfaces and more generally promoting code reuse by making it easier for new code to interact with existing code.

No compile phase

The Jython development cycle does not have a separate compilation phase. Files are compiled if needed during execution, speeding up development.

First-class functions and classes

A *first-class* object can be returned from or passed to a function. In Python, functions, classes, and modules are all first-class objects. Being able to pass these kinds of code objects around can lead to very elegant code designs and increase reuse by allowing classes to "plug" functionality into existing structures. While some of this is technically achievable in Java using either anonymous inner classes or the *java.lang.reflect* package, the Python version is much easier to use. The following two code blocks are roughly equivalent, each creating a function object called someFunc and calling it.

Java:

```
import java.lang.reflect.*;
Class aClass = anInstance.getClass( );
Method someFunc = aClass.getMethod("method", new Class[] {Integer,
String});
someFunc.invoke(anInstance, new Object[] {new Integer(3), "Fred"});
```

Python:

```
someFunc = anInstance.method
someFunc(3, "Fred")
```

Extensive included library

Jython includes most of the Python standard library. Although some of that functionality is duplicated in the Java standard library, much of it is not. Examples include regular expression support (finally coming in JDK 1.4), parsers, network support, unit test frameworks, and much more.

All this additional functionality comes without having to sacrifice integration with existing Java code. Jython code can be compiled to Java *.class* or *.jar* files, and these files can be distributed like any other compiled Java files—the fact that the code was written in Jython can be made completely transparent to the end user.

For Python Programmers

If you are already a Python programmer, you know about the programming features of Python and are probably wondering what you gain from the Java side of the equation. There seem to be at least three important gains.

Extended reach

Using Jython, you can deploy a Python language program in arenas that are simply not possible using CPython. The most notable examples of this are web-based—namely, the creation of applets that will be accepted by mainstream browsers, and the creation of servlets that can be run by Java servlet or J2EE servers.

Ease of distribution

Jython makes it easy to distribute your program as a cross-platform binary in *.jar* format. Although there are binary tools for CPython on different platforms, there is no similar cross-platform tool for CPython.

Tools and libraries

This is the biggest advantage of Jython. Although the Python standard library and available third-party tools are varied and wonderful, Java has benefited from a much larger pool of available tools, particularly enterprise-level tools. The Swing GUI toolkit is more complete and more

cross-platform than any GUI toolkit available for CPython, and is argu-
ably easier to use. Database tools are much more widely available and
standardized in the Java world. There is a large quantity of high-level
tools for XML data. All these libraries and tools can be used from
Jython at least as easily as other Java tools would be able to use them.

The Speed Question

Everybody asks it, at some point. Whenever you try to sell somebody on
using a high-level scripting-style language, the question will inevitably come
up: "Isn't it slow?" As long-time programmers of scripting languages and
other languages that have been branded as slow (including Java), we have a
variety of reasons why raw benchmark speed is less important than it might
seem as a factor in choosing a programming tool. In fact, we'll also argue
that for most of you, most of the time, the speed difference is not going to
hurt at all.

What is the exact magnitude of the speed difference? It's notoriously difficult to get good information about performance across languages. Sometimes, the person compiling the numbers has an axe to grind and has chosen
a task that favors one language. More often, the person compiling the examples has just done a better job optimizing one version over the other. So, any
cross-language speed comparison needs to be taken with a grain of salt.

That said, one of the authors' experience in running identical code under
both Python 2.1 and Jython 2.1a3 (using Sun's JDK 1.3) suggests that CPython takes 75% of the time that Jython does. Jython is about 1–10 times
slower than equivalent Java code, although admittedly useful hard numbers
on this are hard to come by because the exact speed difference strongly
depends on the nature of your application. Programs that spend a lot of time
doing operations on primitive data types will show the largest speed difference between Java and Jython.

Jython performance is heavily dependent on the specifics of the JVM, of
course. Specifically, the Sun JDK 1.4 is expected to make significant
improvements in the performance of Java reflection, and as a result Jython
should make substantial speed gains under JVM 1.4.

Still, up to 10 times slower seems like a big speed difference. And for some
programs and some projects it might be. But for most programs and
projects, the benchmark speed hit will not be as noticeable in practice as you
might think. There are four reasons why the speed loss is not as harmful in
practice as it is in benchmarks.

For a large number of programs, the bottleneck is either user input speed or network latency, and even a large performance hit in these cases is not noticeable to users. Java programs tend to be in this category frequently—if raw speed was the issue, you probably wouldn't be using Java in the first place.

Even for programs in which optimal performance is particularly important, profiling will often indicate that a small number of classes or methods are the bottleneck. In Jython, these areas can be targeted and rewritten in Java so that you get the maximum performance benefit for the minimum effort.

There's what we might call the Peters principle, after CPython core developer, Tim Peters. He has suggested that his Python programs often run faster than his C programs in practice, because development is so much easier in Python that you often wind up with a much better algorithm than you would in C. In particular, common performance enhancements such as caching function results are quite easy to code in Python.

Finally, as in so many aspects of software design, there's a trade off. If each run of your program takes five seconds longer, but you get it to your users three months sooner than you otherwise would have, what's that worth to you? How much value is created in the development time saved? For many projects, three months of programmer time is worth far more than the user time lost if the program is slower. For some projects, of course, the speed is still critical.

As always, the rule is "Make it work, then make it fast." Jython is a fabulous environment for making it work, and if at some point you find that you still need to make it faster, there are mechanisms to try, both within Jython and by converting some code to Java.

The Rest of the Book

The remainder of the book is broadly divided into three sections: an introduction to the Python language, an overview of how Jython and Java interact, and a tour of various important modules and libraries that can assist a Jython programmer.

You will find an introduction to the Python language in Chapters 2 through 5. The goal of these chapters is a brief but thorough tour through the Python concepts you will need to use Jython effectively. Throughout these chapters, we'll be comparing Python types and structures with the nearest Java equivalents. The four chapters build on top of each other. Chapter 2 starts with a description of Python's built-in types and the functionality they offer. Chapter 3 covers Python statements, including simple statements such as assignments, and block statements such as loops and conditionals. This chapter also covers Python's use of whitespace as a block delimiter. In Chapter 4, we show how you combine statements into functions, and how to create modules that can be reused across multiple programs. Chapter 5 describes Python's object-oriented syntax and semantics, again paying particular emphasis to how it differs from Java's object-oriented structures.

In these chapters, we also try to give a description of what is considered good Python programming style. If you are already comfortable programming in Python, it is probably okay if you just skim this section. However, a few Jython specifics are covered in those early chapters, so they're worth looking over.

In Chapters 6 through 8, we'll move to Jython-specific topics. These chapters describe the various ways in which Jython and Java can interact. The goal of Jython is to make the interaction between Java and Jython code as simple as possible, and to allow you to use Java objects as though they were written in Jython. Chapter 6 covers the use of existing Java classes from within Jython. This includes creating instances of preexisting Java classes, and calling methods of those classes. In addition, Jython performs some automatic type conversions between Java and Python types that are covered in this chapter. Chapter 7 moves into the tighter integration between Java and Jython that comes when your Jython class is a direct subclass of an existing Java class. There are some rules for accessing parent class members that you need to know. Chapter 8 takes a closer look at the introspection shortcuts used in this chapter's exercise that allow you to bypass Java's getSomething and setSomething methods. That chapter also covers the Python tools that allow you to dynamically get information about the classes in your system, both Python and Java, while your program is running.

Chapters 9 through 11 discuss using Jython with existing Java and Python libraries. Jython puts you in a unique position with respect to common tools. Frequently, there is a Java solution and a Python solution that are both usable. We've chosen which to highlight on a case-by-case basis, choosing based on ease of use in Jython, existence of documentation, or sheer coolness. Chapter 9 presents several examples using the Swing GUI toolkit. Chapter 10 uses the JDBC database API, the servlet API, and XML tools to give further examples of using existing Java tools. Chapter 11 covers what portions of the Python standard library are available in Jython, and which are particularly useful.

Finally, Chapters 12 and 13 cover advanced Jython topics. Chapter 12 shows how you can use Jython as a scripting language within a Java program by including the Jython interpreter as an object. In Chapter 13, we show how you can compile your Jython code to .class or .jar files that can be run by any JVM or Java engine.

CHAPTER 2

Jython Basics

Before we can show you how to use Jython to improve your interactions with existing Java libraries, we need to give you a tour of the Python language. The next four chapters will act as both a quick tutorial and a quick reference to using Python. In this chapter, we'll show you how to run Jython and use the interpreter, then discuss Python's built-in types.

Python has roughly the same number of built-in types as Java. It has fewer numeric types, but adds powerful collection objects that are much more flexible and useful than their Java counterparts. This chapter will show how to create and use those types.

Running Jython

Jython can be invoked in three ways. It can be run in an interactive interpreter session, it can be run as a batch interpreter session on a specific script file, or the *jythonc* compiler can be run to compile Jython code to a set of Java classes or to a single *.jar* file. Most of these chapters will cover the interpreter; *jythonc* will be covered in Chapter 13. For instructions on obtaining and installing Jython, see Appendix A.

To start an interactive session, run jython from the command line. (On Windows, you can also double-click the *jython.bat* file.) You will see the following:

```
Jython 2.0 on java1.3.0 (JIT: null)
Type "copyright", "credits" or "license" for more information.
>>>
```

This tells you what version of Jython you are using, and what Java Virtual Machine (JVM) is running it. The triple angle-brackets are the Jython command prompt. If you take the system's advice and type **credits**, you will see the following:

```
>>> credits
Jython is maintained by the Jython developers (www.jython.org).
```

Note that the output won't be boldface on your machine—we're just using that throughout the book to make it clear what lines are output.

Within the Jython interactive session, you can enter valid fragments of Jython programs and see the results. You can also assign to variables and use those variables later in the same interactive session. It's easiest to show this with simple mathematical operators. A sample interactive session might look like this:

```
>>> 2 + 2
4
>>>_
4
>>> 2 * 2
4
>>> x = 4
>>> x * 2
8
>>> 1 / 2
0
```

A couple of quick notes about this session are worth mentioning. In the second command line, the special variable _ refers to the most recent value printed to the interpreter. That variable is available only in the interpreter (you can't use it within a script), and is the only cryptic variable shortcut in Python. In the fourth command line (x = 4), we were able to assign to x without declaring it beforehand. The assignment statement did not return a value (as the analogous assignment would in Java). To exit the interpreter, press Ctrl-z under Windows or Ctrl-d under Unix flavors.

The simplest way to run a Jython script is by invoking the jython command with a filename.

```
% jython file <args>
```

The argument list is passed to the Jython script and is accessible via the standard library. A host of other command-line options to the jython command are discussed in Appendix B.

Under Windows, you can associate .py files with *jython.bat* and then run Jython scripts by double-clicking them. The extension .py is typically used on all systems to distinguish Python and Jython scripts.* Under Unix, you can use the sharp-bang trick to select the Jython interpreter at the top of your file—but not quite in the way you'd expect. You need to invoke it as follows:

```
#! /usr/bin/env jython
```

---

* Remember, Jython *is* Python, so though you may have expected a different extension (such as *.jy*), Jython files use the same *.py* extension. So sharing of all compatible code is directly enabled.

This is because *jython* is itself a text script that invokes a *.jar* file, and some Unix flavors require that the target of the sharp-bang be a binary executable. The previous syntax should work just fine on all Unix flavors, assuming that the *jython* executable script is on your search path for programs.

Basic Types

Instead of merely providing the Java set of basic data types, Jython provides Python's rich set of basic built-in data types. Python features the conventional basic types such as numbers and strings, and also powerful generic container types, such as lists, tuples, and dictionaries. This means that in many cases when prototyping or implementing algorithms, you will not need to write your own data structures from scratch, but you can simply use or combine the built-in container types. Java's java.util.Collection classes expose similar features, however, Python container types are much more effectively integrated with the language: they can be created using literal syntax, and many common operations on them can be conveniently expressed with operators. The result is less cluttered code that more directly conveys what operations are being performed. It's the difference between the following lines of Java code:

```java
map = new HashMap();
map.put("one", new Integer(1));
map.put("two", new Integer(2));
map.put("three", new Integer(3));

System.out.println(map.get("one"));

list = new LinkedList();
list.add(new Integer(1));
list.add(new Integer(2));
list.add(new Integer(3));
```

and the following Python code, which creates a similar dictionary and list objects and assigns the same values to them. The exact details of the Python syntax will be explained later in this chapter, but for now, notice that the objects can be initialized in a single line of code.

```python
map = {"one": 1, "two": 2, "three": 3}
print map["one"]

list = [1, 2]
list.append(3)
```

Python is fully object based. There are no primitive types as in Java, so there is no need for the wrapper objects that Java requires to put things such as numbers in container objects. However, Python does make a distinction between the built-in types and user-defined classes. Not all the operations that you can perform on classes can be performed on types. Most significantly, built-in types in CPython cannot be subclassed. In Jython, however, built-in types are implemented differently, and as a result, some operations on built-in types that do not work in CPython may work in Jython. However, subclassing a built-in type is still not guaranteed to work in Jython.

Python's typical terminology for objects and classes is slightly different from Java's. Any data value, built-in or user-defined, is usually called an *object*. Objects in the Java sense are usually referred as *class instances*.

 Version 2.2 of CPython will begin the process of mending the type/class split. At the end of this process, built-in types and user-defined classes will have more consistent and coherent behavior. For example, you will be able to subclass a built-in type. Jython 2.2, when released, will try to follow the new behaviors in this area of CPython 2.2.

Operations on Python objects (built-in or user-defined) are very similar to the manipulation of objects in Java. You can access the attributes exposed by the objects using the dot . operator: *obj.attr*. Methods are invoked by combining the dot operator with the ( ) call operator: *obj.method( )*. You can change the value of an attribute by using the same dot operator access syntax on the left side of an assignment: *obj.mutableAttr = val*. Some objects, such as user-defined classes and class instances, allow new attributes to be added at any time through assignment to an attribute that does not yet exist. The same is also true for the key/value pairs of dictionary mappings. Attribute removal is performed using the del statement: del *obj.attr* for classes and instances and del *obj[key]* for sequences and mappings. Because Python allows operator overloading, any object, even instances of user-defined classes, can be used as the operand of a built-in operator. The next three chapters will more fully explain the meanings of these operations.

Built-in data types and user-defined classes are often placed into categories to help manage the problem of what methods are defined by the type or class. In general, all objects and user-defined classes in a given category implement the same protocol—a given set of attributes, methods, and operator behavior. This is roughly analogous to a Java interface, however, Python categories are not enforced by the interpreter at compile time—they are more of an aid to discussion. A user-defined class is free to define only the operators and methods of a category that will actually be needed.

Categories are also important because the Python standard library methods often use them informally to define input requirements, and you can do the same. So, while describing the built-in types, we will also name and define the expected behavior for the categories to which they belong. Python's basic built-in types can be split into the following categories:

Numbers
　　All numeric types, including integers, floating-point numbers, and complex numbers

Strings
　　Immutable string objects

Sequences
　　Ordered, indexed, array-like collections, in mutable and immutable forms

Mappings
　　Keyed, random-access, hashmap-like collections

Files
　　Operating system external files

Python has a number of more advanced built-in types that you are less likely to manipulate directly. For example, functions are considered a built-in type in Python. The Java value null is represented in Python by the built-in object None. The None object always maps to false, and it is always available through the None identifier.* It should be noted that None is represented as an empty output in an interactive session.

```
>>> None
>>>
```

Python does not have a built-in Boolean type or value. Most values are considered true, with a handful of exceptions (such as 0, or the empty string "", or any empty sequence or mapping). For user-defined classes, it is possible to define specific truth mappings. By default, however, class instances are always treated as true. For further details on truth values see "Conditional Logic" in Chapter 3.

Operators

Table 2-1 presents all the Python operators in decreasing order of their precedence. Each operator binds tighter than the operators in the rows below it. Most of the operators are similar, if not identical, to their C or Java

---

* This is managed internally by creating a binding between a global value and the identifier None in the _builtin_ module, which is always available. As a result, you can just refer to the global value as None from everywhere in Python. You can redefine the identifier if you want, but that's almost certainly a bad idea.

counterpart. Differences will be noted along the way. As usual, parentheses can be used to tweak precedence.

Table 2-1. Operators and precedence

Operators	Description
$(\ldots), [\ldots], \{\ldots\}, \texttt{`}\ldots\texttt{`}$	Tuple/list/dictionary construction, conversion to string representation
$x[i], x[i:j], x.y, x(\ldots.)$	Indexing, slicing, attribute lookup, call operator
$-x, \texttt{\~}y, +x$	Arithmetic negation, bitwise complement, identity
$x * y, x / y, x \% y$	Multiplication/repetition, division, modulo/printf-like formatting
$x + y, x - y$	Addition/concatenation, subtraction
$x << y, x >> y$	Bit-shifts
x & y	Bitwise and
x ^ y	Bitwise xor
x | y	Bitwise or
$<, <=, >=, ==, <>, !=$ is, is not in, not in	Comparison, identity tests, membership
not x	Logical negation
x and y	Logical and
x or y, lambda *argsList*: *expr*	Logical or, anonymous function

The logical operators short-circuit, which means they evaluate their arguments left to right and stop when the value of the operation is determined, like the Java operators && and || do. For the and statement, the first false value will end the evaluation; for the or statement the first true statement will. Boolean operators return the value of the last evaluated argument, unlike Java, which returns a separate Boolean value.

```
>>> "" or "me"
'me'

>>> "she" or "he"
'she'

>>> "" and 0
''
```

The identity test operator is checks whether its arguments are the exact identical object. This is similar to the behavior of the Java == operator, or the base class java.lang.Object.equals method.

Comparison operators, at least for built-in types, consider the content value (the numerical value for number, the character sequence for strings, etc). For container objects, this means that comparison is performed recursively.

When comparing sequence types, the items are compared in order, which is useful for sorting. Dictionaries are sorted by the order of their keys. If the dictionaries are the same length, the sorted key/value pairs are compared. If no other method of comparison is defined, object identity is used. User-defined classes may specifically overload the comparison operators. For Java objects, the underlying java.lang.Object.equals method is used, which, unless redefined, tests for reference identity. Also, in Python, you can chain comparison operators so that 10 < x < 20 is valid and identical to the Java 10 < x && x < 20.

Numeric Types

Python's numeric types will seem familiar to you—in Jython, many are implemented as thin wrappers around Java numeric types.* However, Python's dynamic typing does lead to some slightly different behavior than Java. Because in Python you do not declare the type of a numeric variable statically, each numeric type has a specific mechanism for creating literal constants of that type.

Although Python typing is dynamic, it is also strong—non-numerical values will not automatically be coerced into numerical ones if used in a mathematical operation. For example, both "3" + 3 and 3 + "3" raise TypeErrors. Python mathematical operations where both items are of the same numerical type always return values of the same type. Where the items are of different types, all the operands are coerced to the "highest" or most precise type, and that is the type that is returned.

Python's numeric types are described in the following sections, from lowest or least precise to highest or most precise.

Integer

Integers are bounded integral types. The Jython implementation represents them as Java int values, which means they are 32-bit signed values. Python does not have integral types that correspond to Java's shorter integral types.

Integer literals are made up of digits without a decimal point, and of course they can start with a - or + sign: 123, -5, +14. The sign prefix is actually just an operator, unlike in Java where it is considered part of the literal. An integer literal that begins with 0 (numeral zero) is interpreted as octal, whereas one that begins with 0x or 0X is interpreted as hexadecimal: 0777, 0xff3. A

---

* This may make Jython numbers behave slightly differently than CPython numbers, which are thin wrappers around C numeric types. In practice, however, there is almost no difference.

legal string or any numeric type except a complex value can be converted to an integer by using the built-in function int(*x* [, *base*]). When converting from a string you can supply an optional *base*.

The result of any operation between two integers is always an integer. This can lead to some confusion with division, where the result of integer division is the integral quotient. For example:

```
>>> 1 / 2
0

>>> 3 / 10
0

>>> 10 / 3
3
```

Long

Longs are integral values of arbitrarily long precision, and should not be confused with Java's basic long type. Jython represents them as instances of java.math.BigInteger. Long literals follow the same rules as integer literals, except they end with an l or L: 12L, 123935704750012374274L. A legal string or any numeric type except a complex may be coerced to a long by using the built-in function long(*x* [, *base*]). The result of any operation between an integer and a long is a long. Division of long values behaves like division of integer values.

Float

Floats represent floating-point numbers. Jython represents floats as Java *doubles*, which means they have 64-bit precision. Again, Python does not support the shorter floating-point types that Java does. Any literal number with a decimal point is considered a float—if there is no digit after the decimal point, it's assumed to be .0. So, 3.2, 3., 0.45, and –45.6 are all floats. A floating-point literal may also end with an exponent expression made up of the letter e (or E), followed by an integer with an optional sign, such as: 7e2, 8345.45E-12, and so on. The built-in float() function will coerce values to float from a legal string or any numeric type except a complex. The result of an operation between either of the integer values and a float is a float. You can use this fact to work around integer division where needed by multiplying one of the values by 1.0 before the operation is carried out (you can also coerce one of the arguments using float()):

```
>>> 10 / (3 * 1.0)
3.3333333333333335
```

This example shows one of the attributes of floating point in any language—namely, that it is inexact. In Python, as in any language, you directly test for equality on two floating-point numbers at your own risk.

Complex

Python also includes built-in support for complex numbers. Complex numbers are represented in Jython by a pair of Java doubles representing the real and imaginary parts of the number. Complex literals are written as *real-part* + *imaginary-part*, followed by a lower- or uppercase j. The rules for float literals apply; the real part is optional. The following are both complex literals:

```
3.5 + 1.2j
2.0J
```

You can also create complex numbers by using the built-in function complex(*real, imaginary*), which takes one or two arguments corresponding to the real and imaginary part of the number. The result of an operation between any other numerical type and a complex number is a complex number.

Numerical Functions

Python has several other built-in functions that manage numerical values. These are, for the most part, straightforward.

abs(*number*)
> Returns the absolute value of the argument.

cmp(*object1, object2*)
> Returns 0 to show *object1* equals *object2*, 1 if *object1* is greater than *object2*, and -1 if *object1* is less than *object2*. This function works with any built-in type, not just numbers.

coerce(*number1, number2*)
> Returns a tuple (*result1, result2*) that represents the two arguments coerced to the same numerical type—the more precise of the two.

divmod(*x, y*)
> Returns a tuple of the integer quotient and remainder—i.e., (*x* / *y*, *x* % *y*). The values passed into the function do not have to be integers.

hex(*integer*)
> Returns a string representing the literal value of *integer* in hexadecimal notation.

oct(*integer*)
> Returns a string representing the literal value of *integer* in octal notation.

pow(*base, power [, mod]*)
> Returns *base ** power*. If the optional argument *mod* is passed, the result is equivalent to (*base ** power*) *% mod*.

round(*number, digits=0*)
> Returns the *number* rounded to *digits* number of digits after the decimal point. Even if the number of digits is zero, the result is still a float.

The standard module math defines a number of other useful functions for floating-point numbers, including the full set of trigonometric functions as well as the constants pi and e.

> CPython 2.2 is also beginning a long process of reforming Python's numeric model away from its C origins. Although the changes will not be required until CPython 3.0, they will probably start to be optional, and covered by Jython, before that. CPython 2.2 introduces optional alternate division semantics whereby division of two integers returns a float and creates a separate operator for integer division. CPython 2.2 will also unify integers and longs, and allow all integer values to have infinite precision if needed. In versions before CPython 2.2, integer operations that flow outside the range of integer values raise an OverflowError. In CPython 2.2 and higher, such operations automatically convert the result to a long value.

Sequences: Lists and Tuples

A Python list is a mutable, sequential, heterogeneous collection of objects, which is an impressive mouthful (try saying it 10 times quickly). Let's unpack that meaning one word at a time, going backward:

Collection
> A Python list collects references to multiple objects.

Heterogeneous
> The elements of a Python list do not have to be of any particular type or class. The elements don't even have to be of the same type or class. The elements can be basic types, user-defined classes, or other lists, tuples, or dictionaries (or anything else that might not be covered by that list).

Sequential
> The elements of a Python list are accessible via integer indexes starting at zero and ending at the list length –1.

Mutable
> A Python list can change in place—that is, the objects to which the list refers can be modified without creating a new list. Items can be added or removed from any place in the list. The list's size can vary over time.

In Java terms, lists are most like java.lang.ArrayList, without the limitations on what kinds of objects are in the list or how you might access them. Given the index, list access time is constant, meaning the internal implementation is more like an array than a linked list. Lists are used both where a list-like structure would fit, and in place of fixed-size arrays. Python does not have fixed-size mutable arrays. In Jython, there are tools and features that make it easy to interoperate between Python lists and Java arrays, to enable Jython programs to call Java methods that require arrays. See "Java Arrays and the jarray Module" in Chapter 6.

List expressions are comma-delimited and enclosed in square brackets:

```
[expr, expr, ...]
```

The expressions inside the brackets will be evaluated, and will furnish the elements for the new list. They will be indexed starting from 0. The expression [ ]creates an empty list. Empty lists map to false. Lists can be nested: [1, 2, [3, 4, 5]] is a three-element list, where the third element is also a three-element list.

Sequence Access

Python lists are accessed the same way as Java arrays, by enclosing the index inside brackets. You can also get a copy of a range of elements, a nice feature called a *slice*. Slices are created by placing the start index and the end index of the desired subsequence, separated by a colon. For example, [1:3] returns the sequence elements at index one and index two—note that the start index is always inclusive and the end index is never inclusive. Some examples of list access include the following:

```
>>> L=[0,"zero","one", 1]

>>> L[1]
'zero'

>>> L[1:2] # slicing
['zero']

>>> L[:2]
[0, 'zero']

>>> L[2:]
['one', 1]

>>> L[-2]
'one'

>>> L[-3:-1]
['zero', 'one']
```

```
>>> L[:]
[0, 'zero', 'one', 1]
```

The built-in function len applied to a list returns its length:

```
>>> len(L)
4
```

As you can see from the examples, indexing also works with negative integers. L[-i] corresponds to L[len(L)-i] so that [-1] is the last element of the list, [-2] is the next-to-last element, and so on. The slice notation [i:j] specifies a range of elements, starting with i up to but not including j. Negative slice indexes are interpreted as they would be in a simple access. Both i and j are optional in a slice and default to 0 and the list end, respectively. If the start index is not specified, as in [:3], the beginning of the list is used. Similarly, if the end index is not specified, as in [1:], the end of the list is used. Therefore, L[:] is an idiomatic way to get a shallow copy of L.

An invalid index in a simple access will raise an IndexError exception. Slicing, however, only considers valid indexes in the interval between i and j. In the case where j precedes i you will get an empty list. Slicing handles overflow of indexes on either end without raising an exception, by silently substituting either 0 or the list length, depending on which side has overflowed.

Lists use existing operators for both concatenation and repetition, which create new lists and have a linear cost. Concatenation is written using the + operator. Repetition is expressed through the * operator applied to a list and an integer. The references in the original list are simply repeated; no copying takes place.

```
>>> [0,"zero"] + ["one",1]
[0, 'zero', 'one', 1]
```

```
>>> [ "foo" ] * 4
['foo', 'foo', 'foo', 'foo']
```

The membership test operator in can be used with lists, and has a linear cost.

```
>>> L=[0,"zero","one", 1]
```

```
>>> "one" in L
1
```

```
>>> "ten" in L
0
```

Lists can be manipulated both with assignment and by using the del statement. Assignment can be either to a simple index or to a slice. Assigning to a slice is equivalent to deleting the slice and inserting the new value at the slice start index.

```
>>> L = [0, 0]
>>> L[1] = "zero"
>>> L
[0, 'zero']

>>> L[1:2] = ["zero","one",1]
>>> L
[0, 'zero', 'one', 1]

>>> del L[-1]
>>> L
[0, 'zero', 'one']

>>> L[1:] = [] # equivalent to del L[1:3]
>>> L
[0]

>>> L[1:1] = ["end"]
>>> L
[0, 'end']
```

When an invalid single index is specified on the left side, assignment raises an error. On the other hand, slice assignment will consider an actual range outside the list as 0:0 if the range precedes the first element, and as len(L): len(L) if the range follows the last element.

Sequence Functions and Functions

The following methods manipulate the target list in-place and return None. A new list is not created, nor is a reference to the modified list returned:

append(item)

Adds a single element to the end of the list; similar to the Java method add.

```
>>> L = []
>>> L.append('zero') # appends a single element at the end of the list
>>> L
['zero']
```

You can also append to the end of a list using slice assignment: L[len(L):] = [value]. Similarly, you can prepend to the front of a list using L[:0] = [value].

extend(sequence)

To concatenate a sequence at the end of the target, use the extend method, similar to the Java addAll.

```
>>> L.extend(['one','two',3]) # does the same with an entire sequence
>>> L
['zero', 'one', 'two', 3]
```

remove(*item*)

> You can remove an object from the list by value with the remove method. This method will remove the first occurrence of *item* from the list. If the value is not in the list, a ValueError exception is raised.

```
>>> L = ['zero', 'one', 'two', 3]
>>> L.remove('two')
>>> L
['zero', 'one', 3]
```

sort(*[function]*)

> Python provides a sort method, which by default sorts in ascending order with respect to <. The sort method can take an optional parameter, a two-argument function used for comparing sorted elements, which should return an integer interpreted as follows: negative means <, zero means ==, and positive means >. Using a function slows the sort considerably.

```
>>> L = ['zero', 'one', 'two']
>>> L.sort()
>>> L
['one', 'two', 'zero']
```

reverse()

> I'm sure you can figure out what reverse does....

```
>>> L.reverse()
>>> L
['zero', 'two', 'one']
```

insert(*index, item*)

> Inserts *item* into the list in-place such that *list* [*index*]== *item*.

Some other useful methods and functions on sequences include:

count(*item*)

> This method returns the number of times the item appears in the list.

pop([*index*])

> L.pop is the inverse of append and returns and removes the last element of the list. If the optional *index* attribute is specified, the element that is *index* number of entries to the left of the last element is returned. Together with append, you can use a list as a stack:

```
>>> L.append("one")
>>> L.append("two")
>>> L.pop()
'two'
>>> L.pop()
'one'
>>> L = ['one', 'two']
>>> L.pop(1)
'one'
>>> L
['two']
```

index(*item*)

The built-in method L.index(*item*) returns an integer, corresponding to the index of the first occurrence of *object* in the list, or raises an exception if *object* is not present.

max(*sequence*) or min(*sequence*)

You can use the built-in functions max( ) and min( ) to get the highest or lowest valued item in the sequence.

```
>>> max(L)
'zero'

>>> min(L)
'one'
```

zip(*seq1*, *seq2*, ...)

Two sequences (or more) of the same length can be combined into a single two-dimensional (*n*-dimensional) list using the zip function:

```
>>> zip(L, [0, 2, 1])
[('zero', 0), ('two', 2), ('one', 1)]
```

The elements of the result list are tuples. We will cover them in the next section.

A list value is really just a reference. As with objects in Java, you can store them in many places, but they will all refer to the same object, so the following should be no surprise:

```
>>> cage = []
>>> cameras = [cage] * 4 # one cage, four cameras
>>> cameras
[[], [], [], []]
>>> cage.append("bird") # one bird
>>> cameras
[['bird'], ['bird'], ['bird'], ['bird']]
```

Just four perspectives of the very same bird in the very same cage.

Functional Programming

In Chapter 3 you will see how to iterate over the elements of any sequence using the for statement. In addition, Python offers built-in functions to iterate over a sequence while applying a user-specified function to constructing a new list or value, similar to LISP or other functional programming languages. Despite the fact that Python was not specifically designed to be a functional programming language, it does not ignore some useful functional programming tools, such as these functions:

```
>>> map(lambda x: 2 * x, [1, 2, 3])
[2, 4, 6]
```

The map function can take any one-argument function and a sequence as its arguments. It builds a new list with the results of applying the function to the elements of the sequence in order.

The lambda *argsList: expr* operator produces an anonymous function taking arguments that match the *argsList* specifier and computing the expression. The general form is lambda *arg, arg, ...: expression*. The full details will be covered in Chapter 4. For now it's enough to know that lambda produces something like a function without having to go to the trouble of giving it a name. When called, this function evaluates the expression using the actual values of the arguments.

The general form of map is:

```
map(function, sequence, ...)
```

The function must take a number of arguments equal to the number of sequences passed to the map statement. It is then called repeatedly, building an argument list by picking an item from each sequence and moving along the sequences in parallel. The results are accumulated in the result list, and are the same length as each sequence—calling map does not produce any kind of cross product. So, in the example map(lambda x: 2 * x, [1, 2, 3]), the function is called first with 1, resulting in 2, then with the second element of the list taking in 2 and returning 4, then called with the third element of the list, returning 6. The three return values are collected in a list and returned.

The function filter takes a one-argument function and one sequence and builds a new list, using the elements in the original sequence for which the function evaluates to true and discarding the others:

```
>>> filter(lambda x: x > 0, [-3, 0, 1, -4, 2])
[1, 2]
```

The function reduce computes a single value by applying a two-argument function recursively, with one argument being the last computed value and the next being an element of the furnished sequence moving from left to right. On the first pass, the first and second elements of the list are used. An optional third argument is placed at the beginning of the list as a "seed value" for the computation. An empty sequence raises an exception, unless the optional third argument is specified, in which case that argument is returned. If you're familiar with Smalltalk, this is identical to the collection method inject:into:. For the rest of us, it's easier to see in action than to explain:

```
>>> # compute the number corresponding to the given binary representation
>>> reduce(lambda x, y: 2 * x + y, [1, 1, 0, 1])
13

>>> reduce(lambda x, y: x - y, [1], 10)
9
```

In the first iteration of the first function call, the integers 1 and 1 are passed to the lambda function, resulting in 3. In the next pass, the current result of 3 is passed to the lambda along with the 0 that is next in the list, resulting in 6. The final pass is 6 and 1, returning 13.

Tuples: Immutable Sequences

Tuples are sequences just like lists, but they are immutable. When a tuple is constructed, it gathers a fixed, indexed set of object references. The objects inside the tuple can still be changed if they are of object types that allow mutation, however the tuple itself cannot be changed. Tuples can be used when a constant list is needed. A tuple can be used as a key in a dictionary if all the items in the tuple are hashable, while mutable lists can never be used as a dictionary key.

You can directly construct a tuple using comma-delimited expressions surrounded by parentheses. The expressions are evaluated before being placed in the tuple:

    (expr, expr, ...)

The expression ( ) is the empty tuple, and is a false value. To construct a one-element tuple a comma must be placed after the single element (expr,). The comma is necessary to resolve ambiguity between the tuple expression and an ordinary parenthesized expression.

All the sequence access operations and the sequence membership operator in are supported on tuples:

```
>>> tup=(0,"zero","one", 1)
>>> len(tup)
4

>>> tup[1]
'zero'

>>> tup[1:2] # slicing
('zero',)

>>> tup[-2]
'one'

>>> tup[-3:-1]
('zero', 'one')

>>> tup[:]
(0, 'zero', 'one', 1)

>>> "one" in tup
1
```

Notice that these slice expressions return a sequence of the same type as the original sequence. If you pass in a tuple, you get a tuple as the returned value. Tuples and lists can be converted into each other by using the built-in functions list(seq) and tuple(seq). In either case, the return value is a shallow copy of the given sequence. Both functions can be used with any kind of sequence.

Tuples offer no methods, and all in-place modification operations that are defined on lists raise a built-in TypeError exception. Because Python is a dynamically typed language, types are attached to objects, not to variables, and therefore this kind of improper use of tuples is detected only at runtime.

Strings

Strings are... well, they are strings. Internally, they are immutable sequences of characters, similar to tuples. Python does not have an object analogous to Java's char character type. Characters in Python are just strings of length one. Python does not have a built-in mutable class to take the place of StringBuffer, although one implementation is provided in the standard library. Like Java strings, all Jython strings are in the Unicode character set (this is a difference from CPython). In general, Python provides more complete string functionality than Java.

There are several different ways to construct string literals in Python. String literals can start and end with single quotes or double quotes. In either case, the other kind of quote can be used safely inside the literal:

```
>>> "Ain't Misbehaving"
"Ain't Misbehaving"

>>> 'and I said, "Hi"'
'and I said, "Hi"'
```

Within the quotation marks, special characters are escaped using a backslash. The list of escapes is based on C and is slightly different from Java's escape list. The exact list is in Table 2-2. Unlike Java, backslashes followed by characters not on this list are legal in strings, and are treated merely as normal characters.

Table 2-2. Backslash escapes

Escape character	Meaning	Escape character	Meaning
\\	Backslash (\)	\r	Carriage return
\'	Single quote (')	\t	Tab
\"	Double quote (")	\u*xxxx*	Unicode 16-bit character value *xxxx* (hex)

Table 2-2. Backslash escapes (continued)

Escape character	Meaning	Escape character	Meaning
\a	Bell (ASCII character number 13)	\Uxxxxxxxx	Unicode 32-bit character xxxxxxxx (hex)
\b	Backspace	\v	Vertical tab character
\f	Formfeed	\ooo	Unicode 8-bit character in octal
\n	Linefeed or newline	\xhh	Unicode 8-bit character in hexadecimal
\N{*name*}	Unicode character identified by name		

String literals may also begin and end with either three single or three double quotes. A triple-quoted string may include newline characters (which would ordinarily need to be escaped) or individual quotation marks.

```
"""some
long
string"""
```

A string literal may also have an r or R before the initial quote, to indicate a *raw string*. Inside a raw string, backslash escape does not work and backslashes are treated as normal characters. Quotation marks may be escaped in raw strings, but the backslash stays in the string.

```
>>> r"c:\program files"
'c:\\program files'
```

```
>>> r"\""
'\\"'
```

Notice that the raw string results in a normal string—after the string is created, you can't tell whether it was created using the raw option. Raw strings are just a flavor of string literal. They are often used in regular expressions to keep them from looking even more like random noise.

A u or U may also be placed at the start of a string. In CPython, this is used to indicate Unicode. In Jython, because all strings are Unicode, it has no effect, except for enabling the Unicode-specific escapes (\u, \U, \N) that would otherwise produce an error.* This is for CPython compatibility.

Two string literals placed next to each other are automatically concatenated at compile time. The strings may have different quote literals:

```
>>> "My name is " 'fred'
'My name is fred'
```

---

* Currently, \U is not supported in Jython.

Because strings are just sequences, all the access and slice access rules for lists and tuples apply. The only difference is that the return value is always a string—for a simple access, it's a string of length one; for a slice, it's a string of the requested length.

```
>>> "Hello"[2]
'l'

>>> "Hello"[2:4]
'll'
```

The in membership operator works a little differently for strings than for sequences. The left-side argument to the operator is a one-character string; 'l' in 'hello' is true, while 'x' in 'hello' is false.

The built-in functions str( ) and repr( ) both convert objects to strings. The str( ) function is designed to return human-readable strings, while repr( ) is designed to return machine-readable ones, typically a valid Python expression to construct the value or something of the form '<useful info>'. You can also get the repr of any object by enclosing it in backticks (such as `item`).

String Formatting

Python uses the % operator to perform string formatting similar to the C sprintf. In the simplest form, formatting specifiers are placed in the string, followed by the % sign, followed by a tuple of values (a list cannot be used here, but if there is only one element, it can be used without parentheses). The values are placed in the string left to right with the matching specifiers. The specifier you will use most frequently is %s, which converts the value to a string using the str function. So, for example:

```
>>> "The Cubs have won %s games and lost %s" % (52, 32)
'The Cubs have won 52 games and lost 32'
```

The first format specifier takes the first element in the tuple, the second specifier takes the second element, and so on.

It gets more complicated. First of all, there are other specifier characters, as shown in Table 2-3.

Table 2-3. Python format specifiers

Specifier	Meaning	Specifier	Meaning
%%	Insert a % sign into the string	%i	Signed integer decimal
%c	Character; value must be a single element string or integer	%o	Unsigned octal
%d	Signed integer decimal	%r	Convert to string using repr

Table 2-3. Python format specifiers (continued)

Specifier	Meaning	Specifier	Meaning
%e/%E	Floating point in exponential format	%s	Convert to string using `str`
%f/%F	Floating point in decimal format	%u	Unsigned decimal
%g/%G	Floating point, uses exponential format if the decimal is too wide to fit	%x/%X	Unsigned hexadecimal

There are three optional elements that can be placed between the percent sign and the character signifier. The first is a conversion flag, which can be 0 to pad the space with zeros, or + to put a sign before the value. The second is a minimum field width for the value, which is either a positive integer or an *. If the * is used, the specifier uses the next value of the tuple for the width, then grabs another value for display. After the minimum field width, you can place an optional precision amount by adding a dot followed by the precision. Again, an * can be used, and is handled in the same way as for the minimum field width.

```
>>> "%f" % (1.0/3.0)
'0.333333'

>>> "%i" % (1.0/3.0)
'0'

>>> "%2.2f" % (1.0/3.0)
'0.33'

>>> "%+2.2f" % (1.0/3.0)
'+0.33'
```

Dictionaries can also be used as the righthand side of a string format expression. The syntax will be shown in the discussion of dictionaries, later in this chapter.

String Functions

You can go back and forth between integers and strings using the built-in methods chr( ), which takes an integer value and returns a length-one string, and ord( ), which takes the character and returns the integer value. For Unicode string values, the method unichr( ) takes an integer between 1 and 65535 and returns its associated Unicode character. In Jython, there is no difference between chr and unichr, although for CPython compatibility you should use chr only with arguments in the range 0–255.

The methods count and index discussed for lists and tuples are also defined for strings, as well as the len built-in function. In addition, strings have a large number of standard methods. Most of them are straightforward.

capitalize(*string*)

> Changes the string so that the first word starts with a capital letter, and all other letters are lowercase.

```
>>> "i love trash".capitalize()
'I love trash'

>>> 'HI THERE'.capitalize()
'Hi there'
```

center(*field width*)

> Centers the string inside a string with the given field width.

```
>>> 'x'.center(5)
'  x  '
```

encode(*encoding, [error]*)

> Translates the string to the given encoding. The encoding is the name of a codec, such as 'utf-8'. An optional second argument tells Python what to do on an encoding error. The options are 'strict' (the default, which raises a ValueError exception), 'ignore', and 'replace'.

endswith(*suffix [, start[, end]]*)

> Tests if the string ends with the given string. It takes an optional start and end location to bound the string being tested.

```
>>> 'hello'.endswith('lo')
1
>>> 'hello'.endswith('el', 1, 3)
1
```

expandtabs(*[tabsize]*)

> Replaces each tab character with the number of spaces to ensure that the length of the string after the spaces is a multiple of the given tab size. The default value is 8.

find(*sub [, start[, end]]*)

> Returns the first index in a string where the substring is found, and also takes an optional start and end to limit the search to a slice. It returns −1 on a failure. It is similar to the sequence method index, but does not raise an exception on failure.

```
>>> 'abcdcba'.find('c')
2

>>> 'abcdcba'.find('c', 3)
4

>>> 'abcdcba'.find('b', 3, 5)
-1
```

isalnum( )

> True if the string is not empty and all characters are alphanumeric.

isalpha( )
> True if the string is not empty and all characters are letters.

isdigit( )
> True if the string is not empty and all characters are digits.

islower( )
> True if the string has at least one letter and all letters are lowercase.

isspace( )
> True if the string is not empty and all characters are whitespace (can include tabs and newlines).

istitle( )
> True if the string is not empty and is made up of capitalized words separated by non-letters.

isupper( )
> True if the string has at least one letter and all letters are uppercase.

join(*seq*)
> Converts the given sequence to a string by inserting the target string between each pair of elements. The elements in the sequence must be strings.
>
> ```
> >>> ': :'.join(["one", "two", "three"])
> 'one: :two: :three'
> ```
>
> The join statement is equivalent in eventual functionality to the following for statement:
>
> ```
> result = ""
> separator = ": :"
> sepOn = 0
> for each in ["one", "two", "three"]:
>     if sepOn:
>         result += separator
>     else:
>         sepOn = 1
>     result += each
> ```
>
> However, the for statement creates a new string each time through the loop (because strings are immutable), where the join( ) does not. Because join is often more efficient than the string creation, lists are often created using append and then joined to give the same effect as a Java StringBuffer—preventing the creation of intermediate strings.
>
> ```
> substrings = []
> for each in [1, 2, 3]:
>     substrings.append(str(each))
>
> print ''.join(substrings)
>
> '123'
> ```

ljust(*width*)

> Returns a string of length *width*, starting with the initial string and padding the rest of the length with spaces.

```
>>> 'hi'.ljust(5)
'hi   '
```

lower( )

> Returns a copy of the initial string with all letter characters converted to lowercase.

lstrip( )

> Strips leading whitespace from the string and returns a copy.

replace(*old, new[, maxsplit]*)

> Returns a new string formed by replacing all instances of *old* in the initial string with *new*. If the *maxsplit* parameter is specified, that is the maximum number of replacements performed.

```
>>> 'hello'.replace('l', 'x!')
'hex!x!o'
```

rfind(*sub, [start, [end]]*)

> Analogous to find, but searches from the end of the string, returning the index of the last occurrence of *sub*.

rjust(*width*)

> Analogous to ljust, but puts the padding spaces at the front of the string.

rstrip( )

> Analogous to lstrip, but removes trailing whitespace.

split(*[sep] [, maxsplit]*)

> Returns a sequence formed by breaking the string at each occurrence of *sep*. The characters in *sep* are discarded. If *sep* is not specified or is None, any whitespace character acts as a delimiter. If *maxsplit* is specified, it sets the maximum number of splits performed—the last element gets all remaining characters. In Java, you would use a StringTokenizer to get this functionality.

```
>>> '10-2-1'.split('-')
['10', '2', '1']

>>> '10-2-1'.split('-', 1)
['10', '2-1']
```

splitlines(*[keepends]*)

> Analogous to split, but uses newlines as delimiters. If *keepends* is set to true (the default is false), the line ending is kept at the end of each line.

startswith(*prefix[, start [, end]]*)

> Analogous to endswith, but tests for a prefix at the beginning of the string.

strip( )
>   Removes whitespace on both ends of the string—as if both lstrip and
>   rstrip were called.

swapcase( )
>   Returns a copy of the string where all lowercase characters are upper-
>   case and vice versa.

title( )
>   Returns a copy of the string in title case. Each word in the string starts
>   with a capital letter, and all other letters are lowercase.

```
>>> 'tO kiLl a MoCKingBirD'.title( )
'To Kill A Mockingbird'
```

translate(*table* [, *deletechars*])
>   Returns a new string with all characters in optional *deletechars*
>   removed, and all other characters mapped by ASCII value to their coun-
>   terparts in the 256-character long string *table*. In Jython, translate can
>   also use a dictionary as a table, in which case the keys are the original
>   characters as ordinal integers, and the values are the new characters as
>   length-one strings. If using a dictionary as the table, Unicode characters
>   are available.

```
>>> s = "abc"
>>> d = { ord('a'): '+', ord('c'): '-' }
>>> s.translate(d)
'+b-'
```

upper( )
>   Returns a copy with all letters converted to uppercase.

Mappings and Dictionaries

Dictionaries are perhaps the most commonly used Python data type. Not
only will you use the dictionary data type frequently for all kinds of data
with non-integer keys, but the mapping protocol used for dictionaries is frequently used for other non-dictionary data sets as well.

Dictionaries are mutable, random-access, heterogeneous collections of
objects. Unlike lists, the items in a dictionary are not stored in order;
instead, they are accessed by an arbitrary key specified when the item is
added to the dictionary. Access time should be constant, no matter the size
of the dictionary. In Java terms, dictionaries are similar to instances of java.
util.HashMap.

The keys in a dictionary can be any immutable object, most often strings,
but also including tuples and numbers, and user-defined classes if they correctly override hashing functionality. Lists and dictionaries cannot be used

as dictionary keys. Any item, including other dictionaries, lists, function objects, classes, and user-defined classes, can be a value in a dictionary.

Dictionaries are directly created using a comma-delimited list of pairs of the form *key: value*. The value can be an expression, which is evaluated before being placed in the dictionary. Stylistically, Python designer Guido van Rossum recommends using no space between the key and the colon, and one space between the colon and the value, as shown here:

```
>>> dict = {'one': 1, 'two': 2, 'three': 3}
>>> dict
{'two': 2, 'one': 1, 'three': 3}
```

Notice that Python does not keep the items in the order inserted. The empty dictionary is represented as {}, and it evaluates to false. Dictionaries may be nested such that a dictionary is inserted as a value inside another dictionary.

Dictionary access is just like list access, only using the key instead of an integer index. Assignment to a key that is already in the dictionary changes the value at that key, whereas assignment to a key that is not in the dictionary adds the key and value into the dictionary. Attempting to access a key that is not in the dictionary raises a KeyError exception. Items are removed from a dictionary by using the del statement. All items can be removed from a dictionary at once by using the clear( ) method. You can get the number of key value pairs in a dictionary by using the len statement.

```
>>> dict["one"]
1

>>> dict["two"]
2

>>> dict["three"] = 333
>>> dict
{'two': 2, 'one': 1, 'three': 333}

>>> dict["four"] = 4
>>> dict
{'two': 2, 'one': 1, 'three': 333, 'four': 4}

>>> dict["five"]
Traceback (innermost last):
  File "<console>", line 1, in ?
KeyError: five

>>> del dict["one"]
>>> dict
{'two': 2, 'three': 333, 'four': 4}

>>> len(dict)
3
```

Aside from len, dictionaries do not respond to the methods or operators defined for sequences. Specifically, there is no concept of slicing or concatenating dictionaries. Dictionaries also do not respond to the in operator. You can determine if a key is in the dictionary by using the method has_key( ).

```
>>> dict.has_key('two')
1
```

There are three methods that allow you to convert the dictionary or part of the dictionary to a sequence. You can get a sequence of the keys by using the keys( ) method, a sequence of the values by using the values( ) method, and a sequence of (key, value) tuples by using the items( ) method.

```
>>> dict.keys()
['two', 'three', 'four']

>>> dict.values()
[2, 333, 4]

>>> dict.items()
[('two', 2), ('three', 333), ('four', 4)]
```

If keys( ) and values( ) are called without any changes to the dictionary between them, the lists are guaranteed to match up—the value corresponding to key[0] is value[0], and so on. To put that another way:

```
dict.items() == zip(dict.keys(), dict.values())
```

You can do something similar to concatenating two dictionaries by using the update(dict) method. The argument is another dictionary, and the method inserts each key/value pair in the other dictionary into the initial dictionary. The initial dictionary is changed in place, and if the key already exists in the initial dictionary, it is overwritten:

```
>>> dict.update({'one': 'I', 'three': 'III', 'five': 'V'})
>>> dict
{'five': 'V', 'two': 2, 'one': 'I', 'three': 'III', 'four': 4}
```

You can also see that, like the in-place list modifying methods, update( ) returns None to emphasize that the dictionary itself has changed.

Dictionaries allow copies of themselves to be created using the copy( ) method. The copies are shallow—the underlying items are not copied, only the reference to them is.

Continually testing for has_key before doing a dictionary access to avoid raising exceptions can become sort of tiresome. Python offers two ways around that. The first method, get(key, default=None), returns the value at key if key exists in the dictionary, and returns the default if it does not.

```
>>> dict.get('one')
'I'
```

```
>>> dict.get('six')

>>> dict.get('six', 6)
6
```

In the second example, the get returned None, which doesn't show up at the interactive prompt.

Dictionaries also provide a setdefault(*key, default*=None) method, which is identical to get with the addition that if *key* is not in the dictionary, the pair *key*: *default* is added to the dictionary, changing it in-place.

```
>>> dict.setdefault('one')
'I'

>>> dict
{'five': 'V', 'two': 2, 'one': 'I', 'three': 'III', 'four': 4}

>>> dict.setdefault('six', 'VI')
'VI'

>>> dict
{'five': 'V', 'six': 'VI', 'two': 2, 'one': 'I', 'three': 'III', 'four': 4}
```

Finally, in Python 2.1 or greater, the method popitem( ) returns an arbitrary (*key, value*) tuple, removing that item from the dictionary in the process. This method may be more efficient than creating the entire items( ) sequence at once, provided, of course, that you don't need the dictionary again.

Dictionaries can also be used in string formatting operations in place of tuples. When using dictionaries, the key desired is placed in parentheses in the specifier after the % and before the remainder of the specifier. The dictionary need not be a literal. The keys are assumed to be strings, and quotation marks are not used. For example:

```
>>> "%(two)s plus %(four)s equals %(six)s" % dict
'2 plus 4 equals VI'
```

This can be particularly useful in conjunction with one of three Python built-in methods that return dictionaries based on the current state. The globals( ) function returns a dictionary containing all identifier/value pairs in the current top-level module. The locals( ) method returns a similar dictionary for all pairs local to the current function or method. This should be treated as read-only. The vars( ) built-in is similar, but can take an optional namespace argument (which can be a class instance), in which case it returns a dictionary of all pairs for that namespace. Chapter 4 contains more detail on modules and identifier/value namespaces.

As part of the new iterator features in CPython 2.2, you will be able to write the expression *key in dict*, and it will be equivalent to *dict*.has_key(*key*). Dictionary iterator methods will also be introduced analogous to the existing keys(), values(), and items(). The new methods are called iterkeys(), itervalues(), and iteritems().

Jython Files

Like most scripting languages, Python offers direct support for file access, through the built-in function open and the built-in file type. You don't have to resort to the standard library for basic I/O.

The open function takes both a *filename* and an optional *mode*, opens the file, and returns a built-in file object ready for I/O:

    file = open(filename, mode)

The *mode* flag should be a string: 'r','w','a' means open for reading, writing, and appending, respectively. The flag can have an optional plus sign, such as 'r+','w+','a+'. This indicates that the file has been opened for updating, meaning that both reading and writing are possible. The 'w+' flag truncates the file before updating. With 'a', all write operations happen at the current end of the file. A 't' or 'b' suffix appended to mode means text and binary mode, respectively. In text mode, platform-dependent line-ending conversion from and to '\n' is performed. All input and output operations on files take and return strings. In Jython, where all strings are Unicode, the platform's character encoding is used for converting between byte streams and strings in text mode. In binary mode, Unicode characters are truncated to 8-bit on output, and zero-widening is used on input.

Built-in file objects support the following methods:

close( )
   Close the file. All subsequent operation on the file will fail.

flush( )
   Flush the underlying stream.

read([size])
   Read until the end of the file or up to optional *size* bytes. The read data is returned as a string. If *size* is omitted the whole file is read. Reading past the end of the file will return an empty string.

readline([size])
   Read one entire line until the end of the file or up to optional *size* bytes. Reading past the end of the file will return an empty string. The

returned string contains the trailing newline. If size is specified, a possibly incomplete line may be returned. Reading past the end of the file will return an empty string.

readlines([*sizehint*])

Read from the file using readline until its end or up to *sizehint* bytes. The result is a list of the read lines as strings.

seek(*offset, whence*)

Set the current file's position for the subsequent operations. The default value 0 for *whence* means that *offset* will be interpreted as an absolute position in the file. The other possible values are 1 for seek relative to the current position and 2 for seek relative to the actual end of file.

tell()

Return current file's position.

truncate([*size*])

Truncate the file to the given size or, if no size is given, the current position within the file.

write(*str*)

Write the content of *str* to file. Returns None.

writelines(*list*)

Write the strings in *list* to the file. No line separators are interleaved, to be complementary to readlines.

In Python, using read or readlines to read the entire contents of a file at once is a typical idiom, especially in the common case where the file will easily fit in memory. The following small example shows how to use built-in files, opening a file, then writing to it, then using readlines to return the contents as a list:

```
>>> f = open("foo.txt",'w')
>>> f.write("small\n")
>>> f.writelines(["file\n","foo\n"])
>>> f.close()
>>> f = open("foo.txt",'r')
>>> f.readlines()
['small\n', 'file\n', 'foo\n']
>>> f.close()
```

CHAPTER 3

Jython Control Flow

Control statements include conditionals such as if, and loop constructs such as for and while. They form the structure that holds a program together and shapes its behavior. Although the basics of conditionals and loops are similar across a wide variety of programming languages, each language has its own specific implementation. Coming from Java to Python, you will find the basic statements familiar, but some of the details will be new. In this chapter, we will tour the ways in which Python manages flow of control, including the use of indentation to mark block boundaries.

Statements and Expressions

A Python program consists of a series of *statements*. A statement can be:

- An expression combining variables and operators, which may include function or method calls
- An assignment
- One of several keyword statements, such as if, for, or try

The following are all valid statements:

```
1 + 2 * 3

range(2, 3)

inputFile.close()

if x == None: return
```

In Python, simple statements are normally separated by the end of a line (any operating system's end-of-line combination will work). However, Python will allow a statement to continue beyond the end of a line if there is an open parenthesis, bracket, brace, or triple-quote string. Such a statement can continue over any number of lines until the delimiter is closed. A statement can also be continued to the next line by ending it with a backslash \. The backslash only allows the statement to be continued for one more line; to continue further, another backslash is needed. In most cases, it's considered more readable to surround the expression with parentheses than to end lines with a backslash.

The following are all valid multiline statements:

```
(1 +
 2)

["a", "b",
 "c",
 "d"]

{"x": 1, "y": 2,
 "z": 3}

"""This is a multi-line
string"""

if x > 3 or \
    y > 5: return
```

It's not done often, but you can place more than one simple statement on a line by separating them with a semicolon.

```
t = 1 + 2; length = len(['a', 'b', 'c'])
```

A comment in Python is indicated by a # sign. This indicates that everything to the right of the # will be ignored by the interpreter until the end of the line.

```
#I'm about to increment x
x +=1 #increment x
```

There are no specific multiline comments in Python. However, if a string literal appears by itself anywhere in a Python program, it's treated as a null operation by the interpreter. Therefore, a triple-quote string can be placed anywhere in your program to serve as documentation. Typically, a meaningful string is put at the beginning of a module, class, or function, in which case the interpreter holds on to the string as a *documentation string* or *doc string*.

Assignment

A simple assignment statement in Python looks just like one in Java:

```
x = 3
```

You can also chain assignments as you can in Java. It works, but it's not normally considered good programming style. The following snippet:

```
x = y = 0
```

assigns 0 to both x and y. This is just syntactic sugar, and should not be taken to imply that Python assignment returns a value the way that Java assignment does. In Python, an assignment is a statement, not an operator.

The meaning of an assignment statement in Python is similar to Java. Like Java object variables (and unlike C), variables always hold references to the actual value, not the value itself. An assignment statement creates a new binding between the variable name on the lefthand side of the statement, and the value on the right. The lefthand side of the assignment can be any valid identifier and can be potentially extended with an attribute lookup and/or the subscript operator [] for sequences and mappings. The following are all valid assignment statements:

```
x = 3

anObject.anAttribute = 14

aList[3] = 12

aDict["key"] = 15

anotherList = [1, 2, 3, 4]

anotherList[1:3] = [100]   # now anotherList is [1, 100, 4]
```

Notice from the last example that if you are assigning to a slice, the right-hand side of the assignment does not need to be the same length as the slice it is replacing. In Jython, there is no distinction between Java and Python data types for the purpose of assignment.

The righthand side of the assignment must be an expression that has or returns a value. Keyword statements, such as if or for, are not allowed on the righthand side of an assignment. Identifiers do not need to be declared before being assigned to, however, they must have been assigned to before they are used.

Unpacking Assignment

One thing you can do with assignments in Python that you cannot do in Java is assign an entire sequence at once. If both the left and right sides of an assignment statement are sequences of the same length, the values on the right are assigned to the variables on the left, in order. For example:

```
(a, b, c, d) = (1, 2, 3, 4)
```

After that line of code, a == 1, b == 2, c == 3, and d == 4. This is referred to as an *unpacking assignment*.

The sequences can be either lists or tuples, and they do not have to be literals. In addition, Python will infer a tuple in an assignment statement even without the parentheses, so the previous statement would more frequently be written as:

```
a, b, c, d = 1, 2, 3, 4
```

Actually, because the righthand side is a range sequence, the preceding statement can also be written as follows:

```
a, b, c, d = range(1, 5)
```

Note the slight quirk here:

```
a = 1, 2, 3      #assigns (1, 2, 3) to a

a, b = 1, 2, 3  #ValueError: unpack tuple of wrong size
```

The first line is interpreted as a regular assignment of a tuple to a variable, while the second is interpreted as an unpacking assignment and raises an error because the sequences are different sizes. The sequences can also be arbitrarily nested, as long as the nesting is consistent on both sides. For example:

```
a, [b, c], d = [1, [2, 3], 4]
```

Used sparingly, unpacking assignment can make your code more readable, particularly in cases where the variable names are more meaningful to use than the list index references would be. Unpacking assignment is also useful to manage multiple return values from a function, where the function returns the values as a tuple. It is similarly useful when looping over a sequence of tuples (such as a dictionary items( ) result). Unpacking assignment shouldn't be used to squeeze unrelated assignments together on the same line.

Augmented Assignment

Python supports a full range of augmented assignment operators: +=, -=, *=, and /= as well as the less often seen %=, **=, &=, |=, ^=, >>=, and <<=. The behavior of each augmentation is the same. The expression *x op= y* is functionally equivalent to *x = x op (y)*. So, for example:

```
a += 2       #adds 2 to a

b *= 3 + 5
#multiplies b by 8 (the augmented operation is performed last)
```

However, the intention of augmented assignment is to change x without creating a new binding. Therefore, there are a couple of subtle differences between augmented assignment and standard assignment:

- In the augmented assignment version, x is evaluated once. In the standard assignment version, x is evaluated twice. Usually this is not an issue, but it's possible that evaluating x might have some side effect, or possibly have a different result if evaluated a second time.
- In the augmented assignment version, if x is a mutable type (for example, a list), it is changed in place. If x is not a mutable type (for example, a tuple or an integer), a new value is created and assigned to x. In the standard assignment version a new value would *always* be created and assigned to x.

The second exception becomes important if other variables are bound to the value of x. The following code shows ordinary assignment to two lists:

```
a = [1]

b = a

a = a + [2]

## Now a is [1, 2] and b is still [1]
```

In this code, the plus operator does not change the value of b because the standard assignment creates a new binding for a, while not affecting the binding of b. In the next example, augmented assignment is used:

```
a = [1]

b = a

a += [2]

## Now a is [1, 2] and b is _also_ [1, 2]
```

In the augmented assignment example, the plus operator does change the value of b because no new binding is created. The only thing that changes is the value that both bindings refer to. Again, this happens only because a is a mutable type. If a was immutable (if it was a tuple), as in the next snippet, a new binding would be created in the augmented version, and the value of b would not have changed:

```
a = (1,)

b = a

a += (2,)

## Now a is (1, 2) and b is still (1,)
```

This can be confusing, and whether this behavior is "right" is still a topic of debate on the *comp.lang.python* newsgroup. The behavior is logical, if perhaps sometimes surprising. If possible, Python will attempt to "augment" the variable in place without creating a new value. If that is not possible because the variable is of an immutable type, Python falls back and creates a new value. User-defined classes can choose to support either behavior.

Printing

Python lets you print values to standard output using the `print` statement, which in its simplest form is:

```
print expression
```

The expression is evaluated and printed to standard output followed by a newline. Some examples:

```
>>> print 3
3

>>> print 1 + 2
3

>>> print [3]
[3]

>>> print [3].append
<built-in method append>
```

Multiple expressions can be printed in one `print` statement by commadelimiting them. Python will place a space between each expression. Adding a trailing comma will suppress the newline, as follows:

```
>>> print 1, 2, 1 + 2
1 2 3

>>> print 1; print 2
1
2

>>> print 1,; print 2
1 2
```

Additionally, if you have a file object, you can print directly to that file by using the following syntax:

```
print >> file-object, expression, ...
```

In practice, this looks like the following:

```
>>> file = open("file.txt", 'w')
>>> print >> file, 2
```

Blocks

You might have heard somebody mention once or twice that Python has a nonstandard way of determining the beginning and ending of a block of code. In a way, the use of indentation to mark block boundaries is Python's signature feature—if you know only one thing about Python, odds are that's the one. It seems as though every programmer has an opinion about indentation and whitespace in Python—especially those who have never used it. For most Python users, however, the use of whitespace quickly becomes natural.

Two of the design goals of Python are to have a simple, clean syntax relatively free of typographic symbols with arbitrary meanings, and to provide exactly one preferred way of doing something where possible. In that context, the use of indentation seems not just logical, but also natural. It removes extraneous symbols (think of how many lines in your last Java program consisted of nothing but a closing brace), and makes program layout uniform. In doing so, it makes programs dramatically more readable.

At this point, it's standard to throw out some legal Java coding horror with if and else statements, deliberately misaligned for confusion. That always seems a bit contrived. In fact, if you are following Sun's Java coding standards, you are already used to indenting code the Python way. The point is to encourage the good programming habits you already have, not to force arbitrary restrictions. Most programs are read far more often than they are written, and the readability gains from using Python make understanding and maintaining programs much easier, with little or no cost. And although we all enjoy writing complicated code now and then, most of the time we just want to write good code with as little muss and fuss as possible. Python's use of indentation does a very good job of enabling that.

Enough with the advocacy, here's how indentation grouping works:

- The first line of a file must start in the leftmost column.

- Each statement in a block must begin in the same column. The continuation of a statement onto subsequent lines may start in any column, but the beginning of the next statement must go back to the same column at which the previous statement started. Comments may begin anywhere. For style purposes, line continuations and comments should be indented to best show the logical structure of the code.

- Each of the Python keyword statements and clauses class, def, for/else, if/elif/else, try/except/else, try/finally, and while/else denotes the beginning of a new block. Helpfully, each statement ends in a colon. (All these statements will be discussed in this chapter, except def, which will be covered in Chapter 4, and class, which will be covered in Chapter 5).

- A new block must be indented at least one space from the enclosing block. Standard indentation is four spaces, but legally, you're free to go wild. A tab character is interpreted as enough spaces to bring the total to a multiple of eight. As far as Python is concerned, eight spaces, one tab, or one space and a tab are all equivalent.

- The end of a block is marked by having the next statement after the end of the block begin in the same column as one of the enclosing blocks.

The following example will help make this clear—don't worry about the exact meaning of the code at the moment, all the statements will be explained fully later in this chapter:

```
for x in (1, 2, 3):
    print x                      #indented to start a new block
    for y in (10, 20, 30):
        if y > 10:               #indented to start a new block
            print y              #indented to start a new block
        print x * y              #dedented back to previous block

        #next statement could start here (and be part of the inner loop)
    #or here (and be part of the outer loop)
#or here (and not be part of either loop)

            #but not here (unexpected indent)
    #and not here (dedent to a place with no block)
```

The next statement could begin at either column nine, which would place it under the for y statement, at column four, which would place it under the for x statement, or at column one, which would place it under neither for statement. Notice that it is immediately clear which block the final print x * y statement is a part of.

Remember that although Python interprets tabs as going to the next multiple of eight spaces, different text editors or operating systems may display them differently. This can cause Python code that uses tabs to be very confusing. Setting your text editor to replace tabs with spaces and using the suggested four-space style is highly recommended.

The following block scope possibilities can also be useful:

- A one-statement block can be placed on the same line as the keyword statement. In that case, the block ends at the end of the line. For example:

```
if x > 3: print x
#next line must start here - the if block is complete.
```

Good Python style would recommend that this be done sparingly, generally only when doing so reduces clutter in the code. It should not be used to try and put as much code as possible on one line.

- The interpreter always expects an indented line after one of the keyword statements. Sometimes you need the keyword statement, but you don't need any code in the block. In that case, you can use the pass statement to indicate that the block is a no-op, so it will have no effect. For example:

```
try:
    x / y
except ZeroDivisionError:
    pass
```

The remainder of this chapter will cover most of the statements that require blocks, and provide further examples of how indentation looks in Python.

Conditional Logic

Conditional logic in Python is handled with the if/elif/else statement, which looks similar to its Java counterpart:

```
if expression:
    block
elif expression:      #elif branch is optional, and can be multiple
    block
else:                 #else branch is optional
    block
```

The expression in the if statement is evaluated. If it is true, the block underneath that statement is evaluated. If not, the test expressions of the elif statements, if any, are evaluated in order. The block subordinate to the first expression to evaluate to true is executed. Only one of the if and elif blocks will be evaluated. The elif statement is optional, and there can be as many elif branches as needed. If none of the if or elif expressions is true, the block subordinate to the else clause is executed, if there is an else clause.

Although the two languages are similar, there are some differences between the behavior of an if statement in Python and Java. In Java, the test expression must resolve to a Boolean variable. In Python, the expression may resolve to any value. The values None, 0, the empty string, the empty list, the empty tuple, and the empty dictionary are all considered false. Any other value of a basic type is considered true. Additionally, in Jython, the Java values Boolean.FALSE and boolean false both evaluate to Python false, as do empty instances of the classes Vector, Hashtable, and HashMap or any empty instance of any class implementing the Dictionary, List, Map, or Collection interfaces. User-defined classes can define truth values for themselves.

The mechanism for resolving a dangling else clause is different. In Java, the dangling else belongs to the closest available if statement, as delimited by braces. In Python, the dangling else belongs to whichever if statement starts in the same column.

```
if x == 3:
    if y == 10:
        if z == 15:
            pass
else:
    print x
```

In the previous example, Jython binds the else statement to the topmost if statement. In Java (without the use of braces) it would bind to the inner if statement.

There are some more minor differences between the Python and Java if statements, as well:

- Python adds an elif keyword for handling middle clauses, where Java uses else if. Using else if in Python is a syntax error.
- In Python, it is a syntax error to put an assignment in the test expression because assignment is not an operator—for example: if x = nextItem( ), which is legal in Java if and only if x is of type boolean.
- You do not need parentheses around the test expressions in Python.

Python does not have anything along the lines of Java's switch statement. A series of if/elif statements are typically used if similar functionality is needed. As in any object-oriented language, if you are using a long series of ifs to dispatch based on type or class, you should consider letting OO polymorphism do the work. Also, Python programmers frequently use the combination of first-class functions and dictionaries to handle dispatch. Here is a series of elif statements:

```
if x == 1:
    self.functionOne( )
elif x == 2:
    self.functionTwo( )
else:
    self.functionElse( )
```

Here is the same functionality rewritten to use first-class function objects and a dictionary:

```
dispatch = {1: self.functionOne, 2: self.functionTwo}
func = dispatch.get(x, self.functionElse)
func( )
```

More on first-class functions can be found in the section "Flying First Class" in Chapter 4.

Loops

Python has two loop statements, the more general while statement, and the sequence-specific for statement. The while statement is as follows:

```
while expression:
    block
else:                    # the else clause is optional
    block
```

The meaning of this is nearly identical to the Java while. The expression in the first line of the statement is evaluated. If true, the block subordinate to that line is executed. When the block ends, the first line expression is evaluated again; if it is true, the block is evaluated again, and so on, until the expression evaluates to false, or until the loop is broken.

Within the main block of the while statement, you can include a continue statement, which immediately moves control back to the top of the innermost loop, similar to its Java counterpart. You can also include a break statement, which, again like the Java version, ends the innermost loop immediately and moves forward.

The somewhat confusingly named else clause is optional. It executes exactly once on loop exit if the loop exits normally. If the loop exits because of a break statement, the else block is not executed.

The rules for truth and limitations on the expression are identical to the if statement. Specifically, you can't "set-and-test" by putting an assignment in the expression. Here is one accepted Python idiom for a set-and-test loop:

```
while 1:                    #always true, loop forever
    assignment statement
    if test:
        break
    rest of block
```

Python does not have an analog to the Java do statement. It's considered redundant given the previous idiom. Also, nobody has yet come up with an elegant syntax for it.

The for statement in Python is used much more frequently than while. It is significantly different from the Java for. The for statement in Python is used specifically to iterate over sequences.

```
for variable-name in sequence-expression:
    block
else:                       #the else clause is optional
    block
```

The most important thing in this statement is that the expression in the first line must resolve to a sequence. It can be a list, a tuple, a string (in which case Python iterates character by character through the string), or any object that implements the sequence hook functions (see "Special Methods" in Chapter 5). Each element in the expression is assigned, in order, to the variable name, and the block is executed once for each element. The continue and break statements can be used with the same meaning as in a while loop.

The Python statement for item in seq: is a direct replacement for the convoluted Java idiom:

```
for (Iterator i =  seq.iterator(); i.hasNext(); ) {
    Item item = (Item)i.next();
}
```

The else clause of the Python for statement is executed exactly once at the end of the loop if the loop has terminated without a break. Therefore, the for statement:

```
for x in [1, 2, 3]:
    print x
```

is equivalent to the while statement:

```
aList = [1, 2, 3]
index = 0
while index < len(aList):
    print aList[index]
    index += 1
```

The built-in range( ) function can be used to emulate a "typical" for loop:

```
for x in range(3):
    print x

1
2
3
```

Sequence assignment is also legal in a for statement. A common idiom for iterating of dictionaries is as follows:

```
dict = {1: "one", 2: "two"}
for key, value in dict.items( ):
    print key, " : ", value

1 : one
2 : two
#the order may be different in practice
```

CPython 2.2 introduces explicit *iterators* to Python. An iterator is a new built-in type that responds to the method next( ) by returning a new object. When the iterator is out of items, it raises an exception. Built-in types and functions were adjusted as needed to handle iterators. An iterator on a list, for example, returns the items of the list one-by-one, while an iterator on a dictionary returns the keys of the dictionary one-by-one (with other methods to return iterators of values or key/value pairs). Any user-defined class can use a special method to create an iterator on that class.

In CPython 2.2, for loops are no longer limited to just a sequence. Any item that defines an iterator can be used on the right side of a for statement, including dictionaries, files, or user-defined types.

List Comprehensions

It is a common operation in Python to create a new list from an existing list by applying some function or expression to each element in the original list. The most straightforward way of doing this is by using a for loop. The following code takes a list of strings and transforms it by capitalizing each string:

```
initialList = ['one', 'two', 'three']
result = []
for x in initialList:
    result.append(x.capitalize( ))
print result
```

```
['One', 'Two', 'Three']
```

This example is straightforward, but Python provides a couple of other ways to do the same thing with less typing. One of them is the built-in map( ) function. The map( ) function takes two arguments. The first is a function object, which can be a named function or a lambda expression. The second argument is a list. The returned value is the list formed by calling the function with each element of the list one at a time. The capitalization example would look like this:

```
map(lambda x: x.capitalize( ), ['one', 'two', 'three'])
```

The map version has the advantage of being shorter. However, many Python programmers find it counterintuitive or hard to read. Also, using variables from the surrounding local scope in a lambda is awkward (see "Scoping Rules" in Chapter 4). So, Python 2.0 introduced *list comprehensions* to provide a more Pythonic way of creating lists.

At its simplest, a list comprehension has the form:

```
[expression for variable-name in sequence]
```

and is an exact replacement for:

```
result = []
for variable-name in sequence:
    result.append(expression)
```

where result would be the value of the list comprehension when evaluated. The capitalization example would be written as:

```
print [x.capitalize() for x in ['one', 'two', 'three']]
```

Notice that x is in scope for the expression in the list comprehension. Any other variables in scope can also be used, which is one of the big advantages of list comprehensions over map( ).

The list comprehension statement can be used anywhere that a regular list can be used, specifically including the right side of an assignment statement, or the list in a for statement. Because the pieces of a list comprehension are so similar to regular Python statements, Python programmers use list comprehensions as a very readable way to build lists.

Instead of a variable name in the for clause you can specify an unpacking assignment, just as in the standard for statement. For example, you can create "key: value" strings from a dictionary by doing the following:

```
dict = {1: "one", 2: "two"}
print ["%s: %s" % (key, value) for key, value in dict.items()]
```

['2: two', '1: one']

The output can also be a list of lists, or a list of tuples. If returning tuples, you must put parentheses around the tuple—Python will not infer a tuple within a list comprehension.

A common idiom for sorting based on an arbitrary function can be written with list comprehensions. In this case, we'll sort the list we've been working on by length of string, from longest to shortest.[*]

```
pairs = [(-len(x), x) for x in ["one", "two", "three"]]
pairs.sort()
sortedList = [x[1] for x in pairs]
```

This code is worth breaking down a bit. After the first statement, pairs is equal to [(-3, 'one'), (-3, 'two'), (-5, 'three')]; three tuples with the first element containing -len and the second containing the string. (We use

---

[*] This common Python code recipe is adapted from the Perl technique known as the Schwartzian Transform. Of course, in Perl, it's usually written in one line, for good or for ill. Alex Martelli posted this Python version.

length times -1 because sort( ) normally sorts from low to high.) After the sort, pairs is changed to [(-5, 'three'), (-3, 'one'), (-3, 'two')], taking advantage of the fact that elements in sequences are sorted based on significance. The final list comprehension picks the original objects back out of the list and sets sortedList to ['three', 'one', 'two'].

In cases where the sort() function is particularly involved, the list comprehension idiom can be faster than calling sort( ) with the function as an argument. In the list comprehension version, the function argument is called once per list element; in the sort(func) version, it is called once per comparison.

The basic list comprehension can be extended in two ways. A filter may be added to the end of the statement like so:

```
[expression for variable-name in sequence if test-expression]
```

which translates to:

```
result = []
for variable-name in sequence:
    if test-expression:
        result.append(expression)
```

So, if you wanted only capitalized versions of words with more than three letters, you would write:

```
[x.capitalize( ) for x in ['one', 'two', 'three'] if len(x) > 3]
```

```
["Three"]
```

Again, the variable x is in scope for the test expression.

Multiple for statements can be added to the list comprehension, in which case the for statements behave as if nested. (This is different from what map( ) does if passed more than one list.) An if filter can be applied after any of the for statements. In the case of two for statements, the general form is:

```
[expression for variable-name in sequence if test-expression
            for another-variable in another-sequence if another-test-expression]
```

meaning:

```
result = []
for variable-name in sequence:
    if test-expression:
        for another-variable in another-sequence:
            if test-expression:
                result.append(expression)
```

This is an admittedly contrived example:

```
[(x.capitalize( ), y) for x in ['one', 'two', 'three']
        for y in [10, 20, 30] if len(x) > 3]
```

```
[("Three", 10), ("Three", 20), ("Three", 30)]
```

Stylistically, the best thing to remember about list comprehensions is to keep them short and simple. Complex list comprehensions quickly lose any readability benefit over ordinary for statements—especially because the nested for in a list comprehension statement doesn't have to be indented according to normal Python rules. If the expression part is getting complicated, consider making it a function in its own right and calling the function from the list comprehension.

In general, you should use list comprehensions only if you are going to keep or return the resulting list. You can use them just for a side effect, however in that case, it's likely more readable to use a for statement.

Exceptions

Sometimes errors or other unexpected conditions can happen inside a Python program. As in Java, a Python program can raise and catch exceptions to handle unexpected events gracefully. A Python function does not need to declare the exceptions it throws. In this regard, Python exceptions are similar to Java's RuntimeException. Python's try statement has two forms, neither of which is exactly equivalent to the Java try statement, but that combine to match Java's exception functionality.

The simpler version of the try statement is as follows:

```
try:
    block
finally:
    block
```

This version is used only to ensure that certain statements execute no matter what. Once any exception is raised in the try, control immediately switches to the finally block. If no exception is raised, the finally block is evaluated after the try block is complete. If the try block performs a return while executing, the finally block is still evaluated before the function returns.

If an exception is raised in the try block, then the exception is re-raised at the end of the finally block, so that it can be further processed elsewhere. This version of the try statement does not consume exceptions, but might be used for example, to ensure cleanup of a file or a database connection even in case of an error. In this version of the try, you cannot specify which kinds of exceptions to handle—all exceptions move control to the finally branch.

The second version of the try statement is perhaps more similar to the Java statement you are used to:

```
try:
    block
except exceptions:        #can have more than one of these
```

```
         block
else:                          #the else statement is optional
         block
```

The try block is executed as before. If an exception is raised, each except clause is tested individually to see if the exception matches, for example, is the actual exception class a subclass of the clause exception? The block corresponding to that clause is executed, and the exception is consumed unless specifically re-raised. The *exceptions* part of the exceptions clause can be any of the following:

```
except:
     #catches all exceptions

except exception-type:
     #catches only exceptions of that one specific Python class

except exception-type, instance:
     #as previous, but also binds the raised exception object to instance

except (exception-type, exception-type, ...):
     #catches any exception in the list
```

If no exceptions are raised during the try block, the else clause is executed. Note that if an exception is raised but not caught, that will still keep the else clause from executing. You should also be careful when using the bare except clause without specifying an exception type. Occasionally, a clause will catch an unexpected exception that indicates a bug in the program. Also, a bare except clause muse be the last clause in the statement. A try statement cannot have both an except clause and a finally clause.

To illustrate a try statement in action, the following code shows another way of converting a for statement to a while statement—this is actually closer to the way the Python interpreter manages it (at least in Python 2.1).

```
x = [1, 2, 3]
index = 0
while 1:
    try:
        print x[index]
    except IndexError:
        break

    index += 1


1
2
3
```

The IndexError is raised by the list access when the index reaches 3, causing control to go to the except clause and the loop to break.

Python exceptions are classes. All built-in exceptions are subclasses of class Exception (see Appendix C for a list of them).* Custom exceptions are typically created by subclassing the Exception class.

To throw an exception within your own code, Python provides the raise statement. When a raise statement is encountered, execution moves up the call stack in search of a try statement that can catch the exception. If none is encountered, the top-level process handles it (usually by printing it to the standard error stream). The raise statement has a no argument form—simply raise—that re-raises the current exception, and is therefore valid only within an except block.

When raising a new exception, the first argument to raise is the exception itself. Normally, this argument will be the exception class itself, as in:

```
raise ValueError
```

In this case, Python creates an instance of this exception to actually pass around. Any try statement with an except clause that contains the class listed will catch the exception. If you are raising a custom exception, and especially if that exception takes extra data, you can use an instance as the argument to raise, rather than the class, like so:

```
raise CustomException(args)
```

where the expression is a valid constructor for the custom exception class. Again, any try/except that matches the class name will catch the exception.

Whether you are raising a class or an instance, the raise statement can also take an optional data argument, which is passed to the exception constructor. For example, AttributeError is sometimes passed with the name of the offending attribute, as in:

```
raise AttributeError, attribute
```

This is completely identical to:

```
raise AttributeError(attribute)
```

Java exception types can also be raised from Jython raise statements, and within Jython they behave the same way as native Python exceptions.

Evaluating Code Dynamically

Python offers a couple of methods for accessing the interpreter at runtime to execute or evaluate. Using the interpreter at runtime allows you to create code dynamically and execute it as if it had already been written before the

---

* Prior to Python 1.5, exceptions were merely strings, but that usage is deprecated.

program started. Dynamic execution can be useful in cases where the exact code to be executed is not known when the code is written. For example, it's common for Python programs to have property files that are made of executable Python statements dynamically executed at runtime. In addition, these functions make it easy to include Python interpreter functionality in a Python program.

On the other hand, this functionality is easily abused. Often, possible solutions based on map(), __import__, apply, or reflection are more elegant. There could also be security issues, so you should consider the origin of the code you are executing.

The relevant functionality in Python is captured by one keyword statement and three built-in functions. The keyword statement is exec *code*. The *code* parameter can be either a string made up of a set of valid Python statements or a compiled code object created with the compile function. If *code* is a string, remember that Python indentation rules still apply on the string. The code passed to exec is executed just as though it was passed to the Python interpreter.

By default, the code in exec is executed in the current scope. However, you can specify a specific global or local namespace by using a statement of the form exec *code* in *global[,local]*. The *global* and *local* parameters need to be mappings, and you need not specify both of them. If specified, name references within the *code* will be resolved against these mappings. Assignment inside the code will be executed in the *local* namespace if it is specified, and in the *global* namespace if *local* is not specified. Exceptions raised during dynamic execution are treated as though the code was executed from static text—the exception propagates through the call stack normally. In addition, syntax errors in dynamically executed strings raise a corresponding SyntaxError exception.

The built-in methods that allow dynamic execution are as follows:

compile(*code, filename, kind*)
Compiles the string argument into a compiled code object, suitable for use in exec or eval. The *code* string argument must be valid Python code; however, like ordinary Python code, the existence of variables will not be checked until the code is executed. The *filename* argument is only to give the interpreter a name to use if the compiled code raises an exception. The *kind* string argument is either 'exec' if the string is made up of statements, 'eval' if it is an expression, or 'single'. If the kind is 'single', the compiled code behaves like the interpreter, printing out the resulting value of the statement in the string.

---

eval(*expr[, global[, local]]*)

Evaluates the expression passed as the *expr* parameter and returns its value. The *expr* argument is a string or compiled code object, and must be a Python expression that returns a value—raw statements such as if or print will raise an error. If specified, the optional *global* and *local* arguments define the scopes in which the *expr* is evaluated—if not specified, the scope of the eval function is used, just like the similar arguments of the exec statement.

```
>>> eval("2 + 2")
4
```

execfile(*filename[, global[, local]]*)

Executes all the Python statements in a file specified by *filename*. Does not return a value. If specified, the *global* and *local* arguments define the scope in which the *expr* is evaluated—if not specified, the scope of the execfile function is used, just like the similar arguments of the exec statement.

CHAPTER 4

Modules and Functions

The three basic building blocks of a Python program are *modules*, *functions*, and *classes*. This chapter will discuss modules and functions, while the next chapter will discuss classes. A Python module is a collection of statements that define variables, functions, and classes, and that is the primary unit of a Python program for the purposes of importing code. Importing a Python module actually executes the module. A function in Python is similar to functions or methods in most programming languages. Python offers a rich and flexible set of mechanisms for passing values to functions.

Modules

Python helps you to organize your programs by using modules. You can split your code among several modules, and the modules can be further organized into packages. Modules are the structural units of Python programs. In Java, this structural role is played directly by classes, and there is a strict correspondence between a file's name and the class it contains. In Python, the filename is used only for organization, and does not require specific names to be used for any object within that file.

A Python module corresponds to a source code file containing a series of top-level statements, which are most often definitions of functions and classes. These statements are executed in sequence when the module is loaded. A module is loaded either by being passed as the main script when the interpreter is invoked or when the module is first imported by another module. This is the typical execution model for scripting languages, where you can take a recipe and easily try it out, but in Python the recipe can be more elegantly expressed using an object-oriented vocabulary.

At runtime, modules will appear as first-class *namespace* objects. A namespace is a dictionary-like mapping between identifiers and objects that is used for variable name lookup. Because modules are first-class objects, they can be bound to variable names, passed as arguments to functions, and returned as the result of a function.

Modules are used as the global lexical scope for all statements in the module file—there is no single "global" scope in Python. The value of a variable binding referenced by a statement within a module is determined by looking in the module namespace, or within a local namespace defined within the module (by a function or class definition, for example). The contents of a module are first set up by the top-level statements, which create bindings between a name and a value. Name-binding statements include assignment, import, function definition, and class definition statements. So, although any kind of statement can appear at the top level in a module (there is no such thing as a statement that can appear only at the top level), name-binding statements play a pivotal role.

Unlike Java, all name bindings in Python take place at runtime, and only as the direct consequence of a name-binding statement. This is a straightforward model that is slightly different from the Java model, especially because Python import statements have very different behavior from their Java counterparts. (Jython does have a compilation phase, but it is transparent to the user and no Python name bindings are set there. Jython compiles Python source code to Java bytecode, which is then dynamically loaded and creates the Python bindings at runtime.) A Java import statement merely allows a specific class or classes to be used with unqualified names, while a Python import statement actually executes the imported file and makes available all the names defined with it. A name binding in a module is available to other statements in the module after the binding is created. The dot operator *module.attribute* is used to access variable names bound in an imported module.

One consequence of the module and import semantics of Python is that Python does not force you to use object-oriented programming. You can mix procedural-style or functional programming in your modules when it makes sense to do so. Although it has been said that procedural programming does not make for very reusable code, this is true mostly for large programs written in statically typed programming languages. However, Python is a dynamically typed language, and because functions have the same first-class status of all other values, even straight procedural code can be reusable. With Python's dynamically typed functions, you have the benefits of a generic programming paradigm such as C++ function templates, but with a simpler and more powerful model. In Python, it is easy to write common utility algorithms that take functions as arguments. Functions of this sort are sometimes called "pluggable," and are very easy to reuse.

In the next sections, we will cover how to write function definition statements and how to use functions and import statements for Python modules and Java classes. Object-oriented class definition and semantics will be discussed in Chapter 5. The other name-binding statements, including the assignment statement and the for statement, are covered in "Assignment" and "Loops" in Chapter 3.

Functions

The simplest form of a function definition is as follows:

```
def funid([arg,...]):
    block
```

At runtime this will create a function object and bind it to the name *funid*. When called, the function object will execute the block of statements, which can refer to the variables defined in the argument list. These will be bound to the values of the actual arguments as computed when the function is called. Functions are called in the usual way, through the ( ) call operator:

```
callable-object([expr,...])
```

The calling convention, pass-by-value, is the same as for objects in Java, where the value being passed is the object reference, not the underlying object (this convention is sometimes called pass-by-object-reference). This means that changes to the underlying object will be visible outside the function; however, changes to the variable binding (such as reassigning it within the function) will not be visible outside the function. As in Java, there is no direct support for pure call-by-reference.

There is nothing magical about function objects in Python that enables them to be called using the call operator. As we will see in "Special Methods" in Chapter 5, any Python class can be defined to respond to the call operator, essentially allowing an instance of that class to mimic a function object.

Because Python is a dynamically typed language, there are no type declarations for the arguments or the return value in a function definition statement. Python does not support function overloading, as Java or C++ do (but see "Parameter Passing with Style" later in this chapter for the Python equivalent). A subsequent function definition for *funid*, like any other name-binding statement, will simply rebind *funid* without triggering an error. This is true even if the later binding is just a variable assignment—you cannot have functions and variables with the same name within a Python namespace. On the other hand, a function in Python is fully generic, in that any set of arguments can be passed to it. If the objects passed as arguments do not support the operations performed inside the function, a runtime error will be raised.

All functions return a value, unless they are abandoned because of a raised exception. A return statement:

```
return [expr]
```

can be used to force the return of control to the caller and specify the return value as the one computed by *expr*. In the case of a bare return without an expression, or if the end of a function is reached without returning a value explicitly, the function will return the value None.

In Python, it is also possible to return multiple values from a function by building a tuple on the fly—for example, return head, tail. Then you can use unpacking assignment at the call site or work directly with the tuple.

You also do not need to declare local variables in Python, but of course there are local variables. A variable is treated as local in a function (and more generally as local in any scope) if it is bound for the first time through any of the name-binding statements within the function or scope. Arguments are also local, and they are implicitly bound at call time. You will find more information on scoping rules in the "Scoping Rules" section, later in this chapter.

 CPython 2.2 introduces a special case of function called a *generator*. A generator is defined the same way as a regular function, but instead of a return statement, it uses the new keyword yield *expr*. When a generator is called, it returns a generator object. The generator object supports the *iterator* protocol. When that iterator's next function is invoked, it executes until it encounters a yield statement, at which time it returns the value of the expression in that statement. When the generator object is invoked again from the same scope, it continues execution from the point of the yield, essentially saving the state of all its local variables. The generator runs until it encounters a yield again, or until it exits normally. Generator functions can be placed anywhere iterators can, including the righthand side of a for statement. A generator is called repeatedly until it either raises a StopIter exception, or exits normally.

For example, the following simple generator returns an increasing range of integers one at a time:

```
def generateInts(N):
    for i in range(N):
        yield i
```

Parameter Passing with Style

Python supports many useful features related to parameter passing, through fancier argument specifiers. All these features are absent from Java.

First, you can specify a default value for an argument, which makes the argument optional. Just add the value after the *arg* in the argument list like so: *arg=expr* (by stylistic convention, you do not put spaces around the equals sign in the argument list). The expression is evaluated once and only once when the function definition statement is executed. It is not re-executed every time the function is called. If the expression value is a mutable object (e.g., a list), it is shared by all the function invocations. Therefore, you need to be careful, because any changes you make to the object in place (such as using append( )) are then visible to future function calls. Here is some code that shows a default argument in action.

```
a = 2
def func(x=a):
    print x

func( )
func(1)
a = 3
func( )

2
1
2
```

In this example, the rebinding of a = 3 does not affect the binding in x=a in the function statement, because the x=a binding was executed first and is not re-executed on each function call. A typical idiom that you can use to cope with problems that can arise when trying to use an optional, mutable list argument is to create a new copy of the argument each time:

```
def manip(..., l=None):
    if l is None:
        l = [1,2,3]
    ...
```

A default value can depend only on variable names that are valid in the namespace when the function is defined—it cannot depend on the other arguments to the function. If you make an argument optional, all subsequent arguments in the function must also have default values.

Python has a richer syntax than Java for passing arguments when a function is called. At call time, you can include any argument in the call using the same *arg=expr* style. For example, the function func in the previous example could be called as func(x=3). This is called a *keyword* argument. Keyword arguments can be in any order (but must come after the standard arguments), and their expressions are passed to the appropriate argument.

The keyword argument syntax works for all user-defined functions, but unfortunately does not work for many of the Python built-in functions. You cannot use keyword arguments when calling a Java method from Jython, since ordinary Java compilation causes the loss of variable name information (there is a partial exception for constructors; see "Using Beans in Jython" in Chapter 8). If you have experience with calls to heavily overloaded Java methods with many arguments, you can see that appropriate use of defaults and keyword arguments can increase code readability and clarity for your Python code.

If you end a function's argument list with a name that has a * in front of it, such as *rest, rest captures in a tuple any excess arguments passed to the function. By using this syntax, a function can take a variable number of arguments. You can also have a second catch-all name at the end of your list, with ** in front. The double-star argument captures in a dictionary any keyword arguments that are not already specified in the argument list. If both of these argument types exist in the function, the tuple argument must come first.

Here is a summary of the complete function definition syntax:

```
def funid([arg,...[,*rest[,**kwargs]]])
    block
```

The following function will be used to make the syntax clearer:

```
def func(a, b=0, c="fred", *d, **e):
    print a, b, c, d, e
```

Ordinary arguments are bound left to right and defaults are filled in. Notice that the catch-all arguments are empty:

```
func(1, 2, 3)
func(1, 2)
func(1)

1 2 3 () {}
1 2 fred () {}
1 0 fred () {}
```

Keyword arguments are explicitly bound to the named argument after the ordinary arguments are bound from left to right. At the end of the call, all arguments (except the catch-alls) must have either a default, an ordinary argument, or a keyword argument. In the preceding code, the argument a must be bound either with a keyword argument, or by having the call start with an ordinary argument:

```
func(1, c=3)
func(1, 2, c=3)
func(b=2, a=1)

1 0 3 () {}
1 2 3 () {}
1 2 fred () {}
```

Finally, assuming that all the listed arguments are filled, the catch-all arguments grab any extras:

```
func(1, 2, 3, 4, 5, 6)
func(1, 2, c=12, f="hi", g="there")
func(1, 2, 3, 4, g="there")

1 2 3 (4, 5, 6) {}
1 2 12 () {'g': 'there', 'f': 'hi'}
1 2 3 (4,) {'g': 'there'}
```

Scoping Rules

Function definitions can be nested. The block of statements in a function definition (or class definition) are placed in a local scope in the same way that top-level statements are placed in the global scope. Ordinary control-flow statements and list comprehensions do not introduce new scopes.

From the beginning of time until Version 2.1, Python variable names were resolved this way:

1. If the name is bound by some name-binding statement in the current scope, all usage of that name in the scope refers to the binding in the local scope. This is enforced during the transparent compilation phase. If such a name is used at runtime before it is actually bound, this produces an error.

2. Otherwise, a possible binding of the name in the global scope is checked (at runtime) and if such a binding exists, this is used.

3. If there is no global binding, Python looks in the built-in namespace (which corresponds to the built-in module __builtin__). If this also fails, an error is issued.

Under these rules, there are only three scopes: local, global, and __builtin__. Scopes do not nest. Therefore, a function whose definition is nested inside another function cannot refer to itself recursively because its name is bound in the enclosing namespace, which is in neither the inner function's scope nor the global or built-in scopes. In addition, names in the enclosing namespace, but not in the global namespace, also cannot be used. The following code shows the potential for "gotchas."

```
def outerFunc(x, y):
    def innerFunc(z):
        if z > 0:
            print z, y
            innerFunc(z - 1)
    innerFunc(x)

outerFunc(3, "fred")
```

This code has two name errors that a Java programmer may not be expecting. The use of y in the print statement is a name error because y is only defined in the outerFunc scope, not in the local or global scope. The usual workaround in this case is to change the definition of innerFunc to def innerFunc(z, y=y):, which works but is undeniably awkward. Even with that workaround, the next line containing the call to innerFunc is also a name error for the same reason. In practice, this is not much of an issue (unless you use lambda expressions a lot, there is rarely a reason why functions need to be nested in Python).

With Version 2.2 of CPython, however, new rules will replace the old ones, allowing access from one scope to binding in the enclosing scopes in the way that a Java programmer would expect. The new rules can already be activated in Jython 2.1 and CPython 2.1 on a per-module basis, putting the following __future__ statement before any other statement in the module:*

```
from __future__ import nested_scopes
```

With the new rules, if a name is locally bound in a scope by some statement in that scope, then every use in the scope refers to this binding. If not, the binding is called *free*.

A free name, when used, refers to the binding in the nearest enclosing scope that contains a binding for that name, ignoring scopes introduced by class definition. If no such explicit binding exists at compile time, Python tries to resolve the name at runtime, first in the global scope and then in the built-in namespace.

The practical meaning of the new rule is that when it is created, an inner function gets a frozen copy of any referenced outer bindings (identifiers only—the values are not copied) as they exist at that time. With these rules, it is still impossible for the inner scope code to modify those outer bindings; using a name-binding statement simply creates a new local binding. In this way, Python diverges from most other languages with nested scopes. Under the new rules, the function outerFunc will work perfectly.

Under both sets of rules, you can always force a name to refer to the global/built-in binding, even if it occurs in a more local name-binding statement, by using the global declaration statement:

```
global name[,...]
```

---

* Future statements such as from __future__ import *feature*[,...] are both import statements and directives to the compiler to activate features that will become mandatory in a future release—part of the Python strategy for gradually introducing new features. They should appear before any conventional statements.

Flying First Class

We have already mentioned more than once that Python functions are first-class objects. They can be stored in variables, returned from other functions, and passed around the same as any other object. The function definition statement simply creates such an object and binds it to a name.

It is also possible to create a function object without binding it to a name using the lambda operator, which was briefly introduced in "Functional Programming" in Chapter 2. The syntax of a lambda is a little different from the def statement:

```
lambda args: expr
```

The argument list *args* has the same structure as the argument specifier of a def statement. Because lambda is an operator, not a statement, it can appear inside an expression and produces an anonymous function object. This function can be called like any other function. When called, it evaluates the expression *expr* using the actual values of the arguments and returns the obtained result. Therefore, the following bits of code are equivalent:

```
fun_holder = lambda args: expr
```

```
def fun_holder(args):
    return expr
```

And both versions are called using the syntax:

```
fun_holder(args)
```

We will use functions as first-class objects often throughout this book. However, the full implications for program design of having first-class functions are beyond our scope. We'll limit ourselves to some more reference material and two examples.

Python offers a built-in function that enables you to dynamically call a function object (or any callable object) with a computed set of arguments. This is useful in the case where you do not even know exactly how many or which arguments will be used at compile time. It is also useful at times when your arguments have been calculated in a sequence or dictionary, but the function being called expects the arguments separately. The syntax is:

```
apply(function[, args [, kwargs]])
```

where *args* should be a sequence specifying the positional arguments, and *kwargs* is a dictionary for the keyword arguments. Both are optional. For example, use the same function we used before:

```
def func(a, b=0, c="fred", *d, **e):
    print a, b, c, d, e
```

```
samefunc = func
samefunc(1, 2, 3)

t = (1, 2, 3)
kw1 = { "g": "hi" }

apply(samefunc, t)                #equivalent to samefunc(1, 2, 3)
apply(samefunc, t[:2], kw1)        #equivalent to samefunc(1, 2, g="hi")
apply(samefunc, (1,), {"b": "hi"})  #equivalent to samefunc(1, b="hi")

1 2 3 () {}
1 2 3 () {}
1 2 fred () {'g': 'hi'}
1 hi fred () {}
```

The sequence argument to apply is treated as though the arguments were listed one at a time and left to right. The dictionary argument to apply then works as though each key/value pair in the dictionary was called as a keyword argument.

In Jython 2.0 and later (CPython introduced this in 1.6), you can also pass sequences or dictionaries in the same "exploded" manner that apply uses by placing * for sequences or ** for dictionaries before the argument at call time. The arguments are applied to the function exactly as they would be in apply. So, the apply calls in the preceding code could also be written as:

```
samefunc(*t)
samefunc(*t[:2], **kw1)
samefunc(*(1,), **{"b": "hi"})
```

and would return the same results. This is purely syntactic sugar, but can sometimes be easier to read.

There is also a built-in module operator that defines corresponding functions for all Python operators, such as operator.add for the + operator. By combining apply and operator, you can mimic any set of static actions at runtime using dynamic functions or operators. The typical use of this module is to minimize the need to use lambda statements when using the reduce() function.

The following example shows how to construct a set of function objects dynamically for building some HTML text (in a rather simple-minded way) through the use of a helper function. The example shows how you might use nested function definitions, nested scopes, and first-class functions.

When the outer function is called, it constructs and returns a new function object. Each constructed function deals with a given tag, passed as a parameter to the helper function, and wraps its input between opening and closing versions of the tag, as defined in the outer function. Each constructed tag function can take as input any number of text fragments that will be concatenated and can set arbitrary attributes for the tag, through keyword arguments.

```
from __future__ import nested_scopes

def tag_fun_maker(tag):
    open = "<%s" % tag
    close = "</%s>" % tag
    def tagfunc(*content, **attrs):
        attrs = ['%s="%s"' % (key, value) for key, value in attrs.items()]
        attrs = ' '.join(attrs)
        return "%s %s>%s%s" % (open,attrs,''.join(content),close)
    return tagfunc

html = tag_fun_maker("html")
body = tag_fun_maker("body")
strong = tag_fun_maker("strong")
anchor = tag_fun_maker("a")

print html(body(
    "\n",
    anchor(strong("Hello World from Jython!"),
    href="http://www.jython.org"),
    "\n"))
<html ><body >
<a href="http://www.jython.org"><strong >Hello World from Jython!</strong></
a>
</body></html>
```

The main point of this example is that tag_fun_maker is able to create a function dynamically and return it. The example also parameterizes the created functions using the new nested scope rules, which cause the inner function to act as a lexical closure, able to refer to variables in the outer scopes as they existed when the function was created.

Here is an idiom borrowed from Smalltalk that you might call "do around." Sometimes, you have a resource that needs to be opened, used, and closed in a variety of places, which might cause you to repeat the open and close logic frequently. A typical example is a file.

```
def fileLinesDo(fileName, lineFunction):
    file = open(fileName, 'r')
    result = [lineFunction(each) for each in file.readlines()]
    file.close()
    return result
```

The key here is that you don't have to rewrite the open and close statements each time you use the file. This is a trivial point for files, but if we added error checking or had a more complicated resource, it would be very useful.

Import Statements and Packages

In Python, modules are either built-in (e.g., the sys module) or defined by external files, typically source files with a *.py* extension. Python comes with a set of external modules that form the Python standard library, which is mostly shared between Python and Jython. Most CPython modules written in Python work directly in Jython. The C extension modules for CPython that are written in C and not Python cannot be used from Jython, although some of these modules have been ported from C to Java.

External modules are retrieved from a path, which, like Java's classpath, is a set of directories. In Python, the path is stored as a list of strings in the sys.path attribute of the sys module (e.g., ['', 'C:\\.', 'e:\\jython\\Lib', 'e:\\jython']), which by default should point at the current working directory and at the Python standard library directory. The path can be changed for all your Jython modules by editing the Jython registry (see Appendix B). Also, the sys.path variable can be changed dynamically by Python code.

Python modules can be organized in packages using the directory structure in a manner similar to Java. But a subdirectory of one of the directories in sys.path is considered a package only if it contains an *__init__.py* Python source file and if all its parent directories do as well, up to but excluding the one in sys.path (there is no concrete default/root package in Python). The names of the packages (directories) in the chain down to the bottommost package (subdirectory) are separated by dots to form the qualified name of the package (e.g., foo1.foo2.foo4). A module gets a qualified name by appending its name (the filename without the *.py* extension) to the qualified name of its parent package (a top-level module has no parent package).

Jython 2.1 will also allow *.zip* and *.jar* archive files to be placed on the Python path. The exact specification is still not complete as of this writing (and may change due to a proposal to put similar functionality in CPython 2.2). However, the basic idea is that the files and directories compressed in the archive would be treated exactly as though they were an uncompressed part of the filesystem.

At runtime, first-class module objects are created for modules and packages by loading their *__init__.py* modules. The *__init__.py* file can contain statements that initialize the package, however, it is often completely empty and serves just as a marker. This is different from Java, in which packages do not have first-class status.

When loading a module, Python ensures that all its parent packages are loaded as well. Loading for a module happens once, and the loaded module and package objects are cached in a dictionary stored in sys.modules with their qualified names as keys.

When loaded, a package/module is bound with its name in its parent package's namespace (if there is a parent package). So, at runtime packages and modules are retrieved through normal attribute lookup. In Python, unlike Java, there is no name resolution against packages or of qualified names at compilation time. Name resolution takes place only at runtime. Requests for modules and packages to be loaded can be issued through import statements, which are name-binding statements executed at runtime.

When a module is loaded, and before the execution of its top-level code, the identifier __name__ is bound to the qualified name of the module in the module's global namespace. This allows you to access the name by which the module is called by the outside world. The case of a module passed as main script by directly invoking the interpreter is special; in that case, __name__ is always set to '__main__', and not to the actual name of the module. The following idiom is typical:

```
if __name__ == '__main__':
    ... # code
```

and is often used to put some test code in a library module, or to give it a working mode as a standalone utility. This idiom is roughly analogous to the special main() function in Java.

Import Statements

Import statements always ensure that their targets are compiled and loaded along with all the packages and the qualified name of the target. Moreover, except in the case of the main module called by invoking the interpreter, Jython catches the results of the transparent compilation that takes place when a module foo.py is loaded in the class file *foo$py.class*.

Python offers two different import statements: import and from. They differ in how they place the imported module within the calling module's namespace.

The syntax of import is:

```
import qualmod [as name][,...]
```

If *qualmod* specifies a bare module, this module is bound to its name in the current scope. Otherwise, the top package specified by *qualmod* is bound to its top-level name. For example, import foo.bar ensures that both the package foo and the module foo.bar are loaded and binds the name foo to the foo module object in the current scope. Then bar and its contents are accessible through attribute lookup. With as *name*, the target module (not the top package) is bound to *name*, and the top-level package is not bound at all.

The syntax of from is:

```
from qualmod import name1 [as alias1][,name2 ...]
```

The value of *qualmod.name1* is bound to *name1* in the current scope, or to *alias1* if that is specified. The qualmod itself is not bound in the current scope. These semantics mean that any later rebinding of *qualmod.name1* (for example, by reloading qualmod) will not affect *name1* in importing scope. By using the from statement, the names imported are accessible directly in the calling module without using the dot operator.

There is a special form of from:

```
from qualmod import *
```

This statement takes all the bindings in *qualmod* whose names do not start with '_', and binds them to the very same name in the current scope. If *qualmod.__all__* exists, it should be a list of strings, and then only the names listed there will be considered and bound.

At first, from statements may seem more convenient than import statements because the variable names are accessible directly, and you don't have to continually type the module name. However, you do need to be careful when using from. It is possible that a from ... import * statement could rebind things that you don't want rebound, such as the names of built-in functions. This is especially true if the from statement does not occur at the top of the module. Starting with Python 2.1, a correct __all__ attribute has been added to most modules in the standard library, but you should still pay attention to this problem with your own modules. In Python 2.2, or in Python 2.1 with nested scopes enabled, from ... import * statements are allowed only at the top level of a module because the result of the import is ambiguous in a nested scope if bindings from the imported module shadow an existing reference.

Also, because from statements create new name bindings separate from the module name bindings, you cannot see changes made in the imported module when it is reloaded. Although this is not usually a problem in running code, it can be a significant annoyance if you are developing using an interactive session—you will continually find that modules are not seeing other module changes.

Both import and from work by calling a built-in special function __import__, which looks like this:

```
__import__(moduleName[, globals [, locals [, fromlist]]])
```

Internally, Python converts import and from statements to an __import__ call. The arguments are a string for the fully qualified name of the module to be imported, dictionaries of current global and local namespace bindings, and the list of items to import, if the statement is a from.* If the call is from ... import *, the last argument is ['*']. Then the function imports the module represented by *moduleName* and returns the top-level package if *fromlist* is empty, and the bottom-level package if it is not. The actual binding of names is left to Python and is not performed by the function.

You can call this function directly in your programs to dynamically control module import—for example, to load modules one at a time to a test suite. You can even substitute this function with your own custom import function by rebinding __builtin__.__import__. In Jython, this can also be used to import Java classes and packages.

Importing Java Classes

Jython also allows access to Java classes and packages through the import statements. Jython is able to load classes through the underlying Java Virtual Machine (JVM), both from the Java classpath and from the directories in sys.path. Conceptually, you can think that for the purpose of loading Java classes, the directories in sys.path have been appended to the classpath. This means there is no need to mark Java packages on sys.path with __init__.py modules, because that would make them Python packages.

Python packages and modules take precedence over Java packages. On the other hand, Java classes in a shadowed Java package can still be loaded from the shadowing Python module.

Because it is not possible to ask the JVM directly through a Java API on which Java packages can be potentially loaded, Jython scans the available *.jar* files at startup and scans the candidate directories for Java packages and classes at runtime. The information obtained from *.jar* files is cached between sessions. All this is done to properly interpret import statements that can trigger loading of Java classes or packages. You'll notice that if you add a *.jar* file to your classpath, then the next time you start Jython, you'll see a message that the new file has been identified.

In Java, import statements are a matter of name resolution at compilation time. We have already seen that the Python model is different; import statements, even for packages, bind names to concrete objects at runtime.

---

* The dictionaries are ignored by the built-in version, except for the global bindings used to retrieve the importing package's __name__. This name information is used to implement package-relative imports, a feature whose usage is discouraged. If you call the function directly and want to supply a *fromlist*, {} is a fine placeholder for both.

To fit Java loading in this overall model, Jython creates module-like, unique concrete objects (instances of the internal org.python.core. PyJavaPackage class) for Java packages.

A statement such as:

```
import java.lang
```

will bind java in the current scope to the module-like object for the Java package *java*. Moreover, this namespace object will map lang to the *java. lang* package. You can then access the String class by referring to it as java. lang.String. The Java feature of having the java.lang classes automatically imported does not work in Jython. However, the statement import java will give access to any class in the standard Java library, provided you fully qualify the name (such as java.util.List).

Java classes are wrapped by Jython in objects that mimic both Python-like class behavior and the original Java class behavior. A binding to this wrapper object will be set up by Jython in the module object for the package when import is requested.

All this has implications for the overhead of a statement such as from *javapkg* import *. This kind of statement creates wrappers for all the classes in *javapkg* and binds to them both in the current scope and in the *javapkg* namespace. Although technically, in this special case the wrappers do not load the Java classes immediately, but rather, lazily as needed. However, it is not a good idea to use from *javapkg* import * for Java packages liberally in production code, as one might avoid using import javapkg.* in Java (actually, that's against the Sun coding guidelines in Java, as well). The from *javapakg* import * statement can be a useful feature, for example, when experimenting in an interactive session.

Auto-loading through lookup

In Java you can always refer to a class by using its fully qualified name without the need for a previous import statement. Given what we have explained about Python import statements, this is not true in Jython, but Jython does offer a shortcut.

If you need to refer to your.favorite.UsefulClass, you do not need an import your.favorite.UsefulClass first. You can simply import the top package your with import your, and then you can use attribute lookup to reach your.favorite.UsefulClass and also your.favorite.InvisibleClass, and so on. For example, you can get access to most of the Java classes by merely using the statement import java. Subpackages can then be accessed using the dot operator.

```
import java
x = java.util.Vector
print x
```

This syntax works because in Jython, attribute lookup on a Java package object triggers loading as necessary. Jython behaves the same way for the import of Python packages, but it should be noted that this feature is not offered by CPython, so it is not portable.

Reload

A nice feature of Python is its support for dynamically reloading modules through the reload built-in function:

```
reload(mod)
```

The reload function takes a module *mod* and executes the top-level statements in its (possibly changed) corresponding file, reusing *mod* as global scope, after it has been emptied. The function then returns the possibly altered and reinitialized *mod*. Reload is most frequently used during development, when you might be continually testing a module as you change its source. To have the Python interactive interpreter recognize the changes, you need to reload the module. Reload can also be useful in the context of an application that needs to be dynamically reconfigured or upgraded at runtime.

It should be noted that reload does not operate recursively on the modules imported by *mod*, and that all the bindings to old values originally from *mod* in other modules remain in place. Code has access to the new values after reload only if it uses attribute lookup. Specifically, a module that imported some values from *mod* through from ... import * will keep the unaffected values. Also, instances of a class defined in *mod* will not be affected by the possibly changed definition. Jython also ships with the jreload module that offers some support for reloading Java classes.

CHAPTER 5

Object-Oriented Jython

Python is an object-oriented scripting language. There is a design tension hidden in that description. Object-oriented languages generally have a number of features designed to enforce access control and encapsulation. Scripting languages, on the other hand, tend to avoid such features, reasoning that they are needlessly restrictive and hamper the programmer. If you've ever cursed out other programmers because they hid vital functionality without allowing access, you understand the appeal.

The Python solution to this tangle is a simple and elegant semantic model that enables object-oriented structures to harmonize with the language features already discussed with a minimum of extra syntax. Python's simple, clear, object-oriented semantics allow you to focus on creating the right modular, object-oriented design without having to make compromises in your design to satisfy language requirements.

In this chapter, we will discuss object-oriented programming in Jython, and show how the Python scripting language helps you use Jython to support good object-oriented design principles. There are a number of things that you can do in Python that you cannot easily do in Java, and there are one or two structures that are common in Java but are difficult in Python. We'll also see how to get your own Python classes to behave like the built-in types.

Creating Classes

Classes are created in Python using the aptly named class statement. To declare a class with no parent classes, the general syntax is:

```
class ClassName:
    block
```

The class name can be any legal identifier, although by convention class names are usually capitalized. Like the def statement does with functions, class builds a class object and assigns it to the name provided. The block can be any combination of Python statements. The statements inside a class block are generally (but do not have to be) name-binding statements, meaning assignment statements and def statements.

The most minimal use of the class statement looks like this:

```
class MyClass:
    pass
```

This is a perfectly legal Python statement to create a class. Type it into the Jython interpreter, and then type MyClass, and you'll get something like the following:

```
>>> MyClass
<class __main__.MyClass at 3352458>
```

So, we've created a class. But what exactly has been created internally? In fact, what we've done is create another namespace, in many respects identical to the one created when a module is imported. (As we'll see, Python manages most of its object-oriented structures by creating and manipulating namespaces.) In fact, the new namespace is accessible to the programmer. To get at the namespace associated with a class, you access the special attribute __dict__ using ordinary dot notation.

```
>>> MyClass.__dict__
{'__module__': '__main__', '__doc__': None}
```

Even though you've put nothing in MyClass, Python has made some class meta-information available. The __module__ attribute contains the fully qualified name of the module where the class is defined—in this case, because the class is being defined at the interactive prompt, that is '__main__'. And the __doc__ attribute contains the documentation string for the class. Because we didn't include a doc string, the value is None. These values are also accessible by using the special attributes __module__ and __doc__, respectively.

The class name is always available by using the special attribute __name__.

```
>>> MyClass.__name__
'MyClass'
```

We can now create instances of MyClass. In Python, instances are constructed by calling the class as though it were a function:

```
>>> x = MyClass()
>>> x
<__main__.MyClass instance at 6826866>
```

In creating the new instance, Python creates another namespace, essentially identical in function to the class and module namespaces but with a special relationship to the class namespace that we'll be discussing in detail. Instances have two special attributes. You can refer back to the class itself by using _class_, and you can see the contents of the instance namespace by using the special attribute _dict_. You can also use the built-in method isinstance(object, class) to determine class membership at runtime.

```
>>> x._class_
<class _main_.MyClass at 3352458>

>>> x._dict_
{}

>>> isinstance(x, MyClass)
1
```

The instance namespace is empty because nothing has been put there yet. So far, of course, this is lacking in any functionality because nothing has been added to the class definition.

 CPython 2.2, in late beta as of this writing, contains the beginning of a significant overhaul to the internals of the Python class system. The primary goal of this restructuring is to allow Python built-in types to behave like classes (for example, allowing direct subclassing). Along the way, there are some additional augmentations to the class system. Although the new class structures are optional and will live together with classic classes in CPython 2.2 (you can create classes of either type), it is expected that they will eventually become the default in subsequent releases. It is assumed that Jython will add the features when Jython 2.2 is released. Some of those changes will be noted in this chapter, however the specifics are still being debated as of this writing.

Methods

Behavior within classes is created by defining methods inside classes. Methods are defined using def statements within the class block. The def statement behaves exactly as it would if it was at the top level of a module, only instead of binding the function object to the module namespace, the function is bound to the class namespace. Methods are called using dot notation. The following example contains a more elaborate class description:

```
class MyClass:

    def _init_(self, initialValue=0):
        self.counter = initialValue
```

```
    def incrementCounter(self, amountToIncrement=1):
        self.counter += amountToIncrement
```

This example creates two methods, __init__ and incrementCounter, within MyClass, which we can confirm by looking at the class dictionary:

```
print MyClass.__dict__
```

```
{'incrementCounter': <function incrementCounter at 7519783>, '__module__':
'__main__', '__init__': <function __init__ at 2225008>, '__doc__': None}
```

The functions are now in the class namespace with the special variables. The __init__ function is the first of many special overloading methods that we will see. These methods are hooks that Python uses to allow user-created classes to behave like built-in classes and types. The __init__ method, if it exists, is called on instance creation to initialize the new instance—essentially, it's a constructor. The arguments to __init__ are passed from the constructing call as if you were calling __init__ directly. Therefore, the following code creates a new instance x and sets the counter to 3:

```
x = MyClass(3)
print x.counter
```

```
3
```

Now that x exists, instance methods and variables can be called on it using the dot notation, like so:

```
x.incrementCounter()
print x.counter
print x.__dict__
```

```
4
{'counter': 4}
```

Notice that the __dict__ for x contains only the variable counter, and not the methods. When encountering an attribute expression involving an instance, Python first looks in that instance's __dict__ for the attribute. If the attribute is not found, Python searches the namespace of the parent class (methods are handled slightly differently, as explained later in this section). In this case, incrementCounter is a function object in the parent class, and so the function call is directed to that object, while counter is a data attribute of the instance itself.

You've probably noticed what appears to be an anomaly between the class definition and the class usage. The incrementCounter function is defined with one argument, self, however it is called with no arguments. Similarly, __init__ is defined with two arguments, but we supply just one in the method call. And you may have noticed that we haven't exactly explained how Python knows to put some variables in the instance namespace, but not others.

The trick here lies in what the Python interpreter does when it encounters a method call of the form x.incrementCounter(3). The method call is handled in two parts—first a lookup of the method name, and second a call to the callable object returned by the lookup.

The lookup of a method from an instance is handled slightly differently from an attribute lookup. If the method is not defined in the instance namespace (and it usually isn't), the Python interpreter looks in the class namespace just as it does for attributes. However, rather than return the function object from the class namespace directly, Python returns a *method object*. A method object has two attributes—the function it encapsulates, and the instance it was called with. If the method object is retrieved from a lookup on an instance, the method is said to be *bound*.

In the case of x.incrementCounter(3), the instance namespace for x does not have an entry for incrementCounter. However, the class namespace for MyClass does have a function in that slot. So, the Python interpreter returns a bound method object with the incrementCounter function of MyClass, and the instance x.

Having retrieved a method object from the lookup, Python proceeds to call the method object. A bound method automatically places its instance at the front of the argument list, then calls the encapsulated function with the new, longer argument list. So, the instance call x.incrementCounter(3) results in the actual function incrementCounter being called with an argument list of (x, 3).

By these rules, the first argument to *any* Python method when it is defined is the instance being called. By long-standing and near-unanimous convention, this argument is named self, but the naming convention is not enforced by the interpreter. (It will be enforced by other people who read your code, however.)

Armed with that knowledge, we can now see how attributes are created and modified. In the __init__ method, the line of code assigns to a value in the self object, which is the instance being created—the actual creation happens before __init__ is called. As with any other line of Python code, the assignment self.counter = initialValue creates the variable in a namespace on assignment—in this case, in the instance namespace of the new object. An implication of this is that the self notation is required to access items within the instance. This is different from Java, where the this keyword is not required.

Because we've mentioned *bound* methods, you may be wondering if you can create an *unbound* method. Unbound methods have no attached instance, and they are created by doing a method lookup directly on the class instead of any specific instance. When an unbound method is called, the instance needs to be explicitly supplied in the argument list.

In other words, the following two lines of code are completely identical in functionality, the first using a bound method and the second using an unbound method:[*]

```
x.incrementCounter(3)

MyClass.incrementCounter(x, 3)
```

Methods are first-class objects and can be passed as variable values in either format.

```
unboundMethod = MyClass.incrementCounter
unboundMethod(x, 3)

boundMethod = x.incrementCounter
boundMethod(3)
```

Again, notice that the unbound and bound versions of the method each take a different number of arguments—the unbound version calls the function directly from the class namespace, while the bound version needs to have the instance as its first argument. Attempting to call an unbound method with an instance not of the same class or of a subclass will raise an exception—unbound methods still carry information about their classes with them.

Sometimes people erroneously see the need to explicitly specify the instance in the method argument list as evidence that object-oriented programming is somehow "tacked on" to Python. In fact, the namespace mechanism elegantly unifies objects and modules, giving object-oriented behavior with a bare minimum of syntactic clutter or complicated data structures. Java class implementations are far more complex. The advantage for Python is that the simpler semantic model—everything is essentially a namespace—makes program behavior easy to predict from just a few basic concepts. As for typing self all the time, it is another example of Python gently enforcing good programming practice, by explicitly distinguishing instance and local variables.

---

[*] Actually, they are not identical if you have explicitly re-bound the method name to a new function within the instance namespace—although doing that frequently is not recommended.

Classes, Instances, and Access Control

Python's model for the use of class attributes is substantially different from Java's. In addition, Python chooses not to allow strict language-mandated access control within objects. These features can be surprising to a Java programmer. This section will explain the differences between Python and Java objects, and will offer some reasons why you'll enjoy the Python way.

Class and Static Attributes

So far, we have only seen functions defined within a class block. Variables can also be created inside a class block with ordinary assignment statements. These variables behave like Java static variables. The variable binding belongs to the class object itself, and can be accessed by any instance of the class. You can also access the variable in the class namespace directly by explicitly using the class name and the dot operator.

```
class MyClass:

    instancesCreated = 0

    def __init__(self, initialValue=0):
        MyClass.instancesCreated += 1
        self.value = initialValue

x = MyClass()
print x.instancesCreated
y = MyClass()
print x.instancesCreated
print MyClass.instancesCreated

1
2
2
```

The line instancesCreated = 0 is executed once when the class is defined, and creates the variable in the class namespace. Every time a new instance is created, the MyClass.instancesCreated += 1 line will increment the variable in the class namespace. The constructor also creates an ordinary instance variable named value in the self object. Once the variable instancesCreated is created, it can be accessed either by directly referencing the class name, as in the last line of the previous example, or by referencing the instance, as in the line before that. If referenced through the instance, Python looks in the class namespace only after checking that there is no binding with that name in the instance namespace.

Unlike Java static variables, each instance does not refer statically to the variable. Instead, all instances share access to the same class namespace when an instance lookup fails. An implication of this rule is that if you create an instance attribute of the same name (such as self.instancesCreated in the previous example), the instance attribute will shadow the class variable.

Static methods are a different matter. There is no way in Python to create a direct analog of a Java static method. (You also cannot create an analog of a class method, such as that used in other object-oriented languages, like Smalltalk.) The nature of Python methods explains why. The method call always consumes the first argument of a method for the instance. So, to call a method you need an instance, which rules out both static methods (which don't have an instance) and Smalltalk-style class methods (which use the class rather than an instance). This is less of an issue than you might think, however, because Python does allow top-level functions that are not part of any class. In most cases, that is a suitable alternative for both static or class methods.

 CPython 2.2 will have a mechanism to allow both static methods (methods bound to a class that don't require an instance to be called) and class methods (methods that take a class object as the first argument rather than an instance) to be explicitly created within the class. A more user-friendly syntax is still under discussion as of this writing. Presumably, Jython will pick up the syntax or at least the functionality for the Jython 2.2 release.

Access Control

You have probably noticed the lack of access control keywords such as private and public in the Python examples. In fact, Python offers no explicit support for access control—all attributes and methods are, by Java standards, public. Python does offer a variety of mechanisms to signal the intention to make an attribute or method private, however, any of these mechanisms can be subverted by sufficiently motivated programmers.

The simplest mechanism is one of social agreement. By convention, any attribute or method name that begins with an underscore is flagged as private, or at least "use at your own risk." Although there is no interpreter support for protection here, the underscore indicates to other Python programmers that the attribute or method is not intended for outside use.

If that is not strong enough for you, you can build a slightly higher fence around your private attributes by starting them with double underscores. Inside a class definition, the Python interpreter will name-mangle a name such as __identifier to read _className__identifier. That's underscore, classname, double underscore, identifier name. Within the class, that's not an issue because all occurences of __identifier will also be mangled. However, outside the class, the name is not automatically mangled, so the double-underscore form cannot be used directly to access the identifier—the full mangled version can still be used, though. The following example demonstrates:

```
class MyClass:

    def __init__(self):
        self._private = 1
        self.__reallyprivate = 2

    def printPrivateValues(self):
        print self._private, self.__reallyprivate

x = MyClass()
x.printPrivateValues()
print x._private
try:
    print x.__reallyprivate
except:
    print "No attribute named x.__reallyprivate"
print x._MyClass__reallyprivate

1 2
1
No attribute named x.__reallyprivate
2
```

Within MyClass, both _private and __reallyprivate are available. Outside the class, _private is available, but __reallyprivate is not. The fully mangled form _MyClass__reallyprivate must be used to access __reallyprivate. While this is not exactly bulletproof protection, one would hope that having to type the full mangled name (not to mention probably having to look up the format) would give any Python programmer pause before using the variable.

If you learned OOP in Java, the lack of strict encapsulation in Python probably worries you (especially if you were already worried by the dynamic typing). Python operates on the principle that the programmers will know what they are doing when calling other classes, and bars them as little as possible from using the classes as desired. It's easy to see the potential problems, but the problems occur far less often in actual practice than you might expect, especially with even minimal attention to naming conventions and documentation. For one thing, incorrect use of a class often causes large, obvious, and quickly fixable problems. An incorrect usage that causes subtle, unnoticed bugs is relatively rare in practice. The best way to avoid those bugs is with good unit testing.

In return for the lack of access control complexity, there are many benefits. Code reuse in general is much more easily managed in Python than Java. Specifically, it's easier to subclass when you don't have to worry about what important functionality might have been declared private or, worse yet, final. Unit testing in Python is noticeably easier to manage than Java—even allowing for the fact that Python tests often include tests for type information. In fact, some Extreme Programming gurus suggest that privacy be used very minimally, even within Java, to facilitate testing.

Get and Set Methods

The common Java idiom of having a private attribute coupled with a get method and a set method is rarely seen in Python. This is especially true for the most common Java case, where the get and set are simple one-line functions that do no checking. While it's possible to do something like this:

```
class BadPythonStyle:

    def __init__(self):
        self.__attribute = 0

    def getAttribute(self):
        return self.__attribute

    def setAttribute(self, value):
        self.__attribute = value
```

it's considered highly redundant—in most cases, the Python programmer will just assign to self.attribute without the underscores and expect other classes to use attribute directly. (It's sometimes hard to take Java encapsulation seriously when it encourages, and sometimes requires, a style that allows complete access to an allegedly private attribute.)

However, you will often want to do some specific checking before setting an attribute, or some additional processing before getting one. While you can, of course, create methods for all of this, it is sometimes awkward to have, say, all the class data accessible via attributes, except for one attribute that requires an explicit set method call and a different one that requires an explicit get method call. Python provides two hooks to allow additional processing for attribute access. They are the special methods __getattr__ and __setattr__.

Using __getattr__

The __getattr__ method, if it exists, is called instead of raising an error on any attribute access lookup that fails. It should either return an object or raise an AttributeError. You can use __getattr__ to associate a get function with an attribute name—just remember that the actual attribute in the class must have a different name, because __getattr__ is called only on failed lookups. This admittedly somewhat contrived example uses an accessor function to convert the internal integer to a float:

```
class AssociateFunction:

    def __init__(self):
        self._thing = 1

    def getThing(self):
        return float(self._thing)

    def __getattr__(self, attribute):
        if attribute == "thing":
            return self.getThing()
        else:
            raise AttributeError(attribute)
x = AssociateFunction()
print x.thing
print x.nothing
```

```
1.0
Traceback (innermost last):
  File "C:\Noel\jython book\test.py", line 17, in ?
AttributeError: instance of 'AssociateFunction' has no attribute 'nothing'
```

In this example, the attempted access of x.thing initially fails because the name thing is not bound in the instance or class namespaces. Because of this, __getattr__ is called, and the if statement returns true, calling self.getThing(). Note that when x.nothing is called, the exception is raised as always. The internal attribute cannot also be named thing because then the attribute lookup would not fail. Obviously, in this case the user could call getThing directly. But it's sometimes useful stylistically to ensure that there is an attribute syntax way of getting at the instance's data. Typically, if you were doing this kind of association on a larger scale you would have a dictionary mapping of attributes to functions rather than a long if statement.

Mere function mapping only scratches the surface of what you can do with the __getattr__ function. One common usage of __getattr__ is to simply provide a default value for any errant lookup:

```
class GetAttrExample:

    def __init__(self):
        self.attribute = 3

    def __getattr__(self, attribute):
        return 0

x = GetAttrExample()
```

```
print x.attribute
print x.fred

3
0
```

In this example, __getattr__ is invoked on the attempted access of x.fred and returns zero.

Another common usage is to redirect the access call to a different object. This example uses an internal dictionary to allow dynamic creation of variables that can then be used as though they were attributes:

```
class DynamicAttributes:

    def __init__(self, **args):
        self.vals = args

    def __getattr__(self, attribute):
        return self.vals[attribute]

x = DynamicAttributes(fred="flintstone", barney="rubble")
print x.fred
print x.barney
x.vals["george"] = "jetson"
print x.george

flintstone
rubble
jetson
```

In the previous code snippet, we set up only one explicit attribute—a dictionary called vals. The keyword attributes are dropped directly into the dictionary through use of the ** argument. Any attribute lookup on anything other than vals will go through __getattr__, which redirects to a simple directory lookup. Finally, we can add new items directly to the vals dictionary and have them be usable using attribute syntax. Of course, if the proxy object is as simple as the DynamicAttributes class, you could just write directly to the __dict__ variable rather than use vals or __getattr__.

Using __setattr__

On the flipside, __setattr__ works slightly differently. If it is defined, it is called on every attempt to set an attribute in that class, whether or not the attribute already exists. Also, the actual variable setting within the method __setattr__ should directly access the __dict__ for the instance—attempting an ordinary self.*attribute* attribute set within __setattr__ could result in an infinite loop. And remember, any use of __setattr__ can be easily confounded by having the user of the class bypass it and directly set the __dict__.

One simple use of __setattr__ is to make instances immutable (as long as the users don't access __dict__):

```
class Immutable:

    def __init__(self, **args):
        for key, value in args.items():
            self.__dict__[key] = value

    def __setattr__(self, name, value):
        raise TypeError, "Cannot change values: %s" % name

x = Immutable(one=1)
print x.one
x.one = 2
```

```
1
Traceback (innermost last):
  File "C:\Noel\jython book\test.py", line 12, in ?
  File "C:\Noel\jython book\test.py", line 8, in __setattr__
TypeError: Cannot change values: one
```

All attribute sets for this class are routed through the __setattr__ method, which just raises an exception (using a pass statement is another option; in that case, the class will just silently not change the value of the attribute).

Because __setattr__ is called for all attributes if it exists, if you are redirecting setting by attribute name you also need to ensure that ordinary assignment takes place for unaffected attributes.

```
class SetFunction:

    def __init__(self):
        self.integerAttribute = 12
        self.otherAttribute = "herman"

    def setIntegerAttribute(self, value):
        value = int(value)
        if value < 0:
            value *= -1
        self.__dict__["integerAttribute"] = value

    def __setattr__(self, name, value):
        if name == "integerAttribute":
            self.setIntegerAttribute(value)
        else:
            self.__dict__[name] = value

x = SetFunction()
x.otherAttribute = -3
print x.otherAttribute
```

```
x.integerAttribute = -3
print x.integerAttribute
```

```
-3
3
```

In the SetFunction example, the assignment to integerAttribute is redirected to the setIntegerAttribute function. Two important things to notice about this program are the final line of setIntegerAttribute, which assigns directly to __dict__. If the final line was self.integerAttribute = value, the code would enter an infinite loop. The final two lines of __setattr__ ensure that even if the attribute does not have a special setting function, it can still be set by client code—the assignment to x.otherAttribute takes place here.

 CPython 2.2 will change this setup somewhat. In the new optional class structure in CPython 2.2, the new hook function __getattribute__ is added. This function will always be called on attribute lookup if it exists, instead of being called only after a failed lookup (__getattr__ can still be used as before). More significantly, CPython 2.2 will allow separate individual getter and setter methods to create a specific attribute (even if the attribute doesn't physically exist in the __dict__), reducing the need to have a long if statement in the __getattr__ method.

Inheritance

Python allows a class to inherit from any number of base classes. Jython allows you to additionally inherit from Java classes, but adds the restriction that you can only inherit from, at most, one Java class. You can inherit from a Python class or classes as well as the Java class. You specify the parent class or classes by using a parenthesized list in the class statement, like so:

```
class ChildClass(ParentClass1, ParentClass2, ...)
```

The sequence of parent classes is available at runtime by using the special attribute __bases__ on the class object.

As you might expect, given the description of Python's object-oriented semantics so far, inheritance is managed with a minimum of extra syntax and semantic clutter. Inheriting from a parent class gives two separate but related pieces of functionality. First, and most importantly, the child class gets access to the parent class namespace. This is accomplished by a simple extension to the lookup rule for instances and classes. After looking in the instance and class namespaces, Python will continue to search through the base classes until a binding is found or until it runs out of namespaces. To resolve potential ambiguity among multiple base classes Python searches the base class list depth-first, starting from the leftmost entry in the list and its base classes, then moving right until a binding is found.* This code will hopefully clarify:

```
class LivingThing:
    def isAlive(self):
        print "Living Things are Alive"

class Animal(LivingThing):
    def canMove(self):
        print "Animals can move"

class ProgrammingLanguage:
    def isAlive(self):
        print "Programming languages are not alive"

class Python(ProgrammingLanguage, Animal):
    def isSlithery(self):
        print "Pythons slither"

x = Python()
x.isSlithery()
x.canMove()
x.isAlive()
```

Pythons slither
Animals can move
Programming languages are not alive

In the multiple inheritance example, the class Python inherits from ProgrammingLanguage and Animal. The complete lookup list would be Python, ProgammingLanguage, Animal, LivingThing. This is shown in the print statements, where isSlithery() is found in the Python class, and canMove() is found by moving up the hierarchy and getting to the Animal class. For isAlive(), there is a potential conflict, because the method is defined in both ProgrammingLanguage and LivingThing. However, moving from left to right, the method is found in ProgrammingLanguage first, so that is the method that is called.

As in any programming language, the use of multiple inheritance comes with a warning label because of its potential for code that is hard to understand and maintain. It's best to limit multiple inheritance to small "mixin" classes that add functionality that might be desired by a number of classes not otherwise related (sometimes these are called *aspects*). This is a case where you would often define an interface in Java—in Python, you can

---

* The new class semantics of CPython 2.2 will change this mechanism for new-style classes, but not for classic classes.

inherit code and data, not just claim to inherit the method names.* It's also not unheard of to define a class as just a combination of mixins, and need no additional functionality (especially in something like a GUI framework), which is indicated by just having a pass for the class body:

```
class PrintableTextBox(TextBox, Printable):
    pass
```

The other feature that comes along with inheriting from another class is that the child class can be used wherever the parent class is used. This is similar to the behavior you get as a child class in Java, but in Python there are fewer cases where the interpreter cares what class you are. The most notable is that a subclass instance can be attached to an unbound method of the parent class. So, in the previous code example, you could legally write Animal.canMove(x). In addition, the isinstance(*obj*,*class*) built-in will return true if the instance is of a subclass of the given class. There is also a built-in method issubclass(*class1*, *class2*), which returns true if *class1* is a subclass of *class2*.

Because a Python class can have more than one parent class, there is no analog to Java's super keyword. If you need to get at a parent attribute directly, you need to use the parent class name explicitly; if you need to call a parent method directly, you need to call it as an unbound method and pass the child instance in the instance slot. Most commonly, this needs to be done with __init__. Python does not implicitly call any parents' __init__ method from a child class, mostly because figuring out the right thing in case of multiple inheritance is best left to the programmer. Continuing the animal example earlier in this section, the Python class could be rewritten to call the other isAlive function:

```
class Python(ProgrammingLanguage, Animal):
    def isSlithery(self):
        print "Pythons slither"

    def isAlive(self):
        return Animal.isAlive(self)
```

Special Methods

Python does not have a top-level class in the place of Java's Object class. This is partially because so much of Python's functionality is defined by the basic types and built-in methods, and also because Python is dynamically

---

* Although Python has no direct use for interfaces in the Java sense because all name binding is done at runtime, there is a concrete proposal for an interface-like mechanism that would query whether an object implements a related suite of methods and allow some type safety. To date, nothing has come of the efforts.

typed. Python allows user-defined classes to override default behavior for relevant built-in methods, operators, and keywords through the use of *special methods*. These special methods act as hooks that the Python interpreter uses to call a user-defined instance for its special behavior. We've already seen a few special methods: __init__ is invoked during instance creation, and __getattr__ and __setattr__ are invoked during attribute access. Special method names always begin and end with double underscores. Special methods are always optional—classes that don't define them will just exhibit default behavior.

Using special methods well enables your classes to have the look and feel of Python's built-in types, and allows you the convenience of, for example, using + instead of add( ) for your list-like types.

General Instance Special Methods

The following special methods override behavior common to all Python objects:

__init__(self, *args*...)
Called on instance creation.

__del__(self)
Called when an instance is no longer used, similar to a Java finalizer in that the exact time of the call to __del__ cannot be determined.

__str__(self)
Called by the str( ) built-in and by print. Similar to the Java Object. toString( ). This method is intended to display a human-readable string representation of the object. Must return a string. If this function does not exist, __repr__ is tried.

__repr__(self)
Called by the built-in function repr( ), and also used to represent an object during stack traceback on error reporting and for reporting results in an interactive session. This is supposed to be a machine-readable representation of the object—meaning a Python expression suitable for being used to recreate the object, if possible. Otherwise, is it typically of the form '<*useful info*>'. Must return a string.

__cmp__(self, other)
Generic comparison operator, called whenever a comparison is needed between this object and another. If both instances define different __cmp__ methods, the method of the object on the left side is called. This method should return 0 if self == other, 1 if self > other, and -1 if self < other. Broadly similar to the Java Comparable.compareTo( ), but see the next item for another option.

__lt__(self, other), __le__(self, other), __eq__(self, other), __ne__(self, other), __gt__(self, other), __ge__(self, other)

Rich comparison functions for use with a specific comparison operator. Again, the method for the instance on the lefthand side of the equation is called. The methods are tied to the operators <, <=, ==, !=, >, and =>, respectively, based on the common two-letter representation of each operator. These methods are called in preference to __cmp__ if they exist. These methods can return any kind of value (that's why they are called rich comparisons), or the special built-in object NotImplemented to notify lack of support for a pair of supplied arguments.

If none of the equality methods (__cmp__, __eq__, __ne__) is defined for a class, object identity is used for the equality comparison.

__hash__(self)

Called by the built-in function hash( ), and also used as the hash value for keying within a dictionary. Similar to Java's Object.hashCode( ). The method must be defined such that for two instances x and y, if x == y, x.__hash__() == y.__hash__( ). This should be true no matter which method is used to define equality. Classes that have a __cmp__ method but not a __hash__ method cannot be used as dictionary keys. The hash value must be immutable, usually meaning that the instance is immutable.

__nonzero__(self)

Called to determine the truth value of the object—for example, the line if x: . should return 1 or 0. If this method does not exist, Python tries to call __len__ interpreting a 0 length as false. If that method does not exist, all instances of the class are considered true.

__getattr__(self, name)

Called such that for any attribute lookup x.name is the equivalent of x.__getattr__(name). Only called if the attribute lookup fails using the normal namespace mechanism.

__setattr__(self, name, value)

If defined, called such that an attribute assignment x.name = value becomes x.__setattr__("name", value). Also name is passed in as a string. The actual sets within __setattr__ must go directly to __dict__ to avoid infinite recursion.

__delattr__(self, name)

Called on del obj.name.

__call__(self, args...)

Allows your instance to emulate a callable function object. The line of code obj(args...) is translated to obj.__call__(args...). If this method does not exist, calling the object as a function raises an error.

Sequences and Mappings

The following methods let your class use sequence and mapping syntax for access:

__len__(self)
> Called by the built-in function len( ). May also be called to determine truth value of an object if __nonzero__ is not defined.

__getitem__(self, key)
> Invoked by the line x[key], which triggers the call x.__getitem__(key). If __getitem__ is not defined, x[key] raises a syntax error. For mappings, key can potentially be any object. For sequences, key can be either an integer or a slice object. If an integer key is out of bounds for the sequence, an IndexError should be raised—this allows for loops to behave properly.

> The __getitem__ function is expected to be able to handle as keys both integers and *slice objects*. A slice object is what gets passed to __getitem__ when the sequence is called with slice syntax—for example, list[2:3]. Slice objects can be explicitly created using the built-in function slice(start=0, stop, step=1).

__setitem__(self, key, value)
> Invoked by x[key] = value. The key types are the same as in __getitem__.

__delitem__(self, key)
> Invoked by the line del self[key]. Types as in __getitem__.

__contains__(self, item)
> Called for the membership test item in x. If this method does not exist, membership test is performed by looping through the sequence. Therefore, you need to define this method only if there is a faster or more efficient mechanism for the class.

In addition to the special methods, user-defined classes that emulate sequences or mappings should also override any relevant sequence or mapping methods as defined in the sections "Sequences: Lists and Tuples" and "Mappings and Dictionaries" in Chapter 2.

Numbers

Each binary arithmetic operator has three separate special methods. The basic one is called when the instance is on the left side of the equation. Another version, prefixed with the letter r, is called if the instance is on the right side of the equation, and the object on the left side does not define the operations. A third version, prefixed with the letter i, is called when the instance is on the left side of an augmented assignment using that operation. For example, the + operator defines the special methods __add__, __radd__, and __iadd__. These are called as follows (where y is an object that does not define addition):

```
x + y      # calls x.__add__(y)

y + x      # calls x.__radd__(y) - only if y does not define addition

x += y     # calls x.__iadd__(y)
```

The binary operators and their special methods are displayed in Table 5-1.

Table 5-1. Binary operators and special methods

Operator	Special method
+	__add__(self, other)
-	__sub__(self, other)
*	__mul__(self, other)
/	__div__(self, other)
%	__mod__(self, other)
divmod()	__divmod__(self, other)
**	__pow__(self, other[, modulo])
<<	__lshift__(self, other)
>>	__rshift__(self, other)
&	__and__(self, other)
^	__xor__(self, other)
		__or__(self, other)

To be completely clear, that is bitwise and, xor, and or, not the Boolean operations.

Unary operations have their special methods as well, as shown in Table 5-2.

Table 5-2. Unary operators and special methods

Operator	Special method
-	__neg__(self)
+	__pos__(self)
abs()	__abs__(self)
~	__invert__(self)

The typecast and radix changing functions also have special methods—each of these maps to the built-in operators of the same name (well, the same name without the underscores):

```
__complex__(self)
__float__(self)
__int__(self)
__long__(self)
__oct__(self)
__hex__(self)
```

Finally, the special method __coerce__(self, other) allows you to control the manner in which your instance is typecast in the event it is in an arithmetic operation with a different numeric type. If defined, __coerce__ is tried before the operation overriding methods (__add__, etc.). This method should return a tuple of the two values cast to a common type. If the coercion is undefined, it should return None.

CHAPTER 6
Using Java from Jython

This chapter covers the use of Java classes from Jython code. From Jython, you have access to all the Java classes in all standard libraries, any third-party libraries, and, of course, your own Java code. Jython leverages Python's object-oriented structures and support to integrate smoothly with Java.

Basic Object Usage

In "Importing Java Classes" in Chapter 4, we showed how you can retrieve Java classes using the import statement. The Jython runtime wraps both Java classes and instances inside proxy objects, which offer a natural and intuitive mix between what you expect from Java semantics and what you have learned so far about user-defined Python classes. Using these objects, Jython provides a number of automatic conversions when passing objects back and forth between Jython and Java code.

When using a Java class in Jython, you can, by default, access all inner classes, static fields, static methods, and instance methods—as long as they are defined as public. If you need to get access to protected or private members, you can set the Jython registry option python.security.respectJavaAccessibility = false, an option used mainly for testing. The following code shows how you can import and then use Java classes and methods from the interpreter:

```
>>> from java.lang import System
>>> System.out.println("print would be more pythonic")
print would be more pythonic
```

You construct Java instances the same way you construct Python instances, by calling the class as a function—you do not need to use the Java keyword new. For a non-static inner class *Inner* you would supply an instance *outerInstance* of the outer class *Outer* as the first argument of the constructor—for example, *Outer.Inner(outerInstance, ...)*. You can also obtain an unbound method of a Java class exactly the way you would for a Python class, by attempting to access an instance method from the class—for example, String.startsWith. This code snippet shows how you can create a string and then call its methods in either a bound or unbound manner:

```
>>> from java.lang import String
>>> x = String("Zot")
>>> x.startsWith("Z")
1
>>> String.startsWith(x, "Z")
1
```

The internal result in Jython of creating a Java object is an instance of the class org.python.core.PyJavaInstance that will, for most of your needs, act as a transparent wrapper around the created Java instance. The PyJavaInstance class offers the functionality used to do the automatic mapping between Python data and naming conventions, and Java data and naming conventions.

Once you have obtained a Java instance you can use it like any Jython object. You can retrieve or set the value of its fields, invoke its methods, or retrieve them as bound methods. The methods of Java instances can be passed or returned as first-class objects, just like the methods of native Python classes. There is only one restriction on the use of Java class instances in Jython. You cannot create arbitrary new attributes on an instance of a Java class with an assignment statement, as you can with Python instances. As this code shows, if you try this, you will receive a TypeError. To be able to add arbitrary attributes, you can subclass the Java class with a Jython class, which is the topic of Chapter 7.

```
>>> from java.util import Random
>>> rg=Random(99)
>>> rg.nextInt()
-1192035722

>>> Random.nextInt(rg) # unbound method
1672896916

>>> rint = rg.nextInt # bound method
>>> rint()
1491444859

>>> rint()
-1244121273

>>> rg.x="?"
Traceback (innermost last):
  File "<console>", line 1, in ?
TypeError: can't set arbitrary attribute in java instance: x
```

In Jython, Java methods are first class in both their bound and unbound form, so you can, for example, use the built-in map function to apply a Java method to all the elements of a list. Java offers similar functionality through the *java.lang.reflect* package, but the Java functionality is far more cumbersome to use. Jython does use this reflection package internally to mimic Python functionality.

If you've programmed in Java, you know that you spend a lot of effort on typecasts to convince the Java compiler that the object is of a particular type for the purposes of a particular method call. Because Jython is a dynamically typed language, where data and not variables carry type information, you do not need to use typecasts for this purpose—even when calling a Java method using Java instances.

For a given Java instance *jobj*, the set of methods you can invoke and fields on which you can access is based on the methods reachable by its concrete class, defined in Python as *jobj*.__class__ or equivalently in Java as *jobj*. getClass( ). In other words, you never need to use the common Java idiom of casting an instance down the inheritance hierarchy just to be able to call a specific method.

This code shows another difference between Java class behavior and Jython class behavior:

```
>>> from java.util import Date
>>> from java.lang import Object
>>> Object.toString(Date())
'Thu Aug 23 02:23:31 GMT+02:00 2001'

>>> Object.toString(Object())
'java.lang.Object@29df8a'
```

An unbound method of Python classes (both in CPython and Jython) statically invokes the method based on the class target as it is explicitly stated. However unbound methods of Java classes perform dynamic dispatch based on the runtime Java type of the instance. Therefore, in the previous code sample, Object.toString on a java.util.Date object invokes the java.util. Date version of the toString method, not the original functionality in Object.toString, as you might expect. So, the date is output rather than the generic string method, which would have produced 'java.util.Date@.... This behavior occurs when we invoke the unbound Java method on a wrapped Java instance.

If the instance passed to the unbound method is from a Python class that inherits from a Java class, the behavior is different. The dynamic dispatch stops where the Java code does, resulting in the most specialized Java version of the method being called. This is true even if the Python class overrides the method—the dispatch still stops with the most specialized Java version.

Automatic Type Conversion

To call a Java method or constructor, Jython performs an appropriate set of automatic conversions at runtime between the arguments based on their Python type and the expected types of the method on the Java side. The goal is to allow Java code to be used smoothly and naturally from Jython without the programmer having to spend a lot of time managing data types. These conversions include changing Python built-in data types to the appropriate Java type (integers to `int`, for example). In addition, Java proxy objects created by Jython are unwrapped so that the actual Java class is passed during a method call rather than the Jython proxy instance. The Jython runtime will sometimes need to choose among different overloaded versions of a method. Remember, you cannot use keyword arguments when calling a Java method from Jython, because Java compilation does not keep the necessary argument naming information.

Managing Overloaded Methods

Data conversion and selection between overloaded methods happen at the same time. Table 6-1 summarizes the rules for both. If the overloaded methods have different numbers of arguments, Jython dispatches solely based on the number of arguments. Table 6-1 is used to decide between methods with the same number of arguments. Jython sorts the overloaded methods based on the type signature of the Java arguments. The sort order is the order of the types in Table 6-1, with types higher in the table having precedence over those lower.

Table 6-1. Java-to-Python argument conversions

Java type	Python types and Java wrapped types
`long`	Integer, long, `java.lang.Long`
`int`	Integer, long, `java.lang.Integer`
`short`	Integer, long, `java.lang.Short`
`char`	String (length must be 1), `java.lang.Character`
`byte`	Integer, long, `java.lang.Byte`
`double`	Integer, long, float, `java.lang.Double`
`float`	Integer, long, float, `java.lang.Float`
`boolean`	Integer: 0 is mapped to `false`, nonzero values are mapped to `true` `java.lang.Boolean`
`java.lang.String`	String
`long[]`	General array rule
`int[]`	General array rule

Table 6-1. Java-to-Python argument conversions (continued)

Java type	Python types and Java wrapped types
short[]	General array rule
char[]	General array rule, string (copying conversion)
byte[]	General array rule, string (copying conversion)
double[]	General array rule
float[]	General array rule
boolean[]	General array rule
java.lang.String[]	General array rule
SubFoo (subclass of Foo)	SubFoo, Foo, ...
Foo	Foo, ...
java.lang.Class	Wrapped Java classes or Python classes subclassing a Java class.
java.lang.Integer,	Integer, long, java.lang.Integer,
Other primitive type Java wrapper class	Same conversions as the corresponding primitive types (except for the different priority)
java.math.BigInteger	Long
java.lang.Number	Integer (as java.lang.Integer), long (as java.math.BigInteger), float (as java.lang.Double)
java.io.Serializable	Like java.lang.Object
java.lang.Object	Java wrapped instances/arrays or instances of Python classes subclassing a Java class Integer, long and float as in java.lang.Number case String (as java.lang.String)

Jython then picks the first candidate among the overloaded methods for which an applicable conversion exists from the Python runtime type of the arguments. The order is strictly defined for basic data types and basic arrays, with java.lang.String handled specially, like a primitive type rather than an instance. Other Java classes are ordered using the class hierarchy relationships, with the subclass SubFoo being tried before its superclass Foo. If all else fails, java.lang.Object is tried last.

The following code should make this clearer:

```
public class OverloadExample {

    public void method(long l) {
        System.out.print("long method: ");
        System.out.println(l);
    }

    public void method(int i) {
        System.out.print("int method: ");
        System.out.println(i);
    }
```

```java
    public void method(String s) {
        System.out.print("string method: ");
        System.out.println(s);
    }
    public void method(Object o) {
        System.out.print("object method: ");
        System.out.println(o);
    }

    public void method(Object o1, Object o2) {
        System.out.print("two-argument method: ");
        System.out.println(o1.toString() + " " + o2.toString());
    }

}
```

The next example shows Jython code that touches each overloaded method definition in the preceding code:

```python
import OverloadExample
import java

x = OverloadExample()
x.method(3)
x.method(java.lang.Integer(3))
x.method("3")
x.method([1, 2])
x.method(1, 2)

long method: 3
int method: 3
string method: 3
object method: [1, 2]
two-argument method: 1 2
```

In the first call of this example, a bare Python integer 3 triggers a call to the long method because longs come before ints in the conversion table. To get to the integer method, you need to specifically cast the Python integer to a Java Integer. The cast works to hit the int method because Jython specially converts from the Java primitive type wrapper classes (java.lang.Integer, ...) to the corresponding primitive type (int, ...) but not to other primitive types. Therefore, the typecast argument cannot be converted to long, so the long method cannot be called.

A consequence of this rule is that a method taking a java.lang.Integer would be completely shadowed by the int method, and would not be callable from Jython without explicitly using Java reflection. In general, a method taking a Java basic type will block normal access to a method using the corresponding Java wrapper object. In practice, this kind of overloading is rare and is discouraged.

In the next call of the previous example, the Python string cannot be converted to either integer method, so the string method is called. The Python list falls through both integer methods and the string method, until the Object method is finally called. The two-argument method is called normally, from the two-argument call. If the method is overloaded on multiple arguments, a generalization of this algorithm is used. Overloaded versions are sorted and the first for which applicable conversions exist for all arguments is chosen. When sorting, rightmost arguments count more than leftmost. This means x.meth(int, long) is tried before x.meth(long, int).

A version of a method with the following signature takes precedence over any other:

```
returnType meth(org.python.core.PyObject[] args,String[] kws)
```

No conversion will be performed on the arguments. The class org.python. core.PyObject is the superclass of all classes used by Jython to represent built-in objects internally. (More details about PyObject are in Chapter 12.) Positional arguments followed by the keyword argument values are passed in args, while the keywords are passed in kws. This feature can be used to write Java code that can tightly interoperate with Jython and its internal representation for data or simply mimic Python function calling style. Also, return type can be PyObject to avoid any conversion on the return value.

If the Java class has multiple overloaded constructors, the actual constructor used for a set of supplied arguments is chosen using the same rules used for any method invocation.

Basic Data Conversions

In Table 6-1, each row describes a set of applicable conversions between the Python types listed on the right and the Java type on the left. The conversions from a Java class on the right to a Java class on the left simply involve the unwrapping of a wrapped Java instance. The special cases and rules for Python user-defined classes that subclass a Java class will be treated in Chapter 7, but they are generally treated the same as Java subclasses.

For each allowed conversion into a primitive Java type, there is a similar conversion into the primitive type wrapper class. For example, every type that can be converted into a Java int can be converted to a java.lang. Integer. The only difference is that wrapper classes have a lower priority for the purpose of disambiguating overloaded methods. As we have seen, Java wrapper classes can be converted to primitive Java types, such as java.lang. Integer to int.

Boolean values are a special case. To have a Python object automatically converted to a Java boolean for the purposes of a method call, it needs to be an integer value—0 is false and all others are true. Jython does not apply Python rules for the truth value of other types such as strings, lists, tuples, or dictionaries when converting data types. This is to avoid an ambiguous case where there is an overloaded boolean method in addition to another method—which do you call for an empty string, and should a non-empty string be treated as the string or as true?

Python's None value can be used to pass null to a Java method. It is converted to null for any non-primitive Java type.

When converting Python built-in types to java.lang.Object, such as when passing a value to the collection classes, Jython tries to do something meaningful with the data type you pass. Specifically, it converts to the corresponding Java wrapper type using the list in Table 6-1 for precedence. Therefore, Integer is preferred to Short, and Double to Float. Objects will not be converted automatically to Boolean. If you are not satisfied with the standard conversions you can explicitly construct the needed Java object using the ordinary constructor (from Jython you can use Boolean(1) or Boolean(0)), as in the following:

```
>>> import java
>>> v = java.util.Vector()
>>> v.add(3) # converts to java.lang.Integer(3)
1

>>> v.add(java.lang.Short(3))
1

>>> v.add(java.lang.Boolean(1))
1

>>> v
[3, 3, true]
```

Jython will convert from Python built-in file objects to java.io.InputStream or java.io.OutputStream, if the file was opened for the corresponding mode (reading or writing, respectively).

Converting Arrays

When calling a Java method that requires an array, a conversion to a Java array is automatically performed from Python lists and tuples, as well as from Java array objects created in Jython. In the list/tuple case, the conversion recursively tries to coerce each element to the expected component type of the Java array, using the rules shown in Table 6-1. In practice, this can lead to type exceptions if the objects in the list or tuple are of incompatible classes. A Java array is trivially unwrapped in the same way as any Java instance if the expected Java array has the same type or a supertype (if not, an exception is raised).

The Jython list [1, 2, 3] can therefore be converted to an int[], to a long[], or to a java.lang.Integer[] as needed. You can pass a tuple of Python strings to a method expecting a java.lang.String[]. The automatic conversion actually copies each element of the list in a new array, which means that possible modifications to the array are not reflected back to the original Python list. If a method modifies an array argument or uses it as buffer (e.g., java.io. InputStream.read(byte[] buf)), you need to directly construct a wrapped Java array using the jarray module, which we explain in the next section.

There are special conversions to enable Python strings to be used as byte[] and char[] arrays. In both cases the content of the string is copied to a new array. When the Java method expects a char or Character, a string of length 1 can be passed.

Java Arrays and the jarray Module

Java arrays are wrapped by the Jython runtime in objects that hold a reference to the original Java array and allow you to access it through a part of the Python mutable sequence protocol. Wrapped arrays can be converted to any Java array type compatible with the original type. The conversion simply unwraps the array and passes the original reference. The wrapped arrays are compared, as any sequence would be, considering length and the corresponding elements.

Sometimes, however, you need to create a Java array directly. Most likely, this is because the method you are passing the array to makes changes to the array—the Jython automatic conversions to arrays are just copy conversions and by themselves will not propagate those changes back to the Jython object. Jython supports the construction of Java arrays through the built-in module jarray, which offers two functions.

zeros(length, type)
    Creates and returns a Java array of the given *type* and with the given *length*. The *type* can be either a Java class or one of the strings in Table 6-2 indicating a primitive type. The elements of the new array will have the standard default value, either 0, null, or false.

array(sequence, type)
    Create an array of the given *type* and initialize it with the elements of the given *sequence*. The *type* parameter is evaluated the same way as for

zeros. The new array is filled using the elements in the *sequence* coerced to *type*. If for some element the conversion is not possible, an exception is raised.

Table 6-2 shows the Jython strings that can be passed as the type parameter to the jarray function, and the Java primitive type that results.

Table 6-2. Primitive type strings for jarray

String	Java primitive type
'1'	long
'i'	int
'h'	short
'c'	char
'b'	byte
'd'	double
'f'	float
'z'	boolean

This sample shows the jarray module in action:

```
>>> import jarray
>>> jarray.zeros(5,'i')
array([0, 0, 0, 0, 0], int)

>>> jarray.zeros(3,'z')
array([0, 0, 0], boolean)

>>> import java
>>> jarray.zeros(4,java.lang.String)
array([None, None, None, None], java.lang.String)

>>> jarray.zeros(7,java.lang.Object)
array([None, None, None, None, None, None, None], java.lang.Object)

>>> jarray.array([8,9,2,1],'i')
array([8, 9, 2, 1], int)

>>> jarray.array(['J','y','t','h','o','n'],'c')
array(['J', 'y', 't', 'h', 'o', 'n'], char)

>>> jarray.array(['crystal','ball'],java.lang.String)
array(['crystal', 'ball'], java.lang.String)

>>> jarray.array([2,3j,4],'1')
Traceback (innermost last):
  File "<console>", line 1, in ?
TypeError: can't convert 3j to long
```

As the following code shows, Java arrays created with jarray support Python indexing with assignment and slicing:

```
>>> a = jarray.zeros(5,'i')
>>> a[3] = 2
>>> a
array([0, 0, 0, 2, 0], int)

>>> a[-2]
2

>>> a[2] = 3
>>> s = a[2:]
>>> len(s)
3

>>> s
array([3, 2, 0], int)
```

Also, for ... in ... iteration is supported using Java arrays as the sequence argument. Slice assignment is supported only for byte or char arrays, and the righthand value should be an exact length string:

```
>>> b = jarray.array(['f','a','r'],'c')
>>> b[1:]='oo'
>>> b
array(['f', 'o', 'o'], char)

>>> b[-1:] = 'baz'
Traceback (innermost last):
  File "<console>", line 1, in ?
ValueError: invalid bounds for setting from string

>>> b[-1:] = 'O'
>>> b
array(['f', 'o', 'O'], char)
```

The other sequence operations, such as append( ) and extend( ), are not supported on Java arrays because wrapped arrays are fixed-length sequences (like Python tuples). Wrapped byte and char arrays support a tostring method:

```
>>> b.tostring( )
'foo'
```

The ability to construct Java arrays is usually useful only when calling a method that modifies an array argument or uses it as buffer, e.g., for some I/O operation. Using Python lists and their automatic implicit conversions to arrays results in more Pythonic and flexible programs. The conversions almost always do what you need. However, the fact that a conversion from a list object copies the list content can be quite deceiving in cases where the Java code modifies the array, as this code shows:

```
>>> i = java.io.ByteArrayInputStream("foobaz") # a six-byte stream: 'foobaz'
>>> buf = [0] * 3
>>> i.read(buf) # buf conversion creates a new array which gets lost
3

>>> buf # we expect it to be the 'foo' from the read ([102, 111, 111])
[0, 0, 0]

>>> buf = jarray.zeros(3,'b') # this is the right way
>>> i.read(buf)
3

>>> buf
array([98, 97, 122], byte)

>>> buf.tostring()
'baz'
>>> # but 'foo' (the first 3 bytes of the file) is lost
>>> i.close()
```

In the first part of this code, we expect the buf array to contain the first 3 bytes read from the input stream—namely, 'foo' (or the list of bytes [102, 111, 111]). However, the automatic conversion to the Java byte array that takes place during the i.read(buf) statement creates a copy of buf, and therefore the changes performed to that array in the Java code don't show up in Python. For the next read, we use jarray to directly make buf a Java array—then the read works properly.

Java-to-Python Types: Automatic Conversion

Jython performs a set of automatic conversions from Java types to Jython built-in types for the value returned by a Java method or for the value retrieved by a Java attribute lookup. Table 6-3 shows the conversions. To fit Java void methods into the Python model, Jython makes them return None.

Table 6-3. Result conversions

Java type	Python type
java.lang.Long, long	Long
java.lang.Integer, int	Integer
java.lang.Short, short	Integer
java.lang.Byte, byte	Integer
java.lang.Boolean, boolean	Integer (false maps to 0, true to 1)
java.lang.Double, double	Float

Table 6-3. Result conversions (continued)

Java type	Python type
java.lang.Float, float	Float
java.lang.Character, char	String of length 1
java.lang.String	String
Java class instance	Wrapped Java class instance
java.lang.Class	Wrapped Java class
null	None
Java arrays	Wrapped Java arrays

The conversions shown in Table 6-3 do not apply to constructor methods, which always produce wrapped instances of the Java instance constructed, as shown here:

```
>>> from java.lang import Integer,Boolean
>>> Boolean.FALSE # static field => conversion
0

>>> Boolean(0) # constructor
false

>>> x = Integer(3) # constructor
>>> x.__class__
<jclass java.lang.Integer at 8204046>

>>> import jarray
>>> a = jarray.zeros(1, Integer)
>>> a[0] = x
>>> isinstance(a[0], x.__class__) # fails because of conversion to Python
integer
0
```

For each Java class used, the Jython runtime creates a single wrapper instance using caching. The uniqueness of the wrapping for instances is simulated, in the sense that the operator is is defined in terms of the underlying Java instance references. Java null is always mapped to None.

Jython also performs this automatic mapping on exceptions thrown by Java code called from Jython, so you can simply use the usual Python idiom for catching Java exceptions, as shown in the following code:

```
>>> import java
>>> v = java.util.Vector( )
>>> try:
...     x = v.elementAt(7)
... except java.lang.ArrayIndexOutOfBoundsException,e:
...     print "My Bad", e
...
My Bad java.lang.ArrayIndexOutOfBoundsException: 7 >= 0
```

Collection Wrappers

There is no automatic conversion back and forth between Python dictionaries and the java.util mapping classes (java.util.HashMap, java.util. Hashtable, ...) or between Python sequences and the list classes. The only reasonable automatic implementation would be some kind of copy conversion that would defeat the purpose of converting at all because the copying would prevent changes in the collection from being seen by the Python code.

To make the use of java.util collection classes less cumbersome and more Pythonic, Jython augments the wrapper classes of these instances with minimal support for the sequence or mapping protocol based on the kind of collection.

Jython adds for ... in ... iteration support to the subclasses or implementers of: java.util.Vector, java.util.Enumeration, java.util.List, and java. util.Iterator; and indexed or keyed access and assignment (but no slicing) del[] and len( ) support to the subclasses or implementers of: java.util. Vector, java.util.Dictionary, java.util.List, and java.util.Map.

The following example shows how the Java collection classes can be used in Jython almost as though they were the Python built-in type:

```
>>> from java import util as jutil
>>> h = jutil.Hashtable( )
>>> h['foo'] = 1
>>> h['bar'] = 2
>>> h
{bar=2, foo=1}

>>> h['baz'] = 3
>>> del h['bar']
>>> for x in h.keys( ): # keys is the Java method returning a java.util.
Enumeration
...     print "%s: %s" % (x,h[x])
...
baz: 3
foo: 1
```

Avoiding Name Collisions

In nearly every case, the transition between using Python objects and Java objects is smooth and easy to navigate. However, there are some instances in which the different naming rules between Java and Python can cause some difficulties. Usually, however, there is a workaround, if you approach the needed functionality differently.

One problem that occurs rarely is that Java allows a method and field to have the same name, whereas Python does not. In Jython, the method name will always shadow the field name in cases like this. There is no direct workaround for these cases except for explicitly using Java reflection. However, using the same name for a method and field is considered poor Java style.

In CPython, Python reserved words can never be used as method or variable names. This causes a problem because some Python reserved words are commonly used as method names in Java (such as print). Because of this issue, Jython is a little more flexible about the use of reserved words. In Jython, Python reserved words can be used as identifiers in the few places where they help Java integration. In practice, this means that a Python reserved word can be used as an identifier, in a def statement, after a dot, and in a keyword argument in a calling sequence, but not in an argument specifier definition. Therefore, def print( ): pass, a.print( ), and f(print=3) are valid, but def f(print=3) is not.

The differing semantics of Java and Python classes can lead to occasional name issue problems, which might seem surprising the first time you encounter them. There are almost always workarounds for these problems. For example, the following Java code runs fine (assuming that it's within a method and everything has been imported properly). It will print the names of the two classes.

```
Object o = new Object( );
System.out.println(o.getClass().getName());
java.io.File f = new java.io.File("fred.py");
System.out.println(f.getClass().getName());
```

Attempting to run the analogous code in Jython, however, we see that the Object part works fine, while the File part raises an error:

```
import java
o = java.lang.Object( )
print o.getClass().getName( )
f = java.io.File("fred.py")
print f.getClass().getName( )

java.lang.Object
Traceback (innermost last):
  File "nameclash.py", line 5, in ?
TypeError: getName( ): expected 1 args; got 0
```

In the Object case, the expected is happening—o.getClass( ) returns the class object, and getName( ) returns the name of the class. In the File case, however, the call of f.getClass( ) returns the File class. The next call is interpreted as File.getName( ), and because the Java File class has a getName( ) instance method, File.getName retrieves the unbound form of that method, which effectively shadows the getName method of java.lang. Class. The unbound method expects an instance as an argument—hence the type error, which claims that the method expects an argument.

This issue happens anytime you attempt to use an instance of java.lang. Class to call a method and there is an instance method of the same name in that class. There is one workaround for this problem that will always work, which is to call the Class method using its unbound form, as follows:

```
print java.lang.Class.getName(f.getClass())
```

However, that's a lot of typing, and it's not very readable, so it's worth pointing out that most of the functionality of java.lang.Class is made available by Jython in some Pythonic way. In this case, you can write:

```
print f.getClass().__name__
```

or:

```
print f.__class__.__name__
```

And they will have the same result as the longer line of code.

CHAPTER 7
Inheriting from Java

Inheritance and the resulting reuse of code is a key feature of object-oriented programming, supported both by Java and Python. The ability to create subclasses is vital to the flexible use of an object-oriented library. In particular, many Java libraries are designed so that inheriting their classes or implementing their interfaces is the best way to use them. GUI libraries (AWT or Swing) are prime examples of this.

To allow effective access to preexisting Java code, Jython supports direct inheritance from Java classes. This is done without any additional syntax and with natural extensions of the semantics explained so far.

Extending an existing Java class is as simple as putting the Java class name in the base classes list of a Jython class statement. The following Java code defines a Java class MentalState to be subclassed in Jython:

```java
public class MentalState {

    public int energy;

    public MentalState(int e) {
        this.energy = e;
    }

    public int askEnergy( ) { return energy; }
}
```

The following Jython code actually defines a Jython subclass of MentalState. For the Jython code to work, MentalState must be in the Jython classpath.

```python
import MentalState

class FlexibleMentalState(MentalState):
    pass

if __name__ == '__main__':
```

```
flexible = FlexibleMentalState(3)
print flexible.askEnergy()
```

3

Similarly, implementing an interface is as simple as putting one or more interface names in the base classes list. The only restriction is that a Jython class can only be a subclass of, at most, one Java class. The base class list may contain, at most, one Java class or one Python class that already inherits from a Java class. This is related to the Java single inheritance limitation. The restriction obviously does not apply to Java interfaces; nor does it apply to Python classes. A Jython class can still inherit from any number of pure Python classes, along with the single Java class.

The rest of the chapter will discuss the details of the behavior of the resulting classes. To a large degree, this behavior is what you would naturally expect. To illustrate points, we will dig into how inheritance is implemented under the hood in Jython.

Basic Mechanics

When Jython encounters a class statement at runtime, it creates a Python class object and binds it to the class name. This is still true when there is a Java class or interface among the base class list, and it is still true if a Python class already inheriting from Java is in the base class list. So, in the previous code snippet we still create a Python class FlexibleMentalState. But when the Jython class inherits from a Java class, Jython also dynamically creates a proxy class in Java, which is associated with the Python class.* For the rest of this chapter, we will be referring to this internal Java class as the *proxy* class, to better clarify the distinction between it and the Java class you are actually inheriting from within your Jython code.

When an instance of the Jython child class is created, an instance of the proxy class is also created internally. The Jython child instance holds a reference to the proxy instance, but otherwise it behaves like any Python instance, exposing a __dict__ attribute and allowing the user to set arbitrary attributes. This is one way to get around the Jython restriction of not allowing arbitrary attributes to be created on instances of Java classes. By creating a blank subclass, you can set arbitrary attributes on the subclass. This example illustrates this behavior using MentalState and FlexibleMentalState:

```
>>> import MentalState
>>> mental = MentalState()
```

---

* This proxy class will be dynamically loaded using a dedicated classloader so that it can be discarded by Java when it is no longer needed.

```
>>> mental.joy = 5
Traceback (innermost last):
  File "<console>", line 1, in ?
TypeError: can't set arbitrary attribute in java instance: joy

>>> from flexibleMind import FlexibleMentalState
...
>>> mental = FlexibleMentalState()
>>> mental.joy = 5
>>> mental.__dict__
{'joy': 5}
```

The Java proxy class extends the specified Java parent class. If the Java inheritance is indirect through another Jython class, it will extend the proxy class of that Jython class. The proxy will also implement any Java interfaces in the base classes list. If only interfaces are specified, java.lang.Object is assumed to be the Java parent class.

Attribute or method lookup within Jython on the new instance uses the normal Python rules. If the lookup returns a Java-inherited method or field, this method or field will be accessed through the wrapped proxy instance in the same manner as for other wrapped Java instances described in "Automatic Type Conversion" in Chapter 6. As a result, you have access to the public fields of the Java base class along with the public and protected methods. These snippets show these possibilities using the classes from the previous example:

```
>>> mental.energy = 10
>>> mental.energy
10

>>> mental.__dict__['energy'] = 5
>>> mental.__dict__
{'energy': 5, 'joy': 5}

>>> mental.energy
5

>>> mental.askEnergy()
10

>>> del mental.__dict__['energy']
>>> mental.energy
10
```

Setting an attribute that corresponds to a field inherited from Java will set the field in the Java proxy instance, and will not modify the Python namespace mapping unless you directly manipulate the Python __dict__. For attribute access within Jython, the Python __dict__ values override the Java fields. However, if a method defined in Java is called, then the Java proxy field is retrieved. So, in the previous example, the askEnergy()

method still returns the Java value for energy, even when the variable name has been explicitly bound in the __dict__ on the Python side.

Access to protected fields is currently not supported by Jython inheritance. Generally, this is not a problem with most classes in the standard Java libraries. The standard libraries generally define public access methods rather than protected fields. If you are creating a Java class that you expect to eventually be subclassed in Jython, you need to take this into account and avoid protected fields. A method *foo* that declared final protected is a special case. A method declared this way is still not directly accessible as *jobj*. *foo(...)* but can be accessed using the name *jobj*.super__*foo(...)*, which is a public wrapper method created in the proxy class to call the original protected method.

Internally, the proxy class is defined with public methods that call the corresponding protected methods of the parent class. Because these methods are defined as public, access to protected methods is not limited to the methods of the subclass, as in Java, but is extended to all the Jython code. You may choose to exploit this increased access if you like, but we recommend you don't. The primary benefit is increased flexibility. On the other hand, by doing this you are most likely using the parent class in an unexpected way, and this could cause bugs. Also, this causes a high degree of reliance on the internal mechanism of the parent class. Protected methods are accessible only for a Java class that is being used as a parent class in Jython—if the class is not a parent class, its protected methods are inaccessible.

Java Interoperation and Overriding

An instance of a Python class extending a Java class or implementing a Java interface can be passed back to Java everywhere the Java class or interface is accepted as a method argument or field value. Internally, the proxy class instance is passed back to Java. Here is some code that illustrates this point:

```
public class Therapist {

    public MentalState analyze(MentalState mental) {
        System.out.println("mental state? "+mental.askEnergy());
        return mental;
    }

}

>>> from flexibleMind import FlexibleMentalState
>>> mental = FlexibleMentalState()
>>> mental.energy = -1
>>> import Therapist
>>> therapist = Therapist()
```

```
>>> mental2 = therapist.analyze(mental)
mental state? -1
>>> mental2.energy
-1
>>> mental2 is mental
1
```

In the preceding code, the Java class Therapist, which expects an instance of MentalState, also accepts an instance of the Jython class FlexibleMentalState. The proxy class instance also holds a reference to the corresponding Jython instance—when the proxy class needs to be returned to Jython, its Jython instance is returned.

The next code snippet shows that Jython subclassing is able to override Java methods and implement interface methods. The example subclasses java.awt.Color and implements java.lang.Comparable and overrides the method java.lang.Object.toString.

```
from java.awt import Color
from java.lang import Comparable, System, ClassCastException
from java.util import Arrays

class ComparableColor(Color, Comparable):
    def __init__(self, color):
        Color.__init__(self, color.getRGB())

    def _RGBTuple(self):
        return (self.getRed(), self.getGreen(), self.getBlue())

    def compareTo(self, color1):
        rgb0 = self._RGBTuple()
        rgb1 = color1._RGBTuple()
        return cmp(rgb0,rgb1)

    def toString(self):
        return "#%02x%02x%02x" % self._RGBTuple()
    def __repr__(self):
        return "<co: %s>" % self.toString()

from jarray import array

colors = [Color.green, Color.magenta, Color.orange ,Color.red]

colorsArray = array(colors, Color)

try:
    Arrays.sort(colorsArray)
except ClassCastException:
    print "java.awt.Color does not implement Comparable"

colorsArray = array(map(ComparableColor,colors), Color)

print
```

```
print "ComparableColor does:"
print "unsorted:",
for color in colorsArray:
    print color,
print

Arrays.sort(colorsArray)

System.out.print("sorted: ")
for color in colorsArray:
    System.out.print(color) # uses java.lang.Object.toString
    System.out.print(" ")
System.out.println( )
```

java.awt.Color does not implement Comparable

ComparableColor does:
unsorted: <co: #00ff00> <co: #ff00ff> <co: #ffc800> <co: #ff0000>
sorted: #00ff00 #ff0000 #ff00ff #ffc800

For each method that is declared in the child Jython class and overrides a base class or interface method, the proxy class defines a corresponding Java method.

When the overriding methods of the proxy are invoked, for example, by calling toString( ) or compareTo( ), as shown in the previous code example, they call the Python methods and convert any arguments using the automatic Java-to-Python conversions defined in Chapter 6. The result is automatically coerced back to the expected Java type. The compareTo( ) method defined in Jython is therefore correctly called from the Java Arrays.sort( ) method.

The previous example also shows that you can call the Java parent constructor from Jython with the usual Python idiom—namely, Color.__init__ (self, color.getRGB( )).

The overriding methods of the proxy retrieve and call the Python method with the same name using the Python lookup rules for methods. The reference to the Jython instance in the proxy is used. The extra layer of lookup is necessary to ensure that a Python method correctly overrides a Java parent class method of the same name, both from the perspective of other Python code and from the perspective of other Java code receiving instances of the Python class.

Jython does not check at class creation time whether the Jython class implements all the methods of the implemented interfaces or all abstract methods of the base class. However, calling a non-implemented method produces an error at runtime.

Note that the existence of a single Python method overrides all the possible overloaded Java versions with the same name. Therefore, when overriding a

Java method with multiple signatures, you must either guarantee that only one version is used or write the Python method so that it can deal with all the possible sets of arguments, by using default arguments, a *rest* argument, or explicitly checking for types.

The following example shows a Java class where the behavior method is overloaded. The Jython class behavior method is called for all three versions of the Java method.

```
public abstract class JavaAbstract {

    abstract public void behavior(int j);
    abstract public void behavior(String s);
    abstract protected void behavior(int j,String s);

    public static void testBehaviorInt(JavaAbstract jabs) {
      jabs.behavior(1);
    }

    public static void testBehaviorString(JavaAbstract jabs) {
      jabs.behavior("baz");
    }

    public static void testBehaviorIntString(JavaAbstract jabs) {
      jabs.behavior(1,"foo");
    }

}
```

```
>>> import JavaAbstract
>>> class SnakeClass(JavaAbstract):
...     def behavior(self, *args):
...         print "got: %s" % (args,)
...
>>> snake=SnakeClass()
>>> JavaAbstract.testBehaviorInt(snake)
got: (1,)

>>> JavaAbstract.testBehaviorString(snake)
got: ('baz',)

>>> JavaAbstract.testBehaviorIntString(snake)
got: (1, 'foo')
```

If any overriding Python method raises an exception, the corresponding method of the proxy class tries to coerce it to one of the exceptions declared by the overridden method in Java, or to java.lang.RuntimeException or java.lang.Error, and re-throws the coerced exception. If the exception cannot be coerced, the Python or Java exception will be thrown wrapped as an org.python.core.PyException, a subclass of java.lang.RuntimeException that is used internally by Jython to represent exceptions.

Calling Super Methods and Constructors

If you override a Java-defined public method, you can invoke the original super-class version with the usual Python idiom for calling base class methods: *JavaBase.method*(self, ...). An unbound Java method applied to an instance of a Python class inheriting from Java calls the most specialized Java-defined version of the method.

If you override a protected method *foo*, the original super-class version is accessible as self.super__*foo*(...). Through self.super__*foo*(...) you get access to the most specialized Java-defined version of the protected method, as demonstrated here:

```
public class JavaBase {

  public String one( ) { return "Java-one"; };

  protected String two( ) { return "Java-two"; }

  public static String callOne(JavaBase jb) { return jb.one( ); }
  public static String callTwo(JavaBase jb) { return jb.two( ); }

}

import JavaBase

class SnakeClass(JavaBase):
  def one(self):
    return "snake-one(%s)" % self.super__two( )

  def two(self):
    return "snake-two(%s)"  % JavaBase.one(self)

snake=SnakeClass( )
print JavaBase.callOne(snake)
print JavaBase.callTwo(snake)
```

snake-one(Java-two)
snake-two(Java-one)

In this sample, the static method calls at the end of the Python script call the Python version of the methods callOne( ) and callTwo( ). Within those methods, each uses a different mechanism to call the parent method. If you were to further subclass a Python class *PythonClass* inheriting from Java, you could obtain the Python version of *foo* using the normal Python idiom *PythonClass.foo*(self,...).

Each proxy class created in Jython derives a set of constructors from the public and protected constructors of the Java base class. Each constructor takes the same set of arguments as the corresponding parent class constructor and simply calls that constructor. Normally, the proxy class instance is automatically constructed after the code of the optional Python __init__ method is executed. By default, calling a zero-argument constructor is tried. This means that the zero-argument constructor of a Java parent class, if it exists, is automatically called from Jython when a subclass instance is created. This is different from the normal Python behavior where no parent class constructor is automatically invoked from a subclass.

If you define an __init__ method in the Python class, you can force the Java parent class constructor to be called before the end of the __init__ method. This is done by using the usual Python idiom *JavaParentClass*.__init__ (self,...) and works for both public and protected constructors. The explicit call can also be used if you want to call a constructor of the parent class other than its zero-argument one.

If you call a method or field from the Java base class within the Python method __init__, Jython will attempt to implicitly call the Java zero-argument constructor at that point, to ensure that the Java data is properly initialized before you begin to change it. If the parent class has no public or protected zero-argument constructor, you must be explicit about calling a suitable parent class constructor before using the parent class.

This Java class followed by a Jython subclass traces the various ways that a Java constructor can be invoked from within Jython code:

```
public class JavaBase {
  protected JavaBase() {
    System.out.println("protected JavaBase()");
  }

  private String txt;

  public JavaBase(String txt) {
    System.out.println("public JavaBase(\""+txt+"\")");

    this.txt = txt;
  }

  public void setText(String txt) {
    this.txt = txt;
  }
```

```
  public String getText() { return txt; }

}

import JavaBase
class SnakeClass(JavaBase):
  def __init__(self,opt):
    print "begin __init__"
    if opt == "default":
      pass
    elif opt == "explicit":
      JavaBase.__init__(self)
    elif opt == "force":
      self.setText("snake")
    elif opt == "error":
      self.setText("snake")
      JavaBase.__init__(self)
    else:
      JavaBase.__init__(self,opt)
    print "end __init__"

def try_snake(opt):
  print "*** SnakeClass(%r) ***" % opt
  snake = SnakeClass(opt)
  print snake.getText(), "\n"

try_snake("default")
try_snake("explicit")
try_snake("force")
try_snake("jython")
try_snake("error")

*** SnakeClass('default') ***
begin __init__
end __init__
protected JavaBase()
None

*** SnakeClass('explicit') ***
begin __init__
protected JavaBase()
end __init__
None

*** SnakeClass('force') ***
begin __init__
protected JavaBase()
end __init__
snake
```

```
*** SnakeClass('jython') ***
begin __init__
public JavaBase("jython")
end __init__
jython

*** SnakeClass('error') ***
begin __init__
protected JavaBase( )
Traceback (innermost last):
  File "snake.py", line 29, in ?
  File "snake.py", line 22, in try_snake
  File "snake.py", line 15, in __init__
TypeError: instance already instantiated for JavaBase
```

As you can see in this example, explicitly invoking a base constructor once the proxy class instance has already been constructed raises an error. However, under normal circumstances it's unlikely that you would try to do that.

CHAPTER 8

Reflection and JavaBeans

Chapters 6 and 7 showed how to use and extend existing Java code with Jython. This chapter offers a slightly different perspective on the use of Java code. It explains not merely how to use the Java code, but also how Jython's own use of Java reflection can make working with JavaBeans easier from Jython than from Java. This chapter also shows how Python's own reflection can help you write better code.

Reflection is the ability of an object to find out about its structure, and to operate on that knowledge. Examples include the ability to list all the instance's attributes, and the ability to invoke a method from its name string. In Java, reflection is managed by the *java.lang.reflect* package, which defines objects that encapsulate fields and methods. In Python, reflection is a much more integrated part of the language, with the ability of instances (and other language objects) to provide information about themselves built into the core of the way objects are defined.

Reflection is useful because it allows for more flexible and abstract manipulation of objects. For example, consider a case in which a user may change an object's attributes at runtime from a web form. The result of that change is a series of key/value pairs of the new attributes. Without reflection, you would probably need a large case statement or the equivalent to separately change the appropriate attribute based on the key. With reflection, you can send the object the key and the value in a single statement, and the object will know which attribute to change. The version with reflection is simpler, and has the added benefit that the addition of new attributes requires no further code.

Jython uses reflection in two different ways. The Java reflection mechanisms are exploited to allow Java classes to be accessed using common Python idioms. Using this mechanism, Jython automatically recognizes method names that conform to the JavaBeans naming standard, and associates them with their underlying property or event. Jython uses bean reflection information to enable you to use the bean in a manner and idiom more consistent with

Python style. As a result, in many cases, bean access from within Jython is simpler, clearer, and requires fewer lines of code than the equivalent Java code. In addition, Jython allows access to reflection information using Python's rich set of mechanisms for obtaining and using information about objects. Both kinds of reflection will be discussed in this chapter.

Bean-Based Reflection

Unlike most features in Java, JavaBeans are not specified using a super class or interface. Although there are several auxiliary bean classes in the *java. beans* package to manage bean reflection and whatnot, there is no specific class Bean. Any Java class can be used as a bean regardless of its base class or the interfaces implemented. (Technically, beans are supposed to implement the java.io.Serializable interface. However, that requirement is rarely enforced in practice, and is not enforced by Jython.) Instead of using a base class to define a JavaBean component, the JavaBeans specification presents a coding style for bean classes that ensures that the class will have the proper hooks to be manipulated by a GUI builder or other bean-aware tool. A description of the JavaBeans specification can be found in *Java in a Nutshell* by David Flanagan (O'Reilly), and a complete treatment is in *Developing JavaBeans* by Rob Englander (O'Reilly).

A JavaBean component exposes a set of *properties* that are the attributes that an external object can discover using reflection. The JavaBeans specification sets out a number of ways to explicitly list the properties of a bean. In common practice, most beans (including those defined in Swing and AWT) use the simplest method—a set of naming patterns that define properties. Using this mechanism, a property is specified by defining a *getter* method and/or a *setter* method.

Jython automatically recognizes a property called *propertyName* for access if either of the getter methods—get*PropertyName* or is*PropertyName*—is defined. The property will be recognized for assignment if the setter method set*PropertyName* is defined. All the methods must be public. The setter method takes one argument, which must be the same type returned by the getter method. There need not be an actual field called *propertyName*. Also note that the property name *propertyName* starts with a lowercase letter, but must start with an uppercase letter in the getter and setter methods.

Similarly, a bean declares itself to be a source of an *eventName* event if there are public methods named add*eventName*Listener and remove*eventName*Listener. *eventName* must correspond to a known event class, named *eventName*Event, and a known listener interface, *eventName*Listener. Events are most often used in GUI code. See Chapter 9 for larger examples of using events from Jython.

Example 8-1 shows a simple bean that uses the naming conventions to define two properties, named integerProperty and stringProperty.

Example 8-1. A sample JavaBean

```
public class SampleBean {

    public SampleBean( ) {
        this._integerProperty = 0;
        this._stringProperty = "initialized";
    }

    private int _integerProperty;

    public int getIntegerProperty( ) {
        return this._integerProperty;
    }

    public void setIntegerProperty(int i) {
        this._integerProperty = i;
    }

    private String _stringProperty;

    public String getStringProperty( ) {
        return this._stringProperty;
    }

    public void setStringProperty(String s) {
        this._stringProperty = s;
    }

}
```

Using Beans in Jython

When using the SampleBean class from Jython, we could just call the methods getStringProperty( ) and getIntegerProperty( ). However, as a matter of style, Python programmers tend to prefer a visual separation between attributes and methods, and therefore tend to avoid using one-line methods to duplicate attribute lookup. So, using the Java methods directly is not really in keeping with the spirit of Python. Jython uses reflection to provide access more in keeping with Python style. In Jython, an attribute reference to a bean property of a Java class automatically calls the getter or setter method for that property. The following code shows the use of SampleBean in Jython:

```
import SampleBean
beanInstance = SampleBean( )

print beanInstance.stringProperty
print beanInstance.integerProperty
```

```
beanInstance.stringProperty += " and reset"
beanInstance.integerProperty += 1

print beanInstance.stringProperty
print beanInstance.integerProperty
```

initialized
0
initialized and reset
1

In this code, the expression beanInstance.stringProperty automatically calls beanInstance.getStringProperty( ). Similarly, an assignment such as beanInstance.stringProperty += " and reset" automatically triggers a call to beanInstance.setStringProperty( ). Is this just syntactic sugar? Perhaps, but it is pretty tasty sugar.

In case you were wondering exactly what properties an item defines, the next example shows a Jython function that will print them out:

```
import java.beans
import SampleBean

def printPropertyInfo(beanClass):
    info = java.beans.Introspector.getBeanInfo(beanClass)
    propertyArray = info.getPropertyDescriptors( )
    for each in propertyArray:
        print each.name

printPropertyInfo(SampleBean)
```

integerProperty
class
stringProperty

There is one quirk to this method that you might notice if you've worked with beans before. The listing includes a property class. The property is generated from the getClass( ) method of the java.lang.Object class. However, there is no setter method for class. Usually bean properties are read/write, but the getClass method is still found by the general Jython reflection mechanism and is therefore usable as a bean property. An attempt to set the value of a read-only property such as class will result in an error.

Jython also allows you to include bean properties as keyword arguments in a constructor. Like an ordinary assignment, these arguments trigger the setter function. This is an exception to the rule that you cannot use keyword properties when calling Java methods—in the specific case of constructors, you can. The following sample shows this usage, with the SampleBean from Example 8-1:

```
import SampleBean
newInstance = SampleBean(integerProperty=100, stringProperty="fred")
```

```
print newInstance.integerProperty
print newInstance.stringProperty
```

100
fred

Though the constructor for SimpleBean takes no arguments, the version exposed by the Jython wrapper for the class calls to the setter functions for each keyword argument. You can also use a keyword argument for any ordinary Java field declared as public, although that's rare in most Java code.

Indexed Properties

An *indexed property* of a bean is a property whose value is an array or collection. The value returned from the attribute access of an indexed property can be treated just like any other Python list. The Java class in Example 8-2 declares an indexed property.

Example 8-2. A bean with an indexed property

```
public class IndexBean {

    public IndexBean( ) {
        this._arrayProperty = new String[] {"Zero", "One", "Two"};
    }

    private String[] _arrayProperty;

    public String[] getArrayProperty( ) {
        return this._arrayProperty;
    }

    public void setArrayProperty(String[] ar) {
        this._arrayProperty = ar;
    }

}
```

Use of this bean is shown here:

```
import IndexBean
indexInstance = IndexBean( )
print indexInstance.arrayProperty[1]
indexInstance.arrayProperty[2] = "fred"
print indexInstance.arrayProperty[2]

anotherInstance = IndexBean(arrayProperty=("a", "b", "c"))
print anotherInstance.arrayProperty[1]
```

One
fred
b

The uses of arrayProperty in the previous code work just as you'd hope they would, enabling you to treat the bean property as a Python list—this is a consequence of the rules for dealing with Java arrays. Also notice that when used as a keyword property (or in any situation), Jython can take a tuple or list and convert it to the appropriate array type. The Python-to-Java coercions described in "Automatic Type Conversion" in Chapter 6 are applied. However, there is one way in which the Jython property introspection is different from JavaBeans reflection. Java allows you to create an indexed property with getter and setter methods that take an integer index into the array. Jython does not support simplified access to those methods. You can, of course, access them directly, as shown in Example 8-3.

Example 8-3. A bean with an array property

```
public class IndexBean {

    public IndexBean( ) {
        this._arrayProperty = new String[] {"Zero", "One", "Two"};
    }

    private String[] _arrayProperty;

    public String getArrayProperty(int i) {
        return this._arrayProperty;
    }

    public void setArrayProperty(int i,String s) {
        this._arrayProperty[i] = s;
    }

}

import IndexBean
indexInstance = IndexBean( )

#print indexInstance.arrayProperty[1]
#indexInstance.arrayProperty[2] = "fred"
#print indexInstance.arrayProperty[2]
# does not work! Instead use

print indexInstance.getArrayProperty(1)
indexInstance.setArrayProperty(2, "fred")
print indexInstance.getArrayProperty(2)
```

The ability to pass a tuple into a keyword argument or attribute setter still holds even when the property is not an array. If the property does not expect an array, but rather, a Java class, that class constructor is called with the values of the tuple as arguments. The following example shows a bean that has a property of type java.awt.Dimension:

```
import java.awt.Dimension;

public class DimensionBean {

    public DimensionBean( ) {
        this._dimProperty = new Dimension(0, 0);
    }

    private Dimension _dimProperty;

    public Dimension getDimensionProperty( ) {
        return this._dimProperty;
    }

    public void setDimensionProperty(Dimension d) {
        this._dimProperty = d;
    }

}
```

The next example shows the Jython code that implicitly sets the value of that property by passing a tuple into the constructor:

```
import DimensionBean
dimInstance = DimensionBean(dimensionProperty=(10, 20))
print dimInstance.dimensionProperty
```

java.awt.Dimension[width=10,height=20]

In the Jython code, the Dimension constructor is called with 10 and 20 as the arguments.

Event Properties

Jython bean properties can also be events rather than values. Java beans declare interest in events by defining two methods, add<*eventListener*> and remove<*eventListener*>. Typically, when managing events in a Java program, you define objects that implement the relevant action listener interface, and pass them to the add and remove event methods. Often this is done using anonymous inner classes, in an effort to keep the bean definition and the action code close to each other. However, many people find the inner class syntax hard to remember and read. The alternative, creating a named inner class, sometimes seems like too much code syntax complexity just to define what might be a one-line response to the event. What's really missing from the Java syntax is a simple mechanism for passing a function to the item waiting for the event. Jython uses a bean-based reflection shortcut to allow you to do exactly that.

When a JavaBean component declares an event property by declaring the add and remove methods, Jython searches for the associated Listener interface. When it creates a Jython instance of the bean, Jython adds an attribute with the name of each method defined by the interface. You can then directly assign a Jython function or bound method object to those attributes, and Jython calls that function or method when the event is triggered. The following Java code uses inner classes to terminate the program in response to a button push:

```
JButton close = new JButton("Close Me");
close.addActionListener(new ActionListener( ) {
    public void actionPerformed(ActionEvent evt) {
        java.lang.System.exit(0);
    }
});
```

The Jython equivalent uses Jython introspection to separate the function definition from the widget creation:

```
close = swing.JButton("Close Me",  actionPerformed=self.terminateProgram)

def terminateProgram(self, event):
    java.lang.System.exit(0)
```

The JButton constructor uses bean access to set the actionPerformed property. The actionPerformed property support is added to JButton by Jython because it is defined by the ActionListener interface. The Jython function passed to the property must be callable with one argument at runtime, but as you can see, the function can be passed in the form of a bound method that is defined to expect one argument beyond the implicit self argument—namely, the event object.

The event listener shortcut works great for the common Java case in which you are implementing an anonymous inner class that just defines a short function. If you are actually broadcasting the event to multiple objects, you can call the add and remove listener functions directly. You can also use the append method and the clear method directly with an event property, such as actionPerformed.clear( ) or actionPerformed.append(func). In that case, all functions so appended are called when the event is triggered. Directly setting the event property replaces all of the previously registered functions.

Python-Based Reflection

The Python language offers numerous ways to discover and use information about an object at runtime. Most objects in Python have special attributes that allow access to their inner structure, however, not all these mechanisms work when reflecting on classes originally defined in Java. In addition, a number of built-in functions help with reflection-based tasks.

The most basic reflection task is to get a list of the available attributes from an instance. As shown in "Creating Classes" in Chapter 5, attribute values are stored in the __dict__ special attribute of a class or instance. Python also provides a couple of built-in functions that allow you to access the same information and are considered less rude than accessing another instance's __dict__ attribute directly. (It's generally considered poor design to access another object's special attributes without a very good reason.) The following code shows a sample Python hierarchy, and some of the reflection mechanisms:

```
class ParentClass:
    def __init__(self, parentValue):
        self.parentValue = parentValue

    def speak(self):
        print "I am a parent"

class ChildClass(ParentClass):
    def __init__(self, parentValue, childValue):
        ParentClass.__init__(self, parentValue)
        self.childValue = childValue

    def play(self):
        print "I can play"

childInstance = ChildClass(1, 2)

print "__dict__:", childInstance.__dict__
print "dir:", dir(childInstance)
print "vars:", vars(childInstance)
print "__class__:", childInstance.__class__
print

print "__bases__:", ChildClass.__bases__
print "class __dict__:", ChildClass.__dict__
print "class dir:", dir(ChildClass)

__dict__: {'childValue': 2, 'parentValue': 1}
dir: ['childValue', 'parentValue']
vars: {'childValue': 2, 'parentValue': 1}
__class__: __main__.ChildClass

__bases__: (<class __main__.ParentClass at 3571905>,)
class __dict__: {'__module__': '__main__',
'__init__': <function __init__ at 4133241>,
'play': <function play at 1334165>, '__doc__': None}
class dir: ['__doc__', '__init__', '__module__', 'play']
```

This example shows a few of the Python reflection attributes and methods on the sample class. In addition to the __dict__ attribute, Python provides the built-in functions vars() and dir(). When passed an instance object, vars() returns the instance's __dict__ dictionary, and dir returns a list of attribute names—in other words, __dict__.keys( ). A useful feature of dir and vars is that they are not limited to taking instances as arguments. They also accept classes and modules, and dir also accepts other built-in types such as lists and dictionaries. When called with no argument, they return the namespace of the current local scope.

The __class__ special attribute contains a reference to the class that the instance is created from. Like __dict__, this attribute can be written to at runtime, (the new value must be a class) and will change the class of the instance. Basically, in that case, method lookups are passed to the new class object rather than the old one—changing the class does not affect the contents of the __dict__ dictionary. Use this rarely, and with care—it's a great way to create unreadable, unmaintainable programs. Causing objects to suddenly change class in midstream is bound to confuse anybody who has to read your code, including you.

Class objects also have __dict__ values, and dir and vars work on them as well (vars isn't shown in the example because it's identical to __dict__). In the previous example, the dictionary contains mostly methods, the module name, and a slot for the doc string. Classes have a special attribute, __bases__, which returns a tuple of the parent classes of that class. The __bases__ attribute can also be modified at runtime (but because tuples are immutable, you need to create a new __bases__ tuple and assign it directly rather than appending to the old one).

Notice that because the __dict__ value does not contain parent class functions (because those are determined at runtime during method lookup), there's no direct way to get the complete list of methods defined on a specific class. This example shows a brief function that recursively traverses the __bases__ tuple to obtain that information:

```
def methodsOf(aClass):
    classMembers = vars(aClass).values()
    methods = [eachMember for eachMember in classMembers
            if callable(eachMember)]
    for eachBase in aClass.__bases__:
        methods.extend(methodsOf(eachBase))
    return methods

print methodsOf(ChildClass)
```

```
[<function __init__ at 4133241>, <function play at 1334165>,
 <function speak at 7131111>, <function __init__ at 4546767>]
```

The methodsOf method in this code uses a list comprehension and the Python built-in method callable to isolate functions. The callable method takes any Python object and returns true if it is legal to use function-calling syntax on that object—which means the object needs to be a function, a method, a class, or an instance of a class that defines the __call__ special method. Having taken the list of functions from the called class, the method makes a recursive call for each element of the __bases__ list, and adds the result to the end of the list. Notice that the function is perhaps too simple, as it returns the __init__ method of both the parent and child classes.

Basic built-in types are handled differently from user-defined objects. To get at the methods of a built-in type, you would use the __methods__ special attribute. But to get at the attributes of the type, if any, you would use the __members__ special attribute. Built-in types are handled differently in CPython and Jython. In CPython, an attempt to take the __class__ of a built-in type will result in an error, while in Jython, it will return a meaningful value. The CPython behavior is scheduled to change in CPython Version 2.2.

Built-in types can also be passed to the built-in function type(*object*), which returns a type object that can be used for comparison. To get known objects for the other end of a type comparison, the common idiom is to use empty literal objects—for example, type([1, 2, 3]) == type([]). If you want something that is a little more English-like, you can use the types module, which defines a number of names corresponding to the type objects, such as ListType, IntType, and so on. All user-defined instances are of the type InstanceType. If you want a more fine-grained comparison of the class of an instance, you need to use the built-in methods isinstance(*instance*, *class*) or issubclass(*class*, *class*). The isinstance function will also work on basic types.

Reflecting on Java Objects

Although many of the reflection techniques described in the previous section also work when the target is a Java class instance, the differences between a Java instance as represented in Jython and Python object structures mean that not all of them will work identically. Most notably, Jython instance objects of Java classes do not store attributes in a __dict__ attribute, which means that __dict__ and vars will raise an error if called on a Java object.

The following code shows some reflection mechanisms targeted on the SampleBean class from Example 8-1:

```
import SampleBean

sample = SampleBean( )
print "dir:", dir(sample)
print "__class__:", sample.__class__
```

```
print "\n__bases__:", SampleBean.__bases__
print "class dir:", dir(SampleBean)
print "class vars:", vars(SampleBean)

dir: []
__class__: SampleBean


__bases__: (<jclass java.lang.Object at 726660>,)
class dir: ['__init__', 'getIntegerProperty', 'getStringProperty',
'integerProperty', 'setIntegerProperty', 'setStringProperty',
'stringProperty']
class vars: {'integerProperty': <beanProperty integerProperty type: int at
7560752>, 'setStringProperty': <java function setStringProperty at 2936165>,
'stringProperty': <beanProperty stringProperty type: java.lang.String at
6345067>, 'getIntegerProperty': <java function getIntegerProperty at
5567317>, 'getStringProperty': <java function getStringProperty at 3378396>,
'__init__': <java constructor SampleBean at 6607053>, 'setIntegerProperty':
<java function setIntegerProperty at 4738155>}
```

There are a couple of items in this example that you might not expect. First, the dir method on the instance is defined, but returns an empty list. This is related to the fact that Java instances don't have __dict__ dictionaries—there's nothing from which to get dir values.

The __class__ attribute exists, but should be considered read-only, both for Java instances and instances of a Jython class inheriting from Java. Changing __class__ of a Java class does affect the accessibility of the attributes of the class. The example shows that class objects in Jython for Java classes do have their own __dict__ dictionaries. In addition to the method names, notice that the __dict__ of this class also contains entries for the bean properties that Jython infers from the naming conventions. Because classes do have attribute dictionaries, the methodsOf method defined previously will work on Java classes, as shown here:

```
print methodsOf(SampleBean)
```

```
[<java function setStringProperty at 2936165>, <java function
getIntegerProperty at 5567317>, <java function getStringProperty at 3378396>
, <java constructor SampleBean at 6607053>, <java function
setIntegerProperty at 4738155>, <java function wait at 431216>, <java
function equals at 8092070>, <java function notify at 7309364>, <java
function notifyAll at 5710111>, <java function hashCode at 4168111>, <java
function toString at 180797>, <java function getClass at 1983877>]
```

Active Reflection

Frequently, you want to get or set the value of an attribute, but you don't know which attribute until runtime, when you have the attribute name as a string. This is particularly common in CGI programming, or when dealing

with external databases. In both cases, you deal with a lot of string key/
value pairs. While you could directly access the object's __getattr__
method or __dict__ attribute, you don't have to. Python provides built-in
functions for reflective access to an object: these built-in functions work
with all built-in objects and not only with class instances:

delattr(*object*, *name*)
> Name is a string representing an attribute in the object. Equivalent to
> del *object*.*name*.

getattr(*object*, *name*[, *defvalue*])
> Name is a string representing an attribute in the object. Returns the
> value *object*.*name*, calling the object's __getattr__ special method if
> needed. The optional argument *defvalue* is returned in case *object* has
> no attribute *name*.

hasattr(*object*, *name*)
> Returns true if the object has an attribute called *name* either directly or
> indirectly up the class hierarchy. The class is considered recursively for
> instances and base classes for classes.

setattr(*object*, *name*, *value*)
> Name is a string representing an attribute in the object. Equivalent to
> *object*.*name* = *value*. Calls the object's __setattr__ special method if
> needed.

An inventive use of these functions can make for generic, reusable, and compact code. The following example shows how to define a base class whose
subclasses can execute a bunch of commands expressed as a string plus a set
of arguments, and then undo everything executed so far.

```
class UndoExecutive:

    def __init__(self):
        self._sofar = []

    def perform(self,cmd,*args):
        _sofar.push((cmd,args))
        getattr(self,"do_%s" % cmd)(*args)

    def undo(self):
        while self._sofar:
            cmd,args = self._sofar.pop()
            getattr(self,"undo_%s" % cmd)(*args)
```

The subclasses should define only the appropriate do_*cmd* and undo_*cmd*
methods.

CHAPTER 9
Using Swing

Swing is the Java standard GUI toolkit as of Java 1.2. It offers a number of advantages over the Abstract Windowing Toolkit (AWT) that was in use before Swing was developed. Among those advantages are a more complete and powerful widget set, lightweight widgets that are drawn in Java, custom look-and-feel designs, and a more flexible and useful event model. Swing uses the JavaBeans specification heavily—it's probably the most aggressively "beaned" Java library in existence—to allow Swing components to be easily added to GUI toolkits that allow the programmer to manipulate the interface design via the bean properties. More information on the JavaBean reflection shortcuts used by Jython in this chapter is contained in "Bean-Based Reflection" in Chapter 8.

If you've spent much time programming in Swing, you know two things. First, you know that Swing is very flexible and powerful. Second, you know that it can be verbose, complex, and downright quirky at times. Swing is definitely an area where Jython's simplification and clarity are particularly useful.

The combination of the Python language, the Jython bean access shortcuts, and Swing is hard to beat as a GUI prototyping kit. If you do prototype your Java GUI in Jython, there is a good chance you'll find writing Swing in Jython so much easier that you will wind up keeping the Jython and never translating to Java at all. If you have programmed GUIs in CPython, we think you'll also find that Jython/Swing is an excellent alternative to Tkinter and wxWindows—Swing has more widgets and a more flexible event model, and it is easier to extend.

For a comprehensive look at Swing, we recommend *Java Swing*, by Robert Eckstein, Marc Loy, and Dave Wood (O'Reilly). That book contains everything you'd ever want to know about Swing. For more of a quick reference, try *Java Foundation Classes in a Nutshell*, by David Flanagan (O'Reilly).

Java Versus Jython

For the most part, using Swing is just like using any Java class from your Jython code. Because nearly everything in Swing is a bean property, the access shortcuts can have a dramatic effect on the size and readability of your code. To demonstrate the differences between Java and Jython, here's a short program written in both languages.

The program is a simple counter, shown in Figure 9-1. Pressing the "Inc" button increments the value, pressing the "Dec" button decrements it, and pressing "Clear" returns the value to zero.

Figure 9-1. The counter screen

Example 9-1 contains the Java code to build this program.

Example 9-1. Counter.java

```
import javax.swing.*;
import java.awt.*;
import java.awt.event.*;

public class Counter extends JFrame {

    private JTextField display;
    private int value;

    public Counter(){
        this.getContentPane().setLayout(new java.awt.FlowLayout());
        value = 0;
        this.setTitle("Counter");
        this.setSize(200, 100);

        this.display = new JTextField();
        this.display.setPreferredSize(new Dimension(200, 30));
        this.setDisplay();
        this.display.setHorizontalAlignment(SwingConstants.CENTER);
        this.getContentPane().add(display);

        JButton increment = new JButton("Inc");
        increment.setSize(65, 70);
        increment.addActionListener(new ActionListener() {
            public void actionPerformed(ActionEvent evt) {
                Counter.this.value++;
```

Example 9-1. Counter.java (continued)

```
                Counter.this.setDisplay( );
            }
        }
        );
        this.getContentPane( ).add(increment);

        JButton clear = new JButton("Clear");
        clear.setSize(65, 70);
        clear.addActionListener(new ActionListener( ) {
            public void actionPerformed(ActionEvent evt) {
                Counter.this.value = 0;
                Counter.this.setDisplay( );
            }
        });
        this.getContentPane( ).add(clear);

        JButton decrement = new JButton("Dec");
        decrement.setSize(65, 70);
        decrement.addActionListener(new ActionListener( ) {
            public void actionPerformed(ActionEvent evt) {
                Counter.this.value--;
                Counter.this.setDisplay( );
            }
        });
        this.getContentPane( ).add(decrement);
    }

    private void setDisplay( ) {
        this.display.setText(String.valueOf(value));
    }

    public static void main(String[] args) {
        Counter window = new Counter( );
        window.show( );
    }
}
```

If you are familiar with Swing, Example 9-1 should be rather straightforward. The code creates a new subclass of JFrame, and populates it with a text field and three buttons. Each button has an anonymous inner class registered as a listener that implements the ActionListener interface. That inner class contains the actionPerformed function, which is called by Swing in response to a button click. The functions do something with the value, and then call the function setDisplay( ), which updates the display on the screen.

The Jython code in Example 9-2 is equivalent to the Java code in Example 9-1. It produces the same window with the same functionality.

Example 9-2. jy_counter.py

```python
import javax.swing as swing
import java

class Counter(swing.JFrame):

    def __init__(self):
        swing.JFrame.__init__(self, title="Counter", size=(200, 100))
        self.contentPane.layout = java.awt.FlowLayout()
        self.value = 0

        self.display = swing.JTextField(preferredSize=(200, 30),
                horizontalAlignment=swing.SwingConstants.CENTER)
        self.setDisplay()
        self.contentPane.add(self.display)

        increment = swing.JButton("Inc", size=(65, 70),
                actionPerformed=self.incrementDisplay)
        self.contentPane.add(increment)

        clear = swing.JButton("Clear", size=(65, 70),
                actionPerformed=self.clearDisplay)
        self.contentPane.add(clear)

        decrement = swing.JButton("Dec", size=(65, 70),
                actionPerformed=self.decrementDisplay)
        self.contentPane.add(decrement)

    def incrementDisplay(self, event):
        self.value += 1
        self.setDisplay()

    def decrementDisplay(self, event):
        self.value -= 1
        self.setDisplay()

    def clearDisplay(self, event):
        self.value = 0
        self.setDisplay()

    def setDisplay(self):
        self.display.text = str(self.value)

if __name__ == "__main__":
    Counter().show()
```

The first thing you'll notice in Example 9-2 is that the code is about two-thirds the length of the Java code in Example 9-1. Admittedly, some of the length difference is due to the lack of lines containing a single closing brace. That's not a completely trivial point, though, because that does allow more code on one screen, which is a nice feature during development. You'll find in practice that more complicated Jython/Swing programs show even larger savings for Jython over Java. (And the Java example would be longer if it adhered strictly to the Sun Java coding standards, which suggest importing each class in its own import statement.)

Although we've seen nearly all the Python language constructs in Example 9-2, there are a few new things worth pointing out. The constructor for the counter calls the parent JFrame constructor directly to be able to use Jython keyword shortcuts.

```
swing.JFrame.__init__(self, title="Counter", size=(200, 100))
```

That line of Jython is equivalent to the following two lines of Java:

```
this.setTitle("Counter");
this.setSize(200, 100);
```

More importantly, Jython avoids the use of inner classes by using the bean property event shortcut. So, where the Java code in Example 9-1 uses the following code:

```
JButton clear = new JButton("Clear");
clear.setSize(65, 70);
clear.addActionListener(new ActionListener( ) {
    public void actionPerformed(ActionEvent evt) {
        Counter.this.value = 0;
        Counter.this.setDisplay( );
    }
});
```

the Jython code in Example 9-2 separates the function definition from the widget creation:

```
increment = swing.JButton("Inc", size=(65, 70),
        actionPerformed=self.incrementDisplay)

def incrementDisplay(self, event):
    self.value += 1
    self.setDisplay ( )
```

Hopefully, the comparison between the Java code in Example 9-1 and the Jython code in Example 9-2 demonstrates that Jython Swing code is easy to read and to generate compared with the Java code. The next three examples show slightly larger Jython Swing programs to demonstrate how you can combine Python and Java strengths.

As you use Jython in your own Swing code, keep in mind that the Swing library is large, complex, and not always consistent. The bean tricks go a very long way toward shielding you from that, but there are some corners of Swing that don't always behave as Jython expects—remember, you can always go back and call the Java functions explicitly. Don't be afraid to experiment—it's much faster to update Jython code than it is to update Java code.

A Calculator

Example 9-3 creates a very simple arithmetic calculator in Jython. It shows off the use of a couple of different kinds of layout managers, as well as more examples of event binding in Jython. We show all the code for the calculator in Example 9-3, then discuss it section by section.

Example 9-3. calculator.py

```python
import javax.swing as swing
import java
import operator

class CalculatorFrame(swing.JFrame):

    operators = {"/": operator.div, "*": operator.mul,
            "-": operator.sub, "+": operator.add}

    operatorString = "/*-+="

    def __init__(self):
        swing.JFrame.__init__(self, size=(200, 250), title="Calculator")
        self.keyReleased = self.key
        self.contentPane.layout = java.awt.BorderLayout()
        self.contentPane.add(self.buildDisplayPanel(),
                java.awt.BorderLayout.NORTH)
        self.contentPane.add(self.buildDigitPanel(),
                java.awt.BorderLayout.WEST)
        self.contentPane.add(self.buildOperatorPanel(),
                java.awt.BorderLayout.EAST)

    def buildDisplayPanel(self):
        panel = swing.JPanel(size=(200,100),
                border=swing.border.TitledBorder("Display"),
                layout=java.awt.BorderLayout(0, 10))
        self.topOperand = swing.JTextField(preferredSize=(200,20),
                editable=0, background=(255, 255, 255),
                horizontalAlignment=swing.SwingConstants.RIGHT)
        panel.add(self.topOperand, java.awt.BorderLayout.NORTH)
        self.operator = swing.JTextField(preferredSize=(20, 20),
                editable=0, background=(255, 255, 255))
        panel.add(self.operator, java.awt.BorderLayout.WEST)
        self.bottomOperand = swing.JTextField(preferredSize=(160,20),
                editable=0, background=(255, 255, 255),
                horizontalAlignment=swing.SwingConstants.RIGHT)
        panel.add(self.bottomOperand, java.awt.BorderLayout.EAST)
        return panel

    def buildDigitPanel(self):
        box = swing.Box.createVerticalBox()
        box.add(self.buildDigitRow((7, 8, 9)))
        box.add(self.buildDigitRow((4, 5, 6)))
```

Example 9-3. calculator.py (continued)

```python
        box.add(self.buildDigitRow((1, 2, 3)))
        box.add(self.buildDigitRow((0,)))
        box.add(self.buildFunctionRow())
        return box

    def buildDigitRow(self, digits):
        row = swing.Box.createHorizontalBox()
        for eachDigit in digits:
            if eachDigit != None:
                button = swing.JButton(str(eachDigit),
                        actionPerformed=self.digitPressed)
                row.add(button)
        return row

    def buildFunctionRow(self):
        row = swing.Box.createHorizontalBox()
        row.add(swing.JButton("Clr", actionPerformed=self.clear))
        row.add(swing.JButton(".", actionPerformed=self.decimalPressed))
        return row

    def buildOperatorPanel(self):
        box = swing.Box.createVerticalBox()
        for operator in self.operatorString:
            box.add(swing.JButton(operator,
                    actionPerformed=self.operatorPressed))
        return box

    def digitPressed(self, event):
        self.handleDigit(event.source.text)

    def operatorPressed(self, event):
        self.handleOperator(event.source.text)

    def key(self, event):
        char = event.keyChar
        if char.isdigit():
            self.handleDigit(char)
        elif char == ".":
            self.decimalPressed(event)
        elif char in self.operatorString:
            self.handleOperator(char)
        elif char == "\n":
            self.clear(event)

    def clear(self, event):
        self.operator.text = ""
        self.topOperand.text = ""
        self.bottomOperand.text = ""

    def handleDigit(self, digitChar):
        self.bottomOperand.text += digitChar
```

Example 9-3. calculator.py (continued)

```
    def decimalPressed(self, event):
        if not '.' in self.bottomOperand.text:
            self.bottomOperand.text += '.'

    def handleOperator(self, opChar):
        if self.operator.text:
            opFunc = self.operators[self.operator.text]
            topNum = float(self.topOperand.text)
            bottomNum = float(self.bottomOperand.text)
            result = opFunc(topNum, bottomNum)
            self.topOperand.text = str(result)
            self.bottomOperand.text = ""
        elif self.bottomOperand.text:
            self.topOperand.text = self.bottomOperand.text
            self.bottomOperand.text = ""
        self.displayOperator(opChar)

    def displayOperator(self, opChar):
        if not self.calculationStarted():
            return
        if opChar == "=":
            self.operator.text = ""
        else:
            self.operator.text = opChar

    def calculationStarted(self):
        return self.topOperand.text or self.bottomOperand.text


if __name__ == "__main__":
    CalculatorFrame().show()
```

Example 9-3 starts by importing the necessary modules, declaring a class-level dictionary mapping operator characters to operations, and a string of operator characters.

The __init__ function sets the size and title of the window, then sets a function to be called on key release, using the bean event shortcut. It sets up a border layout and calls further functions to put the display at border north, the digits at border west, and the operators at border east.

The buildDisplayPanel function is pretty straightforward—these items are all read-only, so there are no events to associate. The background color is explicitly set to white (255, 255, 255), because Swing tends to make read-only text fields gray. This also shows that you can set a border and layout from the keyword arguments, and that you can access the SwingConstants as well.

The digit panel uses the Swing Box component. The panel is a vertically aligned box, where each component is a horizontally aligned box. The buildDigitRow function takes a sequence of digits and creates a new button for each, setting the text to the string representation of the digit, and setting the actionPerformed property to the method to be called when the button is clicked—the same method for each button. Similarly, the buildFunctionRow creates a button for the clear and decimal point buttons—each has its own function. Again, the listener shortcut makes this code significantly cleaner than the Java version with inner classes.

The digitPressed and operatorPressed functions are called directly from the action listeners and just grab the text of the source button and redirect to a separate handler function. This is so that the key event handler can call the same functions. The key event handler redirects to one of the four types of events—digit, operator, decimal point, or clear, based on what key was pressed. If the key is unknown, it does nothing. The events are just the ordinary Java event instances, being accessed using bean properties.

Next come the handlers. For simplicity's sake, the application in Example 9-3 doesn't do any separate storage of the numbers outside the display text fields, so the clear function just resets the text fields to the empty string. The handleDigit method merely appends the character to the end of the bottom operand display—much simpler for this application than attempting to manage the operands as an integer. The decimalPressed method does the same append, but only if there is not already a decimal point in the number.

Finally, the handleOperator method has the meat of the operation. If an operator has not already been pressed, it moves the number from the bottom to the top display and holds on to the operator. If an operator is already being held, the program grabs the operation from the operators dictionary, converts the two displays to numbers, performs the operation, and resets the display. A couple of utility functions ensure that the new operator is displayed properly.

The finished calculator is shown in Figure 9-2.

An HTML Browser

One of the cooler features of Swing is the integration of HTML rendering into the widget set. Not only can you use simple HTML tags to format labels, but also the text components are HTML-aware. It's only a few steps from an HTML-aware widget to a simple Swing web browser. Accent on simple: before you start taking on Mozilla and Internet Explorer, remember that the Java Swing component is really intended for things like displaying JavaDoc—nonstandard, complex, or otherwise weird HTML easily confuses it (at least in JDK 1.3). It also only supports the HTML 3.2 specification. This example is presented for demo purposes only.

Figure 9-2. Jython Calculator

Example 9-4 contains the source code that produces the web browser.

Example 9-4. html_browser.py

```python
import htmllib
import formatter
import javax.swing as swing
import java
import urllib


ACTIVATED = swing.event.HyperlinkEvent.EventType.ACTIVATED
ENTERED = swing.event.HyperlinkEvent.EventType.ENTERED
EXITED = swing.event.HyperlinkEvent.EventType.EXITED


class HtmlBrowserWindow(swing.JFrame):

    def __init__(self, urlString="http://www.jython.org"):
        swing.JFrame.__init__(self, title="HTML Browser", size=(800, 600))
        self.contentPane.layout = java.awt.BorderLayout()
        self.contentPane.add(self.buildTopPane(urlString),
                java.awt.BorderLayout.NORTH)
        self.htmlPane = swing.JEditorPane(urlString, editable=0,
                hyperlinkUpdate=self.followHyperlink, size=(400,400))
        self.contentPane.add(swing.JScrollPane(self.htmlPane),
                java.awt.BorderLayout.CENTER)
        self.status = swing.JLabel(" ", preferredSize=(500,20))
        self.contentPane.add(self.status, java.awt.BorderLayout.SOUTH)

    def buildTopPane(self, startUrl):
        label = swing.JLabel("Go To:")
        self.field = swing.JTextField(preferredSize=(500,20),
                text=startUrl, actionPerformed=self.goToUrl)
        button = swing.JButton("Go", size=(100,100),
                actionPerformed=self.goToUrl)
        topPane = swing.JPanel()
```

Example 9-4. html_browser.py (continued)

```
        topPane.add(label)
        topPane.add(self.field)
        topPane.add(button)
        return topPane

    def goToUrl(self, event):
        self.htmlPane.setPage(self.field.text)

    def followHyperlink(self, hlEvent):
        if hlEvent.eventType == ACTIVATED:
            self.htmlPane.setPage(hlEvent.URL)
            self.field.text = hlEvent.URL.toString()
        elif hlEvent.eventType == ENTERED:
            self.status.text = hlEvent.URL.toString()
        elif hlEvent.eventType == EXITED:
            self.status.text = " "

if __name__ == "__main__":
    HtmlBrowserWindow().show()
```

Given what we have already seen in Example 9-2 and Example 9-3, most of this code should be clear. The hyperlinkUpdate function is defined by the HyperlinkListener interface; therefore, it's assignable via a bean shortcut. However, the page property of the htmlPane cannot be set directly from a string in the goToUrl function. In the case of htmlPane the setter function is overloaded to allow both a string argument and a java.lang.URL. In this case Jython recognizes page as a property of type java.lang.URL, but in the general case of overloaded getters and setters, the behavior of Jython is undetermined. The bean specification does not cover this case. To ensure proper behavior, you need to call the getter or setter explicitly, as in Example 9-4. The similar line in followHyperlink does have a URL, but the set call was performed explicitly anyway, for consistency.

Also, the code in Example 9-4 does not handle exceptions—the setPage call that takes a string will throw a MalformedURLException to the console window if the string is not a valid URL. In a more robust production application, you'd probably want to display something in the editor, but for the demo, it wasn't worth cluttering up the code.

The followHyperlink function determines what to do based on constants defined by the event class. An actual click on the link is event type ACTIVATED, which triggers a call to change the page, while ENTERED and EXITED indicate a mouse-over condition and just update the status line. The constants are assigned to shorter forms at the beginning of the code for readability.

Figure 9-3 shows the browser in action on the Jython web site.

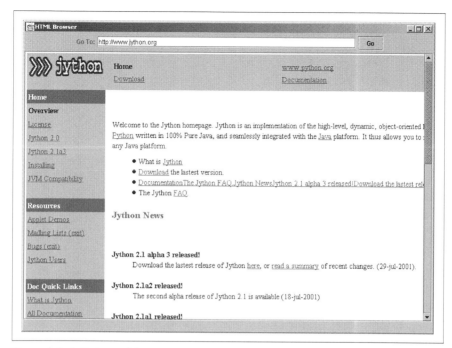

Figure 9-3. A Swing web browser

An HTML Source Browser

The last example for this chapter will demonstrate how to use Swing models in Jython. Swing often uses interfaces such as TreeModel and TableModel to allow you to keep your data separate from the code that does the actual GUI display. This separation is in keeping with the Model/View/Controller pattern for GUI design. In Jython, you can program the data types using Python lists and dictionaries to such a degree that the model and GUI display code approaches the trivial.

Example 9-5 demonstrates how to integrate the Python standard library with Java Swing functionality—in this case the standard Python module *htmllib*, which provides HTML parsing functionality. The program takes an HTML string and converts it to a structured tree representation. Figure 9-4 shows the representation of the Jython home page. As you can see, it displays the nested structure of the HTML tags.

The first step in Example 9-5 is writing the parser to convert the HTML string to a tree representation. While this might seem daunting, the *htmllib* module makes it relatively straightforward. Ordinarily, *htmllib* allows you to create functions named start_*tag* and end_*tag*, which are automatically called when a tag named *tag* is encountered. However, in this case, we want

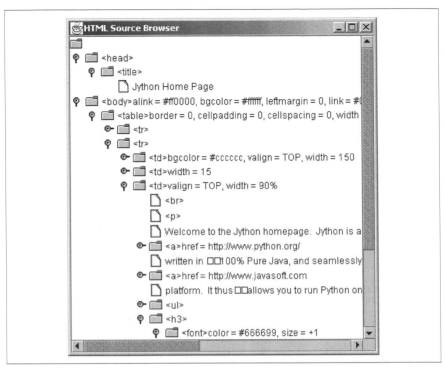

Figure 9-4. HTML source browser

to do the same thing no matter what tag is read, so we override the tag handler function directly. Example 9-5 contains the first part of this program, the HTML parser.

Example 9-5. html_source_viewer.py

```
import htmllib
import formatter
import javax.swing as swing
import java
import urllib

class HtmlTreeParser(htmllib.HTMLParser):

    def __init__(self, initialText = ""):
        htmllib.HTMLParser.__init__(self, formatter.NullFormatter( ), 0)
        self.model = HtmlTagTreeModel( )
        self.tagStack = []
        self.feed(initialText)

    def currentTag(self):
        if self.tagStack:
            return self.tagStack[len(self.tagStack) - 1]

    def handle_starttag(self, tag, method, attrs):
```

Example 9-5. html_source_viewer.py (continued)

```python
        self.starttag(tag, attrs)

    def unknown_starttag(self, tag, attrs):
        self.starttag(tag, attrs)

    def starttag(self, tag, attrs):
        tag = Tag(tag, attrs)
        if not self.model.rootTag:
            self.model.rootTag = tag
        if self.tagStack:
            self.currentTag().addChild(tag)
        self.tagStack.append(tag)

    def handle_endtag(self, tag, method):
        self.endtag(tag)

    def unknown_endtag(self, tag):
        self.endtag(tag)

    def endtag(self, tag):
        poppedTags = []
        while 1:
            poppedTag = self.tagStack.pop()
            if poppedTag.tagString == tag:
                break
            else:
                poppedTag.myParent.addChildren(poppedTag.children)
                poppedTag.children = []

    def handle_data(self, data):
        data = data.strip()
        if data:
            self.currentTag().children.append(data)
```

On initialization, the class calls the parent constructor with some default values (we're not interested here in the formatting capabilities of HTMLParser). The attribute self.model will eventually contain the object that implements Swing's TreeModel interface. We'll keep a running stack of tags being processed, which starts as an empty list. The feed method starts the actual parsing.

Most of the action here is in the starttag, endtag, and handle_data methods. When the beginning of a tag is encountered, HTMLParser calls either handle_starttag or unknown_starttag (the distinction is not important for this program). Both redirect to the starttag method, which makes the new tag a child of the current tag and places the new tag in the stack (the tag argument is the name of the tag, and the attrs argument is a tuple of the name/value pairs in the tag—both are generated by HTMLParser). If the tag is the first to be processed, it sets it as the root of the model.

If HTML were perfectly consistent and all tags had separate starts and ends, all the endtag method would have to do is pop the stack. However, a number of HTML tags, such as img or br, don't have end tags. Ignoring that fact leads to an unbalanced tree, and to tags that are still in the stack at the end of the program. Example 9-5 handles the case pretty simply. The while loop continually pops tags off the stack until the start tag corresponding to the end tag is reached. Any children accumulated along the way are "rolled up" into the parent so that when the start tag is finally reached, it has all the tags beneath it as children, as you would expect. You can see in Figure 9-4, for instance, that the single tags <br> and <p> are both sibling children of the <td> tag—without this loop, <p> would be considered a child of <br>.

When string text is encountered, the handle_data function is automatically called and places that data as a child of the current tag. The recursion makes the children list heterogeneous—it can contain either tags or strings.

Example 9-6 contains the Tag class, which simply provides support for the relationships between tags.

Example 9-6. Tag class for HTML browser

```
class Tag(java.lang.Object):

    def __init__(self, tagString, attrs=[]):
        self.tagString = tagString
        self.children = []
        self.data = ""
        self.arguments = attrs
        self.arguments.sort()
        self.myParent = None

    def addChild(self, newChild):
        self.children.append(newChild)
        if isinstance(newChild, Tag):
            newChild.myParent = self

    def addChildren(self, children):
        for each in children:
            self.addChild(each)

    def argumentString(self):
        stringList = ["%s = %s" % (key, value)
                for key, value in self.arguments]
        return ', '.join(stringList)

    def toString(self):
        string = "<%s>" % self.tagString
        if self.arguments:
            string += self.argumentString()
        return string
```

Example 9-6. Tag class for HTML browser (continued)

```
def __str__(self):
    return toString(self)
```

In Example 9-6, you need to explicitly make Tag a subclass of java.lang. Object, because Swing eventually calls the toString method to display the tag in the tree, using inheritance from Java. That way, Swing receives a proper subclass of java.lang.Object with a properly overridden toString method that delegates its behavior to Jython code. Otherwise, it simply gets the Jython internal representation for a pure Python instance, which includes a more general and, in this case, less useful toString method.

At this point, you may be wondering where the actual Swing code comes in. Be warned—it may seem anticlimactic because having done this part, the Swing-specific code is very short. Of course, keeping the Swing code minimal is generally the goal of a Swing programmer.

First we need a class that implements TreeModel, which was referenced in the HTML parser code in Example 9-5. The TreeModel interface defines eight methods—but we only need to write code for five because the other three are for editable trees. Amazingly, none of the methods in Example 9-7 needs to be longer than one line.

Example 9-7. HTML source browser tree model

```
class HtmlTagTreeModel(swing.tree.TreeModel):

    def __init__(self):
        self.rootTag = None

    def addTreeModelListener(self, listener): pass
    def removeTreeModelListener(self, listener): pass
    def valueForPathChanged(path, newValue): pass

    def getChild(self, parent, index):
        return parent.children[index]

    def getChildCount(self, parent):
        return len(parent.children)

    def getIndexOfChild(self, parent, child):
        return parent.children.index(child)

    def getRoot(self):
        return self.rootTag

    def isLeaf(self, node):
        return (type(node) == type("")) or (len(node.children) == 0)
```

All the tree model methods in Example 9-7 are simple lookups into the attributes of the Tag class—except for isLeaf, which does a type check to catch strings first.

With the model in place, Swing does all the work for rendering the code. All we need to do is put a JTree in the window, as shown in Example 9-8.

Example 9-8. The HTML source browser window

```
class HtmlTreeViewer(swing.JFrame):

    def __init__(self, htmlString="", url=""):
        swing.JFrame.__init__(self, title="HTML Source Browser",
                size=(400, 600))
        if url:
            connection = urllib.urlopen(url)
            htmlString = connection.read( )
        self.parser = HtmlTreeParser(htmlString)
        self.tree = swing.JTree(model=self.parser.model)
        scrollpane = swing.JScrollPane(self.tree)
        self.contentPane.add(scrollpane)

if __name__ =="__main__":\
    HtmlTreeViewer(url="http://www.jython.org").show( )
```

Python's standard *urllib* module lets you treat remote URL addresses as though they were remote files—we can just read the URL text into a string. However, we're ignoring a potential exception to keep the demo straightforward, as discussed earlier. Once the text is in place, a parser instance is created and the model from that parser is passed to the JTree, the JTree is put in a scroll pane, and the scroll pane is put in the window. Voilá!

The examples in this chapter should give you some idea of the power of Jython to build interfaces quickly. The best part of programming in Jython, however, is the interactivity and hands-on feel—which is unfortunately very hard to get across just by showing the finished code example. You'll find that the overhead of making changes is so low that you'll be more apt to experiment with new things, try different features, play with different layouts, and so on. Chapter 10 will show how other Java libraries can be similarly leveraged.

Using Java Libraries

Jython allows you to easily use existing Java library code from within your Jython program. Frequently, the libraries are actually easier to manage from Jython than they are from Java. They may be easier because Jython tools have been written to simplify the library API, or because the Jython reflection shortcuts significantly improve library access.

This chapter showcases three common Java tools—the JDBC database access API, the servlet API, and XML parsing standards—along with strategies for getting the most out of them from within Jython. Although you can use the JDBC database access API directly in Jython, a tool called *zxJDBC* allows for a more Pythonic style of access. The Java servlet API can be programmed directly in Jython with the help of the PyServlet tool. A number of different Java-based XML tools can be used more easily through Jython. We hope that these examples offer you ideas on how to best use other Java libraries.

JDBC and the Python Database API

Database access is an area in which both Java and Python solutions exist. In Java, database access is managed through the JDBC database connectivity classes. JDBC classes work fine in Jython, however their interaction with Python objects and code is a little awkward, in particular because the JDBC classes are not set up to allow Python-style looping through results. The analogous Python functionality is provided by the Python Database (DB) API, which is the standard target for database connectivity within Python.

Using zxJDBC

To use the Python DB API from Jython, you can use the *zxJDBC* package that ships with Jython as of Jython 2.1 (you can also get it at *http://www.ziclix.com/zxjdbc/index.html*). The *zxJDBC* package is a Java implementation of the Python DB API that runs on top of the JDBC classes. If you have a JDBC-compliant driver for your database, you can run *zxJDBC* using that driver. To run *zxJDBC*, the database driver needs to be in your classpath.

The Python DB API is simpler than the Java JDBC, as it contains fewer classes and attributes. A full listing of the API can be found at *http://www.python.org/topics/database/DatabaseAPI-2.0.html*. The discussion in this chapter will focus on the most used features of the DB API, for your convenience.

You start a zxJDBC session when you make a connection by calling the top-level `connect()` function. The `connect()` function and the `paramstyle` attribute are both defined by the database API at the module level.

`connect(jdbcUrl, username, password, driverClassName)`
> Returns a connection object—the exact order and type of the parameters are specific to zxJDBC.

`paramstyle`
> Style of formatting expected for arguments to SQL statements. Styles include:

> `'qmark'`
>> Argument placeholders use question marks; e.g., `where object_id = ?`

> `'numeric'`
>> Argument placeholders use colons followed by integers; e.g., `where object_id = :1`

> `'named'`
>> Argument placeholders use colons followed by argument names; e.g., `where name = :name`

> `'format'`
>> Argument placeholders use C-style formatting directives; e.g., `where name = %s`

> `'pyformat'`
>> Argument placeholders use the Python dictionary syntax for formatting directives; e.g., `where name = %(name)s`

Currently, *zxJDBC* supports only the `'qmark'` style.

Connection Objects

Once you have the connection object, you can use it to control transaction behavior, and to get a cursor object to actually execute SQL statements. Following are the most common methods for connection objects.

```
close( )
```
Closes the connection. The connection is automatically closed when it passes out of scope. The connection will raise an error if used after closing.

```
commit( )
```
Commits the current transaction, if supported. If supported, auto-commit is off by default. In *zxJDBC* you can enable it by setting the autocommit attribute of the connection object to any true value.

```
cursor([dynamicFetch=0])
```
Returns a cursor object, or an object that simulates a cursor. In *zxJDBC*, there is an optional argument, which, if true, returns a dynamic cursor (see the following section).

```
rollback( )
```
Rolls back the current transaction, if supported by the database.

Cursor Objects

The cursor object executes the statements, and allows access to the results. In *zxJDBC*, cursors are either static or dynamic. A static cursor retrieves all its information from the underlying JDBC result set immediately and closes the result set. Although this allows the rowcount parameter to be set in the cursor, this argument can be inefficient. A dynamic cursor keeps the underlying result set and grabs data as needed, which means that the rowcount parameter will not be set. Following are the most commonly used attributes and methods for cursor objects.

```
arraysize
```
Number of rows fetched by a call to fetchmany( ).

```
callproc(procname [, procparams])
```
Calls a stored procedure with the given name and a parameter sequence.

```
close( )
```
Closes the cursor. Further attempts to use the cursor raise errors.

```
datahandler
```
A *zxJDBC*-specific data handler object to manage data types.

```
description
```
A sequence of seven-item tuples, each describing one column of the returned data. Each tuple is of the form (name, type_code, display_size, internal_size, precision, scale, null_ok). If not executed, the value is None.

```
execute(operation [, params])
```
Executes the given SQL statement, with the optional parameters. The parameters are either a mapping or a sequence. The placeholder format to be used in the operation depends on the paramstyle of the driver.

```
executemany(operation, paramseq)
```
Executes the given SQL statement once for each set of parameters in the paramseq. Will use a prepared statement if offered by the database.

```
fetchall()
```
Fetches all returned results as a tuple of tuples.

```
fetchmany([size])
```
Fetches a number of rows from the result equal to the size of the parameter if it is specified, and to the arraysize if it is not.

```
fetchone()
```
Fetches the next row of the result as a tuple.

```
rowcount
```
For a static cursor, the number of rows returned by the query.

As you might imagine, translating data types from the database to Java to Python and back can sometimes be a headache. To get around this problem, you can use the data handler objects provided by *zxJDBC*. By default, the data handler is a generic handler for JDBC 2.0 data types, but specific data handlers are also provided for Informix, Oracle, and MySQL. The constructor for these data handlers takes another data handler as an argument, allowing the handlers to be chained to combine their functionality. The data handler is automatically called when data is collected and smoothes out some data quirks of each database, such as the formatting of dates or the representation of Boolean data.

Example 10-1 shows a simple *zxJDBC* snippet that creates a table, populates it, and then queries it. This example uses MySQL and assumes that the relevant driver class is in the classpath.

Example 10-1. Sample zxJDBC program

```
import com.ziclix.python.sql as sql
dburl, user, pw, drv = ("jdbc:mysql://localhost/test", None, None,
        "org.gjt.mm.mysql.Driver")
db = sql.zxJDBC.connect(dburl, user, pw, drv)

cursor = db.cursor()
cursor.datahandler = sql.handler.MySQLDataHandler(cursor.datahandler)
cursor.execute("""CREATE TABLE IF NOT EXISTS test (
    object_id integer primary key,
    name varchar(100),
    grade float)""")
cursor.execute("DELETE FROM test")
```

Example 10-1. Sample zxJDBC program (continued)

```
cursor.executemany("""INSERT INTO test (object_id, name, grade)
        VALUES (?, ?, ?)""",
        ((1, 'Fred Flintstone', 90.5), (2, 'Zach Paleozogt', 100)))
db.commit()

cursor.execute("SELECT * FROM test ORDER BY GRADE DESC")
print cursor.description

print cursor.fetchall()
```

The output of Example 10-1 is as follows:

```
[('object_id', 4, 11, None, 11, 0, 0), ('name', 12, 100, None, None, None,
1), ('grade', 6, 12, None, 11, 31, 1)]
[(2, 'Zach Paleozogt', 100.0), (1, 'Fred Flintstone', 90.5)]
```

Servlets and PyServlet

Although Java was initially designed to provide web applications on the client using applets, these days you are more likely to see Java deployed on the web server using servlets. The full servlet API is, of course, accessible from Jython. You can create servlets by defining servlet classes and compiling them via *jythonc* in much the same way as you would for applets.

However, you don't have to go through that separate compilation step for servlets. Jython is distributed with a utility class org.jython.util.PyServlet, which allows you to use your Jython servlets in their uncompiled *.py* form. The PyServlet class is not, as you might expect, a parent class for your Jython servlets. Rather, it is the glue between your Jython code and the servlet engine. As far as the servlet engine is concerned, PyServlet is what gets called, and PyServlet manages the calling of the Jython code, through an embedded PythonInterpreter object.

Using PyServlet

The following setup instructions assume Apache Tomcat 4.0 is your servlet engine (it is available from *http://jakarta.apache.org*). Other servlet engines will likely be somewhat different. To set up a Jython servlet application, create a new folder for the application, e.g., *jyserv*, in Tomcat's *webapps* directory. Inside that new folder, you need to create a *WEB-INF* folder (*webapps/jyserv/WEB-INF*), and inside that folder, create a file named *web.xml* (*webapps/jyserv/WEB-INF/web.xml*). So far, this is like any other web application. The *web.xml* file for a Jython servlet needs to look like the one shown in Example 10-2.

Example 10-2. Jython servlet web.xml descriptor file

```xml
<?xml version="1.0" encoding="ISO-8859-1"?>

<!DOCTYPE web-app
    PUBLIC "-//Sun Microsystems, Inc.//DTD Web Application 2.3//EN"
    "http://java.sun.com/dtd/web-app_2_3.dtd">

<web-app>
    <servlet>
        <servlet-name>PyServlet</servlet-name>
        <servlet-class>org.python.util.PyServlet</servlet-class>
        <init-param>
            <param-name>python.home</param-name>
            <param-value>/usr/home/jython-2.1</param-value>
        </init-param>
    </servlet>
    <servlet-mapping>
        <servlet-name>PyServlet</servlet-name>
        <url-pattern>*.py</url-pattern>
    </servlet-mapping>
</web-app>
```

This *web.xml* file binds the servlet name PyServlet with the fully qualified class name for the PyServlet class, sets up a parameter for *python.home*, which should be your Jython home directory (you can set any other Jython registry properties in the same way), and then sets up a mapping such that all *.py* files invoke the PyServlet. For this to work, the *jython.jar* file from your Jython distribution should be copied in the *webapps/jyserv/WEB-INF/lib* folder, which you need to create. This is the simplest place among the various places that Tomcat will let you put the *.jar* file so that it is automatically included in the virtual classpath for the servlet.

Once PyServlet is set up, you can put Jython programs in the *webapps* folder and Tomcat will run them as though they were compiled Java files. However, the Jython file must contain a callable object, such as a class, with the same name as the file itself. The Jython instance returned by that callable object should be a subclass of HttpServlet, and all the subclassing and introspection rules apply. To run a simple "Hello, World" example, put the following code in *hello.py* in the top-level directory of the web application (*webapps/jyserv/hello.py*). Example 10-3 uses get/set introspection to set the content type and grab the output stream, then uses Jython print syntax to write the HTML.

Example 10-3. "Hello, World" servlet

```
import javax.servlet.http as http

class hello(http.HttpServlet):

    def doGet(self, request, response):
        response.contentType = "text/html"
        out = response.outputStream
        print >> out, "<h3>Hello World!</h3>"
```

To run Example 10-3, point your browser to the URL *http://hostname/jyserv/hello.py*. Behind the scenes, the servlet mapping in the *web.xml* file invokes PyServlet. PyServlet uses the name of the file from the URL, and runs the Jython interpreter on that file. Within the file, PyServlet looks for the callable object with the same name as the file. In this case, it finds a class object named hello. Calling the object returns an instance of the class, and PyServlet calls the service method of that instance, which, under the servlet specification, resolves into the call to doGet( ). The code generated by interpreting the hello file is cached, so the interpretation is not rerun every page hit. However, if *hello.py* is changed, the cache is automatically updated.

If naming your class hello offends your sense of naming style, there is a simple workaround—the callable object doesn't have to be the class, it can be a function that returns an instance. If you want to name the class HelloServlet, you just need the following function:

```
def hello( ):
    return HelloServlet( )
```

A simple assignment can also do the trick:

```
hello = HelloServlet
```

You can, of course, access the full servlet specification, including sessions, as well as incoming variables. Example 10-4 prints a string entered from a form, and keeps a running counter of how many times the form has been submitted. The example uses the Python triple-quote syntax along with string formatting to avoid having multiple print >> out statements.

Example 10-4. Form submission servlet

```
import javax.servlet.http as http

class enter(http.HttpServlet):

    def doPost(self, request, response):
        session = request.getSession(1)
        counter = session.getAttribute("counter")
```

Example 10-4. Form submission servlet (continued)

```
        try:
            counter = int(counter)
        except:  # counter is None
            counter = 0
        counter += 1
        session.setAttribute("counter", counter)
        out = response.outputStream
        print >> out, """The string you entered is: %s. <br>
            You have played this game %s times.<hr>""" % (
            request.getParameter("thing"), counter)
        self.doGet(request, response)

    def doGet(self, request, response):
        response.contentType = "text/html"
        out = response.outputStream
        print >> out, """Enter a string: <form method="post">
            <input type="text" name="thing"><input  type="submit">
            </form>"""
```

A Python Template Tool

Python string formatting can also be used as the basis of a simple web-templating tool. A template tool, such as Velocity or WebMacro, allows the web application to separate the HTML display from the creation of the data, by storing the HTML in a file separate from the servlet. The servlet is responsible for creating the data and inserting it in the template. Example 10-5 shows a sample template file using Python string formatting.

Example 10-5. output.ptem template file

```
<html>
<head><title>Jython template page</title></head>

<body>
    <h2>Hello, %(name)s</h2>
    <p>The time is: <b>%(time)s</b></p>
    <p>The date is: <b>%(date)s</b></p>
</body>
</html>
```

The template file in Example 10-5 is just an HTML file with some placeholders, such as %(name)s. As you may have already realized, these placeholders exactly match the Python string formatting syntax when a dictionary is used. Therefore, all that is needed to use this template is a dictionary that has the proper keys. Example 10-6 shows the complete servlet. Again, some error handling has been left off for clarity.

Example 10-6. template.py servlet

```
import javax.servlet.http as http
import time

class template(http.HttpServlet):

    def tempString(self, request):
        fileName = request.getParameter("file")
        try:
            template = open(self.servletContext.getRealPath("/%s.ptem" %
                                                            fileName))
            return template.read( )
        finally:
            template.close( )

    def tempDict(self, request):
        timeTuple = time.localtime( )
        result = {}
        result['date'] = time.strftime("%A, %B %d, %Y", timeTuple)
        result['time'] = time.strftime("%I:%M:%S %p", timeTuple)
        result['name'] = request.getParameter('name')
        return result

    def doGet(self, request, response):
        response.contentType = "text/html"
        out = response.outputStream
        print >> out, self.tempString(request) % self.tempDict(request)
        out.close( )
```

The critical line of code in Example 10-6 is print >> out, self. tempString(request) % self.tempDict(request). This line calls a function to get the template string and a function to get the appropriate dictionary, then merges the two with the string formatting operator. The tempString function gets the filename from an attribute passed into the servlet (as part of a query string, for example), then opens the file and returns its contents to a string. The tempDict function gathers the proper keys, taking the name key from the request parameters and building date and time strings from the current date and time. Calling this servlet with a URL such as *http://localhost:8080/jyserv/template.py?file=output&name=Clark* will correctly fill in the template file.

This servlet could easily be adjusted or subclassed to fill the template from a database or a form submission. What makes this such a powerful technique is its flexibility. By changing the file parameter, the same servlet could manage any number of displays, even an entire application. The displays can also change arbitrarily without changing a single line of code.

Reloading Servlet Modules

One important gotcha to watch out for with Jython servlets has to do with reloading files. Although the servlet file itself is automatically reloaded if changed, if a module imported by the servlet changes, that module is not reloaded. This is particularly annoying if, as suggested by good OO design principles, you keep the servlet functionality minimal and put most of the functionality in associated files. Those of you who are familiar with running servlets in Java already know that one workaround here is to restart the servlet engine, but that can be time consuming in a development environment and not feasible in a production environment. As a partial workaround, especially during development, PyServlet has a reset method that clears the Jython interpreter namespace within PyServlet and causes all files to be reloaded as needed.

To take advantage of this workaround, you need a servlet that calls back to PyServlet (see Example 10-7). In this case, we've called it *reset.py*.

Example 10-7. Resetting a servlet

```
import javax.servlet.http as http

class reset(http.HttpServlet):
    def doGet(self, req, res):
        req.getAttribute("pyservlet").reset( )
        req.getRequestDispatcher("/index.py").forward(req, res)
```

The last line is optional, and redirects to display the *index.py* file.

Jython and XML

It's hard to go more than a week or two these days without seeing some technical article or book explaining how XML is going to enable interprocess communication, solve all your technical problems, and do your laundry. Even for those of you who do not need to communicate between programs in different languages, you can still get benefits out of using XML without wading too deeply into the alphabet soup of X-acronyms. This section will show some simple examples of Jython as a frontend to XML parsers and other tools.

A great deal of XML tools have been developed for both Python and Java, and from Jython you have access to nearly all of these (some CPython tools that depend on C-based libraries, such as the XML tools based on the *expat* parser, you can't use in Jython). This section focuses on the Java tools, but the pure Python package is also useful and might be somewhat easier to integrate with Python tools. The examples in this section use the Xerces parser available from *http://xml.apache.org*. All the examples assume you have placed *xerces.jar* in your classpath.

On the Python side, the PyXML package, which was developed by the Python XML special interest group, is included with Jython Version 2.1 (you can also download and install it from the project page at *http://pyxml. sourceforge.net*). Because SAX and DOM are standards, the Xerces-based examples in this section should be easily ported to using PyXML instead of Xerces.

This section is necessarily brief, and does not cover important but lengthy XML issues such as validation or namespaces, or higher-level XML tools such as XSLT or data binding. For your other XML needs, O'Reilly publishes a wide range of XML books including *Learning XML*, by Erik T. Ray, and *XML in a Nutshell*, by Elliotte Rusty Harold and W. Scott Means. Specific topics of interest to Jython programmers are covered in *Java and XML*, by Brett McLaughlin, and *Python and XML*, by Christopher A. Jones and Fred L. Drake, Jr.

SAX and DOM

At the lowest level, closest to the actual XML parser, there are two different standards for interacting with an XML document. The Simple API for XML (SAX) is a *de facto* standard for event-based parsing, while the Document Object Model (DOM) is the W3C's standard for tree-based parsing. The two standards are different in approach, although generally similar in final outcome. A SAX parser fires events at various important points while parsing in the XML document, such as the beginning or end of a tag. It's up to your program to intercept the important events and convert them into some useful data representation. A DOM parser works through the entire XML document up front and returns a standard tree structure representing the whole thing. Your program then traverses the tree and converts to some useful representation (although sometimes you can just use the DOM tree as is).

A DOM parser is typically slower than a SAX parser and more memory intensive on large files because it must convert the entire file first. A SAX parser, while possibly faster on large files, forces you to manage the state of the document, which can be difficult to deal with if the data is complex. We'll show examples of both processing types on the XML file in Example 10-8, which shows a simple recipe for a peanut butter and jelly sandwich.

Example 10-8. XML recipe file

```
<?xml version="1.0"?>
<recipe>
    <name>Peanut Butter &amp; Jelly Sandwich</name>
    <ingredient amount="1/4" unit="cup">Peanut Butter</ingredient>
    <ingredient amount="1/4" unit="cup">Strawberry Jelly</ingredient>
    <ingredient amount="2" unit="slices">White Bread</ingredient>
    <instruction>
        Place the two slices of bread on a plate.
    </instruction>
    <instruction>Spread the peanut butter on one slice.</instruction>
    <instruction>Spread the jelly on the other slice.</instruction>
    <instruction>Put the slices together.</instruction>
    <instruction>Eat!</instruction>
</recipe>
```

All three programs in the rest of this section (Examples 10-9, 10-10, and 10-11) convert the XML into the following (more or less):

```
Printing a Recipe
Recipe Name: Peanut Butter & Jelly Sandwich
Ingredients:
1/4 cup Peanut Butter
1/4 cup Strawberry Jelly
2 slices White Bread
Instructions
1. Place the two slices of bread on a plate.
2. Spread the peanut butter on one slice.
3. Spread the jelly on the other slice.
4. Put the slices together.
5. Eat!
Enjoy!
```

Admittedly, this example is a little on the contrived side—in a real application, you'd probably be converting the XML to class instances first and then using the class instances to print, thereby gaining a greater separation between the data representation and the code. (Actually, if all you wanted to do was convert from XML to the print representation, XSLT would also work.) Still, the examples will give you a feel for how to use the various tools in Jython. Example 10-9 has a SAX implementation of the XML-to-print tool.

Example 10-9. SAX parsing

```
import org.xml.sax as sax
parserClass = "org.apache.xerces.parsers.SAXParser"

def attrToDict(attrs):
    result = {}
    for i in range(attrs.length):
        result[attrs.getLocalName(i)] = attrs.getValue(i)
    return result
```

Example 10-9. SAX parsing (continued)

```
class RecipeHandler(sax.helpers.DefaultHandler):

    def __init__(self):
        self.ingredientCount = 0
        self.instructionCount = 0

    def startDocument(self):
        print "Printing A Recipe"

    def do_name(self, attrs):
        print "Recipe Name:",

    def do_ingredient(self, attrs):
        attrDict = attrToDict(attrs)
        if not self.ingredientCount:
            print "\nIngredients:"
        self.ingredientCount += 1
        print attrDict["amount"], attrDict["unit"],

    def do_instruction(self, attrs):
        if not self.instructionCount:
            print "\nInstructions:"
        self.instructionCount += 1
        print "%s. " % (self.instructionCount),

    def startElement(self, namespaceURI, localName, qName, attrs):
        method = getattr(self, "do_" + localName, lambda x: None)
        method(attrs)

    def characters(self, chars, start, length):
        print ''.join(chars[start:start+length]).strip(),

    def endElement(self, namespaceURI, localName, qName):
        print

    def endDocument(self):
        print "\n\nEnjoy!"

if __name__ == '__main__':
    reader = sax.helpers.XMLReaderFactory.createXMLReader(parserClass)
    inputSource = sax.InputSource("recipe.xml")
    reader.contentHandler = RecipeHandler()
    reader.parse(inputSource)
```

To use SAX, you create a reader using the XMLReaderFactory class and give it the name of a parser class—in this case, the Xerces SAX parser. We pass the filename to an input source, set a content handler, and parse. The content handler is the class where all the action is. The SAX standard defines a number of different handlers that you create to receive events that happen during parsing. The ContentHandler interface handles events related to the actual XML content—other handlers manage other kinds of XML events such as DTD declarations and errors. The DefaultHandler class from which our RecipeHandler inherits just declares empty versions of all 11 methods in ContentHandler (and the other handlers as well), saving us the effort of having to create them ourselves.

The actual handler methods are called when you might expect from their names. At the start of the document, before any text is processed, the startDocument event is fired. In Example 10-10, we use it to set a couple of state variables. One weakness of SAX is that it does not maintain state between events—any state you need to track needs to be managed in the handler. When creating instance objects, you'll often need to maintain a stack of objects being worked on that corresponds to the XML element hierarchy being processed.

After the tag that starts an element is completed, the startElement function is called with the name information with and without namespace qualifiers, and the attribute list. We avoid a long conditional by defining separate handlers for each type of tag, and dispatching to the correct function based on a getattr lookup of the methods in the handler. Whichever method is returned from the getattr lookup is then called with the attribute list as an argument. Because the attribute list comes in as a simple list, we add a simple utility function to convert it to a dictionary for convenience.

The other complication in Example 10-9 is the characters method. It is called whenever a block of text inside a tag is encountered. Nothing in the SAX specification formalizes how much text is required to trigger a call to this method—it could be called after every character, or only at the end of a block of text, or anywhere in between. The arguments are a list of characters, a start index, and the length of characters included in this call. In this case, we use a slice and a join call to convert the arguments to the desired string.

State management in Example 10-9 makes SAX seem rather complicated, particularly in comparison to the future examples. The need to maintain state while parsing can be difficult for complex XML files. However, sometimes large files or speed requirements or relatively stateless tasks will point you toward a SAX solution.

Example 10-10 solves the same problem using DOM. Again, *xerces.jar* must be in your classpath.

Example 10-10. DOM recipe printer

```
import org.w3c.dom as dom
import org.apache.xerces as xerces
import java.io as io

def printDocument(domDoc):
    print "Printing a Recipe"
    rootElement = domDoc.documentElement
    nameElement = rootElement.getElementsByTagName("name").item(0)
    print "Recipe Name: %s" % nameElement.firstChild.nodeValue.strip()

    print "\n\nIngredients:"
    ingredientNodes = rootElement.getElementsByTagName("ingredient")
    for i in range(ingredientNodes.length):
        node = ingredientNodes.item(i)
        print "%s %s %s" % (node.attributes.getNamedItem("amount").value,
                node.attributes.getNamedItem("unit").value,
                node.firstChild.nodeValue.strip())

    print "\n\nInstructions"
    instructionNodes = rootElement.getElementsByTagName("instruction")
    for i in range(instructionNodes.length):
        node = instructionNodes.item(i)
        print "%s. %s" % (i + 1, node.firstChild.nodeValue.strip())
    print "\n\nEnjoy!"


if __name__ == "__main__":
    parser = xerces.parsers.DOMParser()
    parser.parse("recipe.xml")
    printDocument(parser.document)
```

The main block in Example 10-10 creates a DOM parser and parses the
XML file. This second line causes the entire file to be read into memory and
parsed into a DOM tree structure. The DOM tree structure is stored at
parser.document, and we pass that tree to our printDocument function. In
Example 10-10, because the DOM parsing creates a structure for us, the
printing is simple enough to capture in a single function. In a more complex
application, you might pass the DOM tree to a class constructor.

The DOM tree structure lets you get a set of child elements of a node using
the getElementsByTagName function, which we use once for each type of node
we want to print. The function returns a node list, which is traversable using
the item(*index*) function. In the case of the name tag, because we know there
is just one name, we immediately take the item at index 0. Because the
DOM node lists are not Java collections, we can't iterate over them directly
in Jython, but must range over the indexes.

Text inside a tag is just another kind of child node to DOM. The common idiom for retrieving the text when you know that it's the only child element of the node is the `node.firstChild.nodeValue` series of calls, which returns the text string.

Although the DOM code is shorter and, for this application, somewhat clearer, there is still some awkwardness, especially in that you cannot directly use Python-style looping. Some of that awkwardness obviously could be mitigated if we refactor the repeated code to common helper functions. However, because that's basically what JDOM does in the next section, we decided to leave it to highlight the contrast. DOM is not a Java-specific standard, in that it does not take advantage of Java naming conventions or collection classes that Jython could exploit to make the parsing code more Pythonic.

JDOM and Jython

For XML parsing needs where you want a DOM-style tree but are programming in Java or Jython, JDOM is an excellent choice. JDOM is an open source, DOM-like API specifically for Java and is available at *http://www.jdom.org*. Other than the name, there is no direct similarity or correspondence between DOM and JDOM (and for legal reasons, by the way, JDOM is officially *not* an acronym). As of this writing JDOM is in late beta, but the changes should not affect this code example much. To run the example, the *jdom.jar* file from the download must be in your classpath (in addition to Xerces or some other XML parser).

The big advantage of using JDOM over SAX or DOM for you as a Jython programmer is that JDOM was specifically designed as a Java API. It uses Java collection classes and Java naming conventions. This means that the full force of Jython reflection and interoperability with Java can be used on JDOM in ways that are not available with plain DOM. To see the result, look at Example 10-11, the same recipe printer we've already seen in SAX and DOM, this time using JDOM.

Example 10-11. JDOM recipe printer

```
import org.jdom as jdom
import java.io as io

def printDocument(jdomDoc):
    print "Printing a Recipe"
    rootElement = jdomDoc.rootElement
    nameElement = rootElement.getChild("name")
    print "Recipe Name: %s" % (nameElement.textTrim)
```

Example 10-11. JDOM recipe printer (continued)

```
    print "\n\nIngredients:"
    for node in rootElement.getChildren("ingredient"):
        print "%s %s %s" % (node.getAttribute("amount").value,
                node.getAttribute("unit").value, node.textTrim)

    print "\n\nInstructions"
    counter = 1
    for node in rootElement.getChildren("instruction"):
        print "%s. %s" % (counter, node.textTrim)
        counter += 1
    print "\n\nEnjoy!"

if __name__ == "__main__":
    builder = jdom.input.SAXBuilder()
    doc = builder.build(io.FileInputStream("recipe.xml"))
    printDocument(doc)
```

Example 10-11 is even shorter and clearer than the DOM code in Example 10-10, although the basic structure is the same. The main block builds the JDOM document by creating a JDOM SAXBuilder and passing it an input stream on the file. JDOM builds the document from the SAX parser events.

Notice that in the JDOM example, we can do a for loop directly on the list of child nodes, instead of having to use the range function. Also notice that this isn't always a complete win—in the instructions section, we now have to maintain a separate counter because we don't have the index any longer.

In general, you will probably find that JDOM is more convenient than DOM in cases where you'd like to work with the XML in a tree structure. In fact, JDOM in Jython lets you use more Python structures than the PyXML implementation of DOM (which is necessarily limited to the DOM methods).

The three sections of this chapter show three different mechanisms for dealing with Java tools in Jython. The *zxJDBC* tool defines an overlay that allows you to use Python constructs and translates them in the background to the Java equivalents. In the Servlet example, PyServlet allows you to embed Jython code in a Java context without compilation, making it easy for you to use the Java constructs from Jython. JDOM is an example of a Java toolkit whose conformance to Java naming conventions makes the tool easy to use and clear in Jython. We hope that these examples will provide some guidance as you try to use other Java tools from your Jython code.

CHAPTER 11

Jython Standard Library

The philosophy behind Python is "Batteries included." As a result, Python ships with more than 100 standard modules that cover all kinds of functionality, from file manipulation to network protocols to unit testing to encryption, and so on. As we've seen, in addition to containing the majority of the Python standard library, Jython also includes another set of "batteries"—the standard Java API.

This chapter shows how to use a few of the most useful elements of the Python library from Jython. We chose the modules for this chapter for two reasons. Some modules, such as os or sys, are so commonly used in Jython that you'll need them for nearly anything you write. Others, such as re or unittest, offer functionality that is either not implemented or awkwardly implemented in the Java API. We did not include modules that had obvious Java counterparts (such as math or random), or if they were covered elsewhere in the book (such as exception or operator), or if they were considered less than essential. The CPython documentation contains full documentation on all CPython modules at *http://www.python.org/doc/current/modindex.html*— but see the next section for a sense of which modules will work with Jython. In addition, you can also see *Python Standard Library*, by Fredrik Lundh (O'Reilly), for additional samples of how the different modules are used.

Using Python Modules

Using a Python module is usually as simple as the import *modulename* statement. Most Python modules that are written in Python work just fine in Jython. In fact, it's a good idea to keep a recent CPython version around—you can often use new CPython modules just by copying them to Jython's */Lib* directory, or simply put a pointer to the CPython distribution's */Lib* in the Jython registry's python.path. Often the thing to do is to just try out the module, and see if it works.

A few types of modules will not run under Jython. These include:

Modules that are targeted at a specific platform
CPython defines a lot of modules with specific functionality for Unix, Mac OS, Windows, IRIX, or what have you. For the most part, these depend on a tight integration with the underlying operating system, and as such, they don't run under Jython. Examples include Unix-specific modules such as pipes, Macintosh-specific modules such as macspeech and waste, and Win32-specific modules such as _winreg.

Modules that contain functionality not included in a JVM
A similar category to the above. Some standard CPython modules depend on operating system calls that are not available under Java. The most notable of these is os, which actually does run in Jython, but is missing much of its functionality. Another example is the stat module.

Modules implemented in C
A number of common CPython modules are implemented in C rather than Python, either for a speed boost or because the module is a C wrapper around an external C library. The C modules, or any modules that depend on them, will not run in Jython. Examples include the xml. expat modules, which depend on the *expat* parser, and telnetlib, which depends on the C select module (which so far has not been ported to Jython). Some of these modules, notably cPickle and md5, have been reimplemented in Java and are available in Jython.

There are also a number of modules whose functionality may be better provided by Java API classes. For example, the design of the Python threading module is based on the Java Thread and Runnable classes. In Jython, it may be easier to just use the Java classes directly unless portability to CPython is important.

System and File Modules

The sys module contains a number of always-available variables and functions having to do with the state of the Jython environment in which the Jython script is running. Much of a Jython program's interaction with the external operating system is managed through the os and os.path modules. The os module is essentially a clearinghouse for operating system calls and file manipulation, while os.path specifically manipulates filenames. As you might imagine, the limitations of Java interactions with the underlying system mean that none of these modules contains all the functionality of their CPython counterparts.

The sys Module

The sys module is the standard location for information about the Jython execution environment in which the script runs, including command-line arguments, and path information. Many of the values in the sys module can be set before Jython is invoked using the Jython registry, as shown in Appendix B. The content of the Jython registry is available in the variable sys.registry.

The most important values exposed by the sys module (all of which can be manipulated at runtime by Jython) are as follows:

argv

> Contains a list of the command-line arguments passed to the script when invoked. Under normal circumstances argv[0] is the name of the script itself (or '-c' if the script is invoked via the -c command-line option). If running in the interactive interpreter, argv is the empty list.

maxint

> The maximum integer that can be held in an int value. In Jython, that is 2147483647, or 2**31 –1.

modules

> A dictionary whose keys are strings representing the names of modules, and whose keys are the modules themselves. All currently loaded modules are in this dictionary, unless they are deliberately manipulated by the program. Removing a module from this dictionary does not automatically force a reload of that module. A subsequent import will force the reload, or you can rely on the reload( ) built-in function.

path

> The list of directories searched by Jython for modules. In Jython 2.1 and higher, entries on this list may be .zip or .jar files, which are treated as though they were expanded in place. One can also specify a subdirectory packed inside the archive such as foo.jar/Lib. The first entry in the list is always the directory of the script being executed—that directory is always searched first.

platform

> The name of the platform being run. In Jython, it's always a string of the form 'java1.3.0', where the word java is followed by the Java version number extracted from Java property java.version. So, sys. platform[:4] == 'java' is a common idiom for checking whether a script is running under Jython.

prefix

> The directory where the Jython installation lives. It is set to the value of the python.home Jython property. For example, under Windows with a default installation, the value is 'C:\\jython-2.1'.

stdin, stdout, stderr

> References to the system's standard input, output, and error streams, which can be used as file objects. You can assign these. For stdout and stderr, all you need is an object that defines a write(*string*) method. The original streams are always available at __stdin__, __stdout__, and __stderr__ if these are overridden.

version, version_info

> The version attribute contains a string representation of the current version number for Jython, and version_info breaks it into a tuple. Jython also has a sys.hexversion, which is guaranteed to always increase with version numbers.

```
>>> import sys
>>> sys.version
'2.1a3'
>>> sys.version_info
(2, 1, 0, 'alpha', 3)
>>> sys.hexversion
33620131
```

The sys module also exposes a couple of useful functions:

exc_info( )

> Returns a tuple of values about the current exception being handled (returns None if no exception is being handled). The tuple is of three elements: the type of the exception, the argument passed to the exception, and a traceback object. The traceback object can be manipulated by the traceback module to print an error message based on the exception.

exit(*arg*)

> Exits Jython with the specified exit code. You can also assign a value to the attribute sys.exitfunc. The value is a no-argument function object, which is automatically called when Jython exits.

Jython also makes a few functions available in the sys module to manage Java classes and packages. To know about Java packages, Jython scans all the *.jar* files and directories on *classpath* and *sys.path*. Although your Java classloader setup may allow you to load other classes that are not present in those locations, imports of them in Jython will fail unless Jython is specifically informed about the package's existence. The following functions force Jython to scan other locations not on either path, or to inform it about new packages. Information about packages acquired through these functions is not cached across sessions. These functions do not set up a classloader to access them. For an import to succeed from a nonstandard location, there must be both an appropriate classloader and a Jython call to one of these functions.

add_classdir(*directory*)
> Adds the given *directory* to the list of places checked by Jython for Java packages and classes.

add_extdir(*jardir*)
> Forces Jython to scan all *.jar* or *.zip* files in *jardir* for Java packages and classes.

add_packages(*package*)
> Adds the Java package *package* to the list of Java packages known by Jython.

The os Module

The os module is intended to provide cross-platform access to operating system functions such as file and directory functions, and process management. If you've done much cross-platform Java coding, you can already see a problem in implementing this in Java. The Java runtime simply doesn't allow full access to the underlying operating system process management, nor does it allow you to do everything with files that the native operating system typically can do. As a result, the Jython implementation of os is significantly weaker than the CPython one, essentially consisting only of file manipulation utilities, most of which are a thin wrapper around java.io. File actions. Unlike some of the other module listings in this book, the listing in this section is a complete listing of Jython's os functionality—functions not defined here are not defined in Jython.

If you really need full os functionality in Jython, there is a separate project called jnios, which implements the complete CPython os functionality using the Java Native Interface (JNI). Complete download information is available at *http://jnios.sourceforge.net/*. Appendix B explains how to set up Jython so that jnios is installed as the built-in version. As of this writing, it's not clear how much effort has been going into maintaining jnios, but there have been recent discussions on the *Jython-dev* mailing list about folding more of this functionality into Jython proper. For example, starting with 2.1, Jython properly supports os.environ and os.system. The Jython version of os defines the following values:

altsep
> In CPython, an alternative character that can be used for path separation. In Jython, set to None.

curdir

> The string constant used by Java to indicate the current directory—typically '.'.

environ

> A dictionary intended to hold environment variables. Under the major platforms (Mac, Windows, and Unix flavors), Jython fills it with the values from the system environment. Otherwise, it starts off empty but could be used as a placeholder for values.

linesep

> The line terminator string for the given platform as given by java.lang. System.getProperty('line.separator').

name

> The name of the specific operating system os module being run—in Jython, it's always 'java'.

pardir

> String constant used for the parent directory—typically '..'.

path

> A separate module, usually referred to as os.path, which contains functions for manipulating pathnames.

pathsep

> The string constant used by the operating system to separate elements in a path list, as defined by java.io.File.pathSeparator.

sep

> The character used by the operating system to separate elements of a path within a single filename, as defined by java.io.File.separator.

The Jython os module defines the following functions, all of which raise an OSError if something goes wrong during the actual system call.

_exit(*arg=0*)

> In Jython, it calls java.lang.System.exit(arg).

getcwd( )

> Returns the pathname of the current working directory.
>
> ```
> >>> os.getcwd( )
> 'C:\\jython-2.1a3'
> ```

listdir(*path*)

> Returns a list of all files in the given path. The files are not sorted, and the directory itself and parent directory are not included. A direct call to Java's java.io.File.list( ) method.

makedirs(*path*)

> Creates the directory named by *path*, and any parent directories that don't already exist.

mkdir(*path*)

    Creates the directory named by *path*. All parent directories must exist.

remove(*path*), unlink(*path*)

    Synonyms for the same function. Deletes the file if *path* refers to a file; otherwise, raises an exception.

rename(*path, newpath*)

    Renames the file *path* to *newpath*.

rmdir(*path*)

    Removes the directory *path*. Raises an exception if *path* is not a directory, or is not empty.

stat(*path*)

    Returns a tuple of information about *path*. The Jython implementation returns only some of the values of the CPython version. The tuple is of the form (0, 0, 0, 0, 0, 0, size, mtime, mtime, 0), where the three nonzero values are the size of the file and its last modification time (which is included twice).

system(*command*)

    Under the major platforms (Mac, Windows, and Unix flavors), should properly execute command (*string*) in a subshell.

The os.path module

The os.path module contains a number of utility functions for dealing with path and filenames. Again, some of the features of the CPython version cannot be replicated in Java. Two functions defined in CPython are not currently defined in Jython: sameopenfile and samestat. In both cases, this is because the function depends on operating system behavior not contained in the JVM. Two functions that answer Boolean questions always return false in Jython because the JVM cannot make the determination: islink and ismount. Two functions, splitdrive and normcase, that change behavior in CPython based on the underlying operating system behave in the same way on all platforms in Jython—which may mean that they won't behave the way that you want. The function splitdrive(*pathname*), which in CPython splits the path into drive letter and the rest of path, in Jython always has the empty string as the drive letter (which is not consistent with CPython under Windows). Similarly, the function normcase(*pathname*), which under CPython and Windows converts the pathname to all lowercase, does nothing with the pathname in Jython.

The following os.path functions behave the same in Jython and CPython. Equivalent calls are given as they would be written in Jython with Jython shortcuts. For example, we'll show the call as the Jython java.io. File(*pathname*).absolutePath rather than the Java (new File(*pathname*)). getAbsolutePath( ).

abspath(*pathname*)
>   Returns the absolute path of *pathname*, equivalent to java.io. File(*pathname*).absolutePath.

```
>>> os.path.abspath('fred')
'C:\\jython-2.1a3\\fred'
```

basename(*pathname*)
>   Returns the final component of the pathname, equivalent to java.io. File(*pathname*).name.

```
>>> os.path.basename('/jython-2.1a3/test.py')
'test.py'
```

commonprefix(*listOfPathnames*)
>   Returns the longest possible common prefix of the pathnames in the list, working character by character. It is possible that the resulting common string is not a pathname that actually exists in the system if the common prefix ends in the middle of a pathname element.

```
>>> os.path.commonprefix(
['/jython-2.1a3/test.py', '/jython-2.1a3/Lib/unittest.py'])
'/jython-2.1a3/'
```

exists(*pathname*)
>   Equivalent to java.io.File(*pathname*).exists( ).

dirname(*pathname*)
>   Returns the portion of the pathname that describes the directory.

```
>>> os.path.dirname('/jython-2.1a3/Lib/unittest.py')
'\\jython-2.1a3\\Lib'
```

expanduser(*pathname*)
>   If the pathname begins with a tilde (~), and the tilde is either the entire string or is followed by a path separator, expands the tilde to the current user home directory. Unlike CPython, does not handle the case where the pathname begins with ~*username*.

```
>>> os.path.expanduser('~')
'C:\\Documents and Settings\\nrappin'
>>> os.path.expanduser('~nrappin')
'~nrappin'
```

gethome( )
>   Returns the current system property for user home directory.

getsize(*pathname*)
   Returns the size of the file at the given *pathname*.

getuser( )
   Returns the current system property for username.

isabs(*pathname*), isfile(*pathname*), isdir(*pathname*)
   Booleans that check whether the given *pathname* is an absolute path, a file, or a directory.

join(*pathpart, *pathparts*)
   Concatenates a series of path pieces together, inserting a path separator between them. If any of the parts are absolute, the concatenation starts over, beginning with the absolute part.

```
>>> os.path.join('jython-2.1.a3', 'Lib', 'unittest.py')
'jython-2.1.a3\\Lib\\unittest.py'
```

normpath(*pathname*)
   Normalizes the pathname by collapsing duplicate or redundant path separators to a single separator. If the path separator is a backslash, also converts forward slashes to backslashes.

```
>>> os.path.normpath('jython-2.1a3/.//Lib//unittest.py')
'jython-2.1a3\\Lib\\unittest.py'
```

samefile(*pathname1, pathname2*)
   Returns true if both pathnames refer to the same file, as tested by the paths having the same canonical path.

split(*pathname*)
   Returns a tuple of the form (*dir, file*) where the last element of the tuple is everything following the final path separator, and the first element is everything else. The final separator itself is not in either element.

```
>>> os.path.split('jython-2.1a3/lib/unttest.py')
('jython-2.1a3\\lib', 'unttest.py')
```

splitext(*pathname*)
   Similar to split, but separates between the filename and its extension.

```
>>> os.path.splitext('jython-2.1a3/lib/unttest.py')
('jython-2.1a3/lib/unttest', '.py')
```

walk(*pathname, function, argument*)
   For each directory in *pathname* (including *pathname*, if it is a directory) and recursively for all subdirectories encountered, calls the specified *function* with three arguments (*argument, dirname, files*), where *argument* is the parameter passed to walk, *dirname* is the name of the directory being acted on, and *files* is the list of files in the directory.

File Pattern Matching with glob

Jython allows you to perform a pattern match to obtain a list of filenames using the glob module. The glob module defines one function, conveniently also named glob. To use the function, you pass it a string path pattern. In addition to the normal elements of filenames, the pattern can contain the special character *, which matches any number of zero or more characters; ?, which matches exactly one instance of any character; and a range of characters contained in brackets, such as [a-m]. The return value is a list of the complete pathnames of all files whose names match the pattern. Here is an example of the use of glob:

```
>>> import glob
>>> glob.glob('/jython-2.1a3/Lib/d*.py')
['\\jython-2.1a3\\Lib\\dircache.py', '\\jython-2.1a3\\Lib\\dospath.py', '\\
jython-2.1a3\\Lib\\dumbdbm.py']

>>> glob.glob('/jython-2.1a3/Lib/[a-b]*.py')
['\\jython-2.1a3\\Lib\\anydbm.py', '\\jython-2.1a3\\Lib\\atexit.py', '\\
jython-2.1a3\\Lib\\base64.py', '\\jython-2.1a3\\Lib\\bdb.py',
'\\jython-2.1a3\\Lib\\binhex.py', '\\jython-2.1a3\\Lib\\bisect.py']
```

Regular Expressions

Regular expressions are powerful text pattern-matching tools most commonly associated with the Unix command grep and the Perl scripting language. Python's regular expression support is managed through the re module. In Jython, re is implemented using a Java port of the sre engine module used by CPython, so the regular expression syntax is the same across both Pythons. JDK Version 1.4 will eventually add regular expression support to the core Java libraries—that version will, of course, also be accessible from Jython.

The re Module

A regular expression pattern is simply a string, usually called a *pattern*, which may contain a number of special characters. You use a regular expression against a target string or set of target strings with the goal of determining if the pattern is matched by any portion of the target string. Ordinary characters in the pattern match exactly against ordinary characters in the target. The special characters in the pattern can be used to make the match more flexible. The re module provides for several different operations on a pattern and a target string. These functions will be demonstrated first without the special characters to make it easier to see what's going on. Some of these functions return instances of the MatchObject class, which contains detailed information about the match.

findall(*pattern, string*)
> Returns a list of all the segments of *string* that match *pattern*, such that the matches do not overlap.
> ```
> >>> re.findall("ll", "Hello, Allan")
> ['ll', 'll']
> ```

match(*pattern, string[, flags]*)
> Tests to see if *string* matches the pattern at the beginning of the target string only. If not, returns None. If so, returns a MatchObject.
> ```
> >>> re.match("ll", "Hello")
>
> >>> re.match("He", "Hello")
> org.python.modules.sre.MatchObject@6ee404
>
> >>> match = re.match("He", "Hello")
> >>> match.start()
> 0
> >>> match.end()
> 2
> ```

search(*pattern, string[, flags]*)
> Similar to match, but tests for a match anywhere along the string, and returns a MatchObject corresponding to the first one found.
> ```
> >>> match = re.search("ll", "Hello")
> >>> match.start()
> 2
> >>> match.end()
> 4
> ```

split(*pattern, string, [maxsplit=0]*)
> Similar to the string method split: returns a list of elements of *string*, using *pattern* as the delimiter. By default, the elements matched are not included in the returned list; however, if the pattern is enclosed in parentheses, the delimiters will be included in the list. If *maxsplit* is not zero, it denotes the maximum number of splits that will occur, and the remainder of the target is included as the last entry in the list.
> ```
> >>> re.split("ll", "Hello, Allan")
> ['He', 'o, A', 'an']
>
> >>> re.split("(ll)", "Hello, Allan")
> ['He', 'll', 'o, A', 'll', 'an']
>
> >>> re.split("ll", "Hello, Allan", 1)
> ['He', 'o, Allan']
> ```

```
sub(pattern, repl, string[, count=0]),
subn(pattern, repl, string[, count=0])
```
Both of these functions replace all matches of the pattern in the target with *repl*. The replacement argument can be either a string or a one-argument function. If it is a function, the function is called on each matching segment (represented as a MatchObject) and the result of the function is used as the replacement. If it is a string, back-references to groups in the pattern can be inserted. The *count* argument, if greater than zero, limits the number of replacements that can occur in the target. The only difference between sub and subn is their return value—sub returns the replacement string, and subn returns a tuple, (*string, replacement_count*), where *replacement_count* is the number of replacements made, as shown here:

```
>>> re.sub("ll", "xx", "Hello, Allan")
'Hexxo, Axxan'

>>> re.subn("ll", "xx", "Hello, Allan")
('Hexxo, Axxan', 2)
```

Both match and search take an optional *flags* argument. There are four different flags in Jython, as defined in Table 11-1. Each flag has a short and long representation. The flags are constant integer values, and to combine them, you can use bitwise or (|). CPython defines additional flags for Unicode and local support, which are always on in Jython and, therefore, redundant.

Table 11-1. Regular expression flags

Short form	Long form	Meaning
I	IGNORECASE	Performs a case-insensitive pattern match. Lowercase and uppercase versions of the same character match each other.
M	MULTILINE	Changes the behavior of the ^ and $ special characters to match at the beginning and ending of each line rather than the beginning and ending of the entire string.
S	DOTALL	Changes the behavior of the special character . so that it matches anything, including a newline character.
X	VERBOSE	Allows more readable expressions—whitespace in the pattern is generally ignored, and you can use # to insert comments until the end of the line.

Match Objects

The match and search functions both return MatchObjects. Match objects encapsulate information about the specific match, and are particularly useful when the regular expression pattern has defined specific groups within the pattern by using parentheses. You can determine where in the string the match occurred by using the start( ), end( ), and span( ) methods. The start and end functions return the index of the target string where the match began or ended, and span returns both values as a tuple. All three functions take an optional integer argument corresponding to one of the parenthesized groups—if the argument is there, the functions refer to that group only.

To get at the text of a specific parenthesized group, use the group( ) function, which takes one or more integer arguments. If there is one argument, the string corresponding to that group's part of the match is returned. If there is more than one argument, a tuple containing each argument's string is returned. Another function, groups( ), returns a tuple of all the parenthesized groups in the match. The following snippet shows the MatchObject functions in action:

```
>>> result = re.search("(1)(1)", "Hello")
>>> result.span( )
(2, 4)
>>> result.span(1)
(2, 3)
>>> result.span(2)
(3, 4)
>>> result.group(1)
'1'
>>> result.groups( )
('1', '1')
```

Regular Expression Objects

The re module defines one other useful class, *regular expression objects*. A regular expression object encapsulates a regular expression pattern. Regular expression objects are created using the compile(*pattern,* *[flags]*) function, which, as you might expect, takes in a string pattern and optional flags and returns a regular expression object. All the functions defined in re (and listed earlier in this section) are also defined as methods of a regular expression object. This example shows the use of findall as a method of a regular expression object:

```
>>> regex = re.compile("ll")
>>> regex.findall("Hello, Allan")
['ll', 'll']
```

There are a few particularly useful reasons to define a regular expression object instead of using the raw pattern string functions. If the regular expression is particularly complex, you can enhance readability by defining the regular expression object separately from where it is used and giving it a name. And if you are using regular expressions, you'll probably need all the readability help you can get. Also, the regular expression object has a flags attribute. The flags attribute can be set using the flags described in Table 11-1, and the defined flags are kept with the pattern and can be modified at runtime. The match and search methods for regular expression objects have optional *pos* and *endpos* arguments. If defined, these arguments limit the part of the target string that is searched for the match to the substring between *pos* and *endpos*. This example shows how you can loop through a target string and get all the match locations in the target, instead of just the first:

```
import re
pattern = re.compile("ll")
target = "Hello, Allan"
lastLocation = 0
while 1:
    result = pattern.search(target, lastLocation)
    if not result: break
    print result.span( )
    lastLocation = result.end( )
```

(2, 4)
(8, 10)

Compiling pattern strings to regular expression objects can speed up your program if you use the expression more than once. When you call one of the re functions that require a string, the first thing that Jython does is compile the string. Working with an already compiled expression object saves that step. (For your convenience, both CPython and Jython automatically cache the compiled forms of regular expressions, even when they are not explicitly compiled with a small cache that is cleared when it is full. Depending on your usage patterns this cache can be enough to give you the compilation speedup.)

Special Characters

Using regular expressions just to match exact strings of characters is a bit of overkill, because there are simpler string methods that do the same thing. The flexibility, power, and cryptic mystique of regular expressions come from the variety of non-exact matches you can specify using special characters. Table 11-2 defines the most commonly used regular expression characters. Notice that backslashes are frequently used in regular expressions, but under normal Python string usage, the backslashes themselves would need to be escaped. This issue results in a lot of double backslashes, and often truly undecipherable regular expressions. To avoid this problem, use Python raw strings by prefixing the initial quote with r—for example, r'\w\w'.

Table 11-2. Regular expression special characters

Character	Meaning
.	Matches any character except a newline. Matches a newline if the DOTALL flag is set.
^ or \A	Limits the match to occur only at the beginning of the string. If specified with ^, and MULTILINE is set, will match at the beginning of any line. Placed at the beginning of the pattern.
$ or \Z	Limits the match to occur only at the end of the string. If specified with $ and MULTILINE is set, will match at the end of any line. Placed at the end of the pattern.
*	Matches against zero or more of the preceding character, character set, or parenthesized group. By default, is *greedy*—will grab as many characters as possible as long as the pattern still matches. Following the * with a ? makes it *non-greedy*, matching as few characters as possible for a match.
+	Matches against one or more, but not zero, of the preceding character, character set, or parenthesized group. Is also greedy, and can be made non-greedy by appending a ?.
?	Matches against exactly zero or one instance of the preceding element. Is greedy by default, but can be made non-greedy by appending a second ?.
\	Used to escape special characters that need to occur literally in the target string. Also introduces character sets described later.
[]	Defines a character set, such as [aeiou]. A range can be specified, such as [a-z] for lowercase letters. Multiple ranges can be specified: [a-zA-z] matches all letters. Some special characters do not work inside brackets. Preceding the set with a ^ only matches values not in the set.
|	In the expression a|b, indicates that either a or b can be part of a valid match. The subexpressions are tested left to right, and the leftmost that leads to a match is used.
( )	Creates a group. The portion of the match that falls between the parentheses is stored. The string can be retrieved later in the regular expression by using a *index*, where all groups in the string are indexed left to right, starting at 1. The index can also be used in a match object to retrieve information about the specific group.
\b	Matches the empty string at the boundary between words. The boundary is the whitespace or non-alphanumeric character preceding or following a sequence of alphanumeric characters. The start and ending of the string are also considered boundaries.
\d	Matches any digit, identical to [0-9].
\s	Matches any whitespace character, including space, newline, carriage return, and tab.
\w	Matches any alphanumeric character. In English, this is the set [a-zA-z0-9_]. In other locales, this is dependent on characters defined as letters for that locale.

The special characters \b, \d, \s, and \w can all be negated (that is, only match characters not in the set) by using the letters in uppercase, \B, \D, \C, and \W.

Regular expressions tend to get complex pretty quickly. Therefore, we're including a couple of simple examples to show how the special characters work. The Python cod in Example 11-1 matches strings that represent real numbers, where a real number is defined as one or more digits, followed by a literal dot, followed by zero or more digits. Notice in the code that the regular expression requires that there be a decimal point so that it won't match an integer string. Sometimes it is easier to incorporate that kind of special case into the regular expression, but frequently it makes sense to test for simple special cases outside the regular expression match to keep the pattern as simple as possible.

Example 11-1. Digits regular expression

```
>>> import re
>>> digits = re.compile(r"(\d+)\.(\d*)")
>>> result = digits.search("2.345")
>>> result.groups()
('2', '345')

>>> intResult = digits.search("2")
>>> intResult == None
1
```

Another simple regular expression utility fixes variable names that are in mixed case, such as mixedCase, by inserting a space between lowercase and uppercase letters. As Example 11-2 shows, the regular expression finds those boundaries, and the loop around it inserts a space in the string and looks for the next match.

Example 11-2. Fixing mixed case with a regular expression

```
import re
def fixMixedCase(thing):
    regex = re.compile("[a-z][A-Z]")
    pos = 0
    while 1:
        match = regex.search(thing, pos)
        if not match:
            break
        pos = match.start() + 1
        thing = thing[:pos] + ' ' + thing[pos:]
    return thing

print fixMixedCase("fixMixedCase")
print fixMixedCase("aVariableName")
```

fix Mixed Case
a Variable Name

Alex Martelli reviewed this text and pointed out that the fixedMixedCase function could also be written as a one-liner using back references:

```
def fixMixedCase(thing):
    return re.sub('([a-z])([A-Z])', r'\1 \2', thing)
```

Whether the one-line version is more or less readable than the longer version probably depends on how much experience you have with regular expressions.

Serialization and Pickling

Serialization is the ability to transform objects into a byte stream from which they can be reconstructed. Serialization allows you to store objects out to disc and read them back at a later time, send them over a socket connection, and so on. It can be used for persistence or for interprogram communication. Java offers a serialization facility using special object I/O streams. For Jython objects to take advantage of this facility, you can use the normal Java java.io.ObjectOutputStream for output, however you must use the Jython-specific org.python.util.PythonObjectInputStream to read the object in, as shown here:

```
import java.io as io
import org.python.util as util

class TestClass(io.Serializable):

    def __init__(self, value=0):
        self.value = value
        self.message = "Serialized"

    def toString(self):
        return "Message: %(message)s value: is %(value)s" % self.__dict__

instance = TestClass(3)

outFile = io.FileOutputStream("test.ser")
outStream = io.ObjectOutputStream(outFile)
outStream.writeObject(instance)
outFile.close()

inFile = io.FileInputStream("test.ser")
inStream = util.PythonObjectInputStream(inFile)
readInstance = inStream.readObject()

print readInstance.toString()
```

Message: Serialized value: is 3

If you do not use the PythonObjectInputStream, you will get a runtime error, because the ordinary Java ObjectInputStream has difficulty finding and recreating the dynamically loaded proxy classes used for Jython's Java inheritance when trying to deserialize the object. The PythonObjectInputStream manages proxies correctly, and will also work on deserializing ordinary Java objects. Python classes must be defined at the top level of a module other than the main script to work with serialization under Jython.

Python also has its own object serialization technique, called *pickling*. The pickle module defines classes for reading and writing objects. The following example shows pickling in action, using the same TestClass from the previous example:

```
import pickle

class TestClass:

    def __init__(self, value=0):
        self.value = value
        self.message = "Serialized"

    def __str__(self):
        return "Message: %(message)s value: is %(value)s" % self.__dict__

instance = TestClass(3)

outFile = open("test.pickle", "w")
pickle.dump(instance, outFile)
outFile.close()

inFile = open("test.pickle")
readInstance = pickle.load(inFile)

print readInstance
```

Message: Serialized value: is 3

The important part of this code to point out is not the class definition, but what the program does after the class is defined. After opening the file, the program calls the dump method defined in the pickle module. This causes the object to be serialized to the file *test.pickle*. Then the process is reversed, and the readInstance variable is loaded from the pickle file using the load method.

There are two changes that can be made in this example to make it run faster. First, you could import the cPickle module instead of pickle. The cPickle module takes its name from the fact that the CPython version of the module is implemented in C rather than Python. The Jython version is, of course, implemented in Java, but the name is kept for compatibility purposes. To make this work in the previous example, change all three instances of the word pickle to cPickle.

Another pickle speedup comes from using binary format. The binary pickle format is somewhat more compact than the text format. The text format is much easier to read in a debug or development situation, however. To use the binary format, pass an optional third value of 1 to the dump method.

Also, remember that the file needs to be opened in binary format. Using both speedups, the code becomes:

```
import cPickle

class TestClass:

    def __init__(self, value=0):
        self.value = value
        self.message = "Serialized"

    def __str__(self):
        return "Message: %(message)s value: is %(value)s" % self.__dict__

instance = TestClass(3)

outFile = open("test.pickle", "wb")
cPickle.dump(instance, outFile, 1)
outFile.close()
inFile = open("test.pickle")
readInstance = cpickle.load(inFile)

print readInstance
```

Message: Serialized value: is 3

Both the pickle and cPickle methods also define dumps and loads, which are identical to the dump and load methods, except that they return the pickled object as a string instead of writing it to a file.

There are only a few restrictions on what can be saved using pickle. The less commonly used built-in types, such as compiled code types, cannot be pickled. An attempt to pickle an "unpicklable" object will raise a PicklingError exception. Class instances can be pickled only if the classes are defined at the top level of a module different from the main script, and the class name is available when the class is unpickled. Each attribute of the class instance must itself be "picklable" for the instance to be "picklable." Top-level functions can also be pickled. However, Java objects cannot be pickled, and unpickling cannot properly restore the Java fields of a Jython class that subclasses from Java.

When the class is unpickled the __init__ method is, by default, not re-called on the instance. If you want __init__ to be called when the object is loaded, you can define a special method called __getinitargs__. The method should return a tuple, which is then passed as the arguments to __init__. Both pickle and PythonObjectInputStream automatically trigger the import of the necessary module when a Python class instance is deserialized and its module has not already been imported.

Unit Testing with PyUnit

Unit testing is an important part of ensuring the reliability of a program. Having a lightweight test framework that makes it easy to write and run automated tests can save you hours of time poking through debugger output. And, as those of you who have used extreme programming methods know, writing the tests before and while you write code can lead to particularly clean and elegant programs.

As with many other areas in Jython, unit testing offers a Java-based solution and a Python-based solution. The Java solution, JUnit, is available online at *http://www.junit.org*. The Python solution is based on JUnit and is called PyUnit, written by Steve Purcell. PyUnit comes with Jython distributions of 2.1 or later. If you are using an earlier distribution, PyUnit is available at *http://pyunit.sourceforge.net*. This section will focus on PyUnit because it comes with Jython and is a little easier to set up with Python code.

PyUnit can, of course, be used to test pure Java classes from Jython given the smooth Java/Jython integration. Test writing in Jython is generally faster because of dynamic typing. As a result, you may decide to use Jython to test a program that is otherwise written completely in Java.

Simple Tests

PyUnit's structure is a hierarchy with three levels: *test*, *test case*, and *test suite*. A test is any Python-callable object. Sometimes, you'll just want to run a test to see if the code completes without error. More frequently, you'll make assertions in the test function that will cause the test to fail if the assertions are not met.

This example shows a simple test for the len function of string, written using PyUnit's most basic constructs:

```
import unittest
class StringTest(unittest.TestCase):
    def runTest(self):
        self.assertEqual(4, len("hello"))

if __name__ == '__main__':
    runner = unittest.TextTestRunner()
    runner.run(StringTest())
```

Even though the system is called PyUnit, the module to import is called unittest. There is no class for individual tests in PyUnit (as you'll see, you'll most likely run them in bunches), but you can override the runTest method of the TestCase class to make a class that runs one test. Within the test, we use the TestCase method assertEqual, which raises an AssertionError if the two arguments are not equal.

To run the test, you create an instance of TextTestRunner and call its run method with an instance of the test case class—as you'll see, there are more advanced ways of doing that, as well. The PyUnit framework runs the test. The tests can also be run from the interactive prompt—just make sure to reload all dependent modules before running. PyUnit also comes with a graphical interface. However, it is written in the tkinter toolkit, and therefore it won't run under Jython. A Swing version of the interface should be available in either the Jython distribution, the PyUnit distribution, or the web site for this book.

Obviously, the test in the previous example fails, and PyUnit gives the following message:

```
F
=========================================================================
FAIL: runTest (__main__.StringTest)
-------------------------------------------------------------------------
Traceback (most recent call last):
  File "unit_test_one.py", line 4, in runTest
    self.assertEqual(4, len("hello"))
  File "C:\jython-2.0\Lib\unittest.py", line 273, in failUnlessEqual
    raise self.failureException, (msg or '%s != %s' % (first, second))
AssertionError: 4 != 5
-------------------------------------------------------------------------
Ran 1 tests in 0.010s
FAILED (failures=1)
```

The top line of the failure message is a representation of each test run—an F for failure here. The other options are E for error (any exception other than an assertion failure), and a plain dot to indicate passage. Each failure or error generates an error message, which includes the actual error and the Python traceback that came along with it.

Fixing the error gives the following success message:

```
.
-------------------------------------------------------------------------
Ran 1 tests in 0.010s
OK
```

PyUnit defines a number of convenience methods for testing specific cases, which are generally easier to use than the assert statement because they define more readable messages when they fail. (Unlike CPython, Jython does not have an optimized mode where assert statements are removed.) Most methods are defined positively as assert conditions and negatively as fail conditions—the two forms are identical (internally, the assert versions are set equal to the fail version). All the methods take an optional message argument that is printed along with the traceback on failure. The methods are shown here:

```
fail(self, msg=None)
```
Fails immediately. Useful for creating custom constructs.

```
failIf(self, expr, msg=None)
```
Fails if the *expr* is true.

```
failUnless(self, expr, msg=None)
assert_(self, expr, msg=None)
```
Fail if the *expr* is false.

```
failUnlessEqual(self, first, second, msg=None)
assertEqual(self, first, second, msg=None)
assertEquals(self, first, second, msg=None)
```
Fail if *first* is not equal to *second*.

```
failIfEqual(self, first, second, msg=None)
assertNotEqual(self, first, second, msg=None)
assertNotEquals(self, first, second, msg=None)
```
Fail if *first* is equal to *second*.

```
failUnlessRaises(self, excClass, callableObj, *args, **kwargs)
assertRaises(self, excClass, callableObj, *args, **kwargs)
```
Call *callableObj* with *args* and *kwargs*. Fail if an exception of class *excClass* is *not* raised. Used to test code that should raise an exception.

Tests in Groups

The real advantage to using PyUnit comes when you want to run dozens, hundreds, or even thousands of tests at a time. Usually, you will want to run a number of tests together against the same set of data. A common environment used for a series of tests is called a *fixture*. In PyUnit, you can use test cases to define a fixture and run tests against it, as shown here:

```
import unittest
import ftplib
class FtpTest(unittest.TestCase):

    def setUp(self):
        self.host = "ftp3.sourceforge.net"
        self.ftp = ftplib.FTP(self.host)
        self.ftp.login()

    def tearDown(self):
        self.ftp.close()

    def testPwd(self):
        self.assertEqual("/", self.ftp.pwd())

    def testWelcomeStatus(self):
        self.assertEqual("220", self.ftp.getwelcome()[:3])
```

PyUnit calls the setUp method before each test is run, and calls the tearDown method after each test is complete. In the previous code sample, the setup gives an open FTP connection to test, and the teardown closes it. However, because we've now defined two test methods, the test-running solution we used previously will no longer work—there's no runTest method. When more than one test is desired, a test suite needs to be created. This can be done explicitly by creating a test suite instance and adding each test one by one:

```
if __name__ == '__main__':
    runner = unittest.TextTestRunner()
    stringSuite = unittest.TestSuite()
    stringSuite.addTest(FtpTest("testPwd"))
    stringSuite.addTest(FtpTest("testWelcomeStatus"))
    runner.run(stringSuite)
```

Notice that each individual test is run with a clean instance of the TestCase. However, adding tests this way is tedious in the extreme. For the common case of creating a suite with all the methods in a TestCase that start with "test," PyUnit provides a shortcut:

```
if __name__ == '__main__':
    runner = unittest.TextTestRunner()
    stringSuite = unittest.makeSuite(FtpTest)
    runner.run(stringSuite)
```

The makeSuite method automatically adds each test to the suite. There is an optional argument to change the prefix used. The tests are run in order of the cmp function, which normally means in sorted order of their names—it's considered bad practice to write a test that depends on the order in which tests run.

It's highly recommended that each PyUnit module contain a top-level function called suite that returns a suite for that module. If that exists, there's a shortcut for creating and running the TextTestRunner explicitly: the main() function.

```
def suite():
    return unittest.makeSuite(FtpTest)

if __name__ == '__main__':
    unittest.main()
```

Example 11-3 shows the unit tests used to verify the HTML parser used in the tree example in "An HTML Source Browser" in Chapter 9. Notice that assertions commonly tested together are factored out into non-test methods. Not only does this refactoring increase readability, but it also ensures that each assertion is made each time.

Example 11-3. Unit testing the HTML parser

```
import unittest
from html_source_viewer import *

class HtmlSourceViewerTest(unittest.TestCase):

    basicText = '''<html><head><title>Test Page</title></head>
            <body>
            <h2 align='center'>This is my test page</h2>
            <table border='1' align="left"><tr><td>0</td><td>1</td></tr></table>
            <ul><li>fred<li>barney<b>is</b>a friend</ul>
            <a href="www.jython.org">jython</a>
            </body>
            </html>'''

    def setUp(self):
        "Create the HtmlParser and model"
        self.htmlParser = HtmlTreeParser(self.basicText)
        self.model = self.htmlParser.model

    def testStackComplete(self):
        "Ensure that everything is off the stack after parsing"
        self.assertEqual(0, len(self.htmlParser.tagStack))

    def assertTag(self, tag, expectedName, expectedChildren, arguments=[]):
        "Assert that a tag has expected values"
        self.assertEqual(expectedName, tag.tagString)
        self.assertEqual(expectedChildren, self.model.getChildCount(tag))
        self.assertEqual(expectedChildren == 0, self.model.isLeaf(tag))
        self.assertEqual(arguments, tag.arguments)

    def assertLeaf(self, leaf, expectedString):
        "Assert that a leaf has expected values"
        self.assertEqual(expectedString, leaf)
        self.assert_(self.model.isLeaf(leaf))

    def testRoot(self):
        "Test that the root is set correctly"
        root = self.model.getRoot()
        self.assertEqual(2, len(root.children))
        self.assertTag(root, "html", 2)

    def testHead(self):
        "Test that the head tag is set correctly, first test of traversal"
        root = self.model.getRoot()
        headTag = self.model.getChild(root, 0)
        self.assertTag(headTag, "head", 1)
        titleTag = self.model.getChild(headTag, 0)
        self.assertTag(titleTag, "title", 1)
        titleString = self.model.getChild(titleTag, 0)
        self.assertLeaf(titleString, "Test Page")
```

Example 11-3. Unit testing the HTML parser (continued)

```
    def testBody(self):
        "Test the main body tag -- first test of attributes"
        root = self.model.getRoot()
        bodyTag = self.model.getChild(root, 1)
        self.assertTag(bodyTag, "body", 4)
        headerTag = self.model.getChild(bodyTag, 0)
        self.assertTag(headerTag, "h2", 1, [("align", "center")])

    def testTable(self):
        "Test the table tag -- multiple attributes, and traversal"
        root = self.model.getRoot()
        bodyTag = self.model.getChild(root, 1)
        tableTag = self.model.getChild(bodyTag, 1)
        self.assertTag(tableTag, "table", 1,
                [("align", "left"), ("border", "1")])
        trTag = self.model.getChild(tableTag, 0)
        self.assertTag(trTag, "tr", 2)

    def testUl(self):
        "Test the ul tag -- single tags, and interspaced text and tags"
        root = self.model.getRoot()
        bodyTag = self.model.getChild(root, 1)
        ulTag = self.model.getChild(bodyTag, 2)
        self.assertTag(ulTag, "ul", 6)
        for i in [0, 2]:
            liTag = self.model.getChild(ulTag, i)
            self.assertTag(liTag, "li", 0)
        bTag = self.model.getChild(ulTag, 4)
        self.assertTag(bTag, "b", 1)
        self.assertEqual(["is"], bTag.children)

def suite():
    suite = unittest.makeSuite(HtmlSourceViewerTest)
    return suite

if __name__ == '__main__':
    unittest.main()
```

When the test in Example 11-3 is combined with the code in Examples 9-7 and 9-8, PyUnit will produce a clean unit test.

CHAPTER 12

Embedding Jython Inside Java

In the previous chapters we described how to build entire programs in Jython that are executed using the Jython interpreter. From a program being executed by the Jython interpreter you can access existing Java code within external libraries. You can write your entire program in Jython and use only preexisting Java libraries. Alternately, your program can be a hybrid of Java and Jython—for example, data crunching or graphics and visualization code in Java for performance reasons, and connecting logic and user interface code in Jython.

There is another way to use Jython. You can embed a Jython interpreter within your Java program. That interpreter could then execute Jython code and interact with the state of the parent Java program. The embedded interpreter can be used to manage various kinds of customization of the parent program. For example, you could write a system management framework that allows users to define responses to system events in Jython. You could create programmatic filters with all the power of the Python language to enhance, for example, an email client. You could use Jython for macro functionality in nearly any kind of program, or as a mechanism to separate game logic from a game engine.

While you could create an ad hoc solution or language for each of these problems, embedding a Jython interpreter has several advantages. If you are using Jython as your internal scripting language, you don't need to spend time building an interpreter, plus you get access to the entire Jython standard library. It's an excellent general solution, unless you are a better language designer than Guido van Rossum—and we don't think many people are. (And even if you thought you were, you'd still have to contend with more than a decade of language enhancement and usage from the entire community.)

We have seen in Chapter 3 that you can programmatically invoke Jython fragments inside Jython using the eval function. Embedding the Jython interpreter gives you this same functionality from within a Java program. Embedding is particularly useful in the case where you have a preexisting Java code base, or for some external reason you need to deploy a code base written mostly in Java. In particular, you may need your program to start up and deploy like a pure Java program, and can't or don't want to use a Jython program compiled with *jythonc*. In some cases, embedding is useful if you want an interpreter session with a startup or environment different from the normal interpreter setup. You might also use embedding when you're writing an add-on for a preexisting Java framework or program.

Setting Up an Interpreter

To execute Jython code from within a Java program you must create an instance of the class org.python.util.PythonInterpreter. The class has a simple interface, which allows you to execute Jython code passed to the interpreter. You can also manipulate the namespace of the interpreter in which the code is executed, which is an important mechanism for communicating with the Jython code.

In an embedded Jython program, you will frequently want to manipulate the interpreter data from the Java side, but using the Jython internal data types. To do this, Jython provides a common superclass for all Jython data types, org.python.core.PyObject. Most internal Jython types are implemented as subclasses of PyObject—for example, PyInteger, PyString, PyList, PyDictionary, and PyStringMap. In this chapter we look at some of the features of PyObject and the subclasses. For further reference on the internals of these objects, you can examine their source code and the *javadoc* documentation that is bundled with Jython. As a general rule, you should try to manage Jython data on the Jython side because the Python data mechanisms are far less likely to change than the internals of PyObject.

To embed Jython in a Java program, the Jython runtime needs to be loadable by Java, which means that *jython.jar* must be in the classpath of the application, or otherwise loadable. You need the entire *.jar* file because the PythonInterpreter class depends on the rest of the Jython runtime. All other Java classes referred to in this chapter whose names are prefixed with Py are in the *org.python.core* package unless otherwise specified.

Before you create an interpreter, you need to initialize the Jython runtime state as stored in the PySystemState class. Three methods perform that function (all Java examples in this section assume that you have imported the *org.python.core.** and *org.python.util.** packages):

```
public static void PySystemState.initialize( )

public static void PySystemState.initialize(java.util.Properties
preProperties, java.util.Properties postProperties, String[] argv)

public static void org.python.util.PythonInterpreter.initialize(java.util.
Properties preProperties, java.util.Properties postProperties, String[]
argv)
```

The initialize method in PythonInterpreter merely calls the three-argument method in PySystemState. The no-argument method in the first line of the previous code snippet is equivalent to the three-argument call:

```
PySystemState.initialize(System.getProperties( ), null, new String[] {""})
```

The initialize method sets up the global state of the Jython runtime—it's also the first Jython-specific call made when you invoke the Jython interpreter the standalone way. The global state includes global options and the contents of the sys.registry. To create the values of the sys.registry for the runtime, Jython finds the systemwide Jython registry file as specified in Appendix B. Options are then applied in the following order: first, the properties in the preProperties argument to the initialize method; second, the properties specified in the registry file; and third, the properties in the postProperties argument. This set of arguments allows you to specify properties that have either a lower or higher priority than the Jython registry. It is typical to use System.getProperties( ) for preProperties. A typical use of postProperties is shown when the Jython interpreter is launched standalone—the options read by parsing the command-line options are passed to the interpreter in that argument. The final argument to initialize, the argv argument, is used as the default value to initialize the value sys.argv.

To create an embedded interpreter you can use one of the constructors of the PythonInterpreter class:

```
public org.python.util.PythonInterpreter( )
public org.python.util.PythonInterpreter(PyObject dict)
public org.python.util.PythonInterpreter(PyObject dict, PySystemState
systemState)
```

All these constructors create a Python module named main, which uses the dict argument as its namespace. If dict is null or not supplied, a newly constructed and empty instance of PyStringMap is used. The module namespace is used as the global scope for all the code directly executed through the created interpreter. You should note that this main module is not put in the sys.modules module cache. The dict argument must be a member of one of the PyObject subclasses that implement a Jython mapping object. Typically this is either PyDictionary or PyStringMap. PyStringMap is an optimized version of PyDictionary that accepts only string keys.

The systemState argument should be an instance of PySystemState and will be visible to the code run through the interpreter as the Python built-in module sys. If the systemState is not specified or is null, a global instance of PySystemState (which is shared among all interpreters) will be used. In particular, all interpreters using the common state will share the module cache sys.modules and the module search path sys.path. This may not be what you want, so to avoid sharing, you need to call the two-argument constructor with an explicitly created PySystemState:

```
PythonInterpreter interp = new PythonInterpreter(null, new PySystemState())
```

The interpreter has methods that allow you to change the value of the standard streams sys.stdout and sys.stderr in the attached PySystemState instance (note that the PySystemState might be the shared one mentioned in the last paragraph) using the methods setOut and setErr. These methods are overloaded, with versions taking a java.io.OutputStream or a java.io.Writer. Otherwise, by default sys.stdout wraps the Java value System.out and sys.stderr wraps the Java value System.err.

Executing Code

The methods in PythonInterpreter for executing Python code mimic the Python built-ins presented in "Evaluating Code Dynamically" in Chapter 3:

```
public PyObject org.python.util.PythonInterpreter.eval(String s)

public void org.python.util.PythonInterpreter.exec(String s)
public void org.python.util.PythonInterpreter.exec(PyObject code)

public void org.python.util.PythonInterpreter.execfile(String s)
public void org.python.util.PythonInterpreter.execfile(java.io.InputStream
s)
public void org.python.util.PythonInterpreter.execfile(java.io.InputStream
s, String name)
```

The Java eval method works like the Python eval built-in. It takes as an argument a string that should be a valid Python expression, evaluates it, and returns the obtained result. In the Java case, the return value is of type PyObject, although of course the runtime type of the value is likely to be one of the subclasses. Remember that the string must be an expression—a statements that is not an expression, such as print, will raise an error.

The exec methods defined previously allow the interpreter to execute a suite of Python statements at once. They mimic the functionality of the Python exec statement. The string s must be a syntactically valid chunk of Python code. This includes whitespace—the indentation of s must follow Python rules. The version of exec with a PyObject argument expects a Jython internal compiled code object. Should you wish to use this version, you can obtain a code argument for this using the built-in function compile, which has the following Java-side declaration:

```
public static PyCode org.python.core.__builtin__.compile(String data, String
filename, String type)
```

PyCode is the PyObject subclass from which all internal code representations inherit. The combination of __builtin__.compile and the exec version, which takes a code object, is useful when the Jython code will need to be executed more than once. In this case, you essentially cache the compiled code, eliminating the need to recompile the string each time it is executed.

The execfile methods execute the code from a file like the Python built-in function execfile. The version taking a string expects a valid file pathname (something that can be passed to a Java File constructor). The other versions read the source code from an already constructed java.io. InputStream. The optional string argument name identifies the source of the file for the purposes of reporting the source of the error if an exception is raised.

This code shows a complete, if simple, example of the steps needed to create an embedded Jython interpreter:

```
import org.python.core.*;
import org.python.util.*;

public class PyInterpTest {
    public static void main(String[] argv) {
        PySystemState.initialize();
        PythonInterpreter interp = new PythonInterpreter();
        PyObject value = interp.eval("2 + 2");
        System.out.println(value);
    }
}
```

The PyInterpTest goes through the steps of embedding the interpreter as specified in this section—it initializes the system state, calls the constructor, then calls the eval method with the valid Python string 2 + 2, gets the value, and prints it out. It does, as expected, print out 4 to the standard out stream. Remember that *jython.jar* must be specified on the classpath when compiling and executing the code with java. The same is true for the other examples in this chapter. Here are sample command-line invocations for Windows and Unix:

```
>rem Windows
>javac -classpath \jython21\jython.jar PyInterpTest.java
>java -cp \transit\jython-2.1b1\jython.jar;. PyInterpTest
4

$# Unix flavors
$javac -classpath ~/jython21/jython.jar PyInterpTest.java
$java -cp ~/jython-2.1b1/jython.jar:. PyInterpTest
4
```

Accessing the Interpreter Namespace

Being able to run a Jython interpreter is of limited value without the ability to pass data back and forth between the interpreter and the rest of your Java code. Although the eval statement does return a value, you might also want to run an entire Jython script using exec and then examine the data by variable name. Fortunately, Jython allows you to retrieve and set values in the global namespace for the interpreter.

To access the value of a single binding, PythonInterpreter defines two versions of the get method. The one-argument version, get(String name), returns the value in its Jython internal form as a PyObject subclass instance. If name is not bound in the interpreter, null is returned. The two-argument version get(String name, Class javaclass) returns a Java object. Before returning the value, Jython attempts to coerce the PyObject to the class specified in the javaclass argument. The coercion rules defined in "Automatic Type Conversion" in Chapter 6 are used. This method throws a NullPointerException if the name is not bound. If the coercion cannot be performed, a PyException (which wraps a Jython TypeError) is thrown.

You can access the entire global namespace for the interpreter through the getLocals() method. The getLocals method returns the PyObject dictionary used for the namespace, which is either a PyStringMap or a dictionary object passed to the constructor when the interpreter was created.

You can also add or modify values in the interpreter namespace using the set method. There are two forms of the set method. The first form, set(String name, PyObject value), takes a value that is already in a Jython internal type. The second form, set(String name, Object value), takes a Java type and coerces it to a PyObject using the rules in "Automatic Type Conversion" in Chapter 6.

This Java code demonstrates the manipulation of the interpreter namespace. The *namespace_test.py* file referenced in the next example contains a single line: language = "Jython".

```
import org.python.core.*;
import org.python.util.*;

public class PyNamespaceTest {
    public static void main(String[] argv) {
        PySystemState.initialize();
        PythonInterpreter interp = new PythonInterpreter();
        interp.execfile("namespace_test.py");
        Object value = interp.get("language", String.class);
        System.out.println(value);
        interp.set("embedded", "1");
        interp.exec("print embedded");
    }
}
```

Jython
1

In PyNamespaceTest, we set up an interpreter as we did in PyInterpeterTest previously. The execfile statement runs the *namespace_test.py* file, which just assigns the value "Jython" to the variable named language. We then use the get statement to retrieve that value as a Java String object, and print it to standard out. Then, the code uses the set statement to set a variable named embedded to the value 1, which we confirm by executing the statement print embedded from the interpreter, printing the value 1.

Using PyObjects

The PyObject class offers an interface to the Python behavior of the object with methods that match the names of the standard special methods (such as __str__ and __len__, as described in "Special Methods" in Chapter 5). Subclasses implement their behavior by overriding these methods. Jython performs Python operations on the instances by calling these methods.

The most useful methods for use during embedding are the data access methods. We will focus on these methods. Most of the other methods mimic the Python names, and the Jython *javadoc* has more detail. Existing limitations about the immutability of some Python objects or setting of arbitrary attributes are still valid even when you are trying to manipulate the internal representations directly from inside Java. In other words, you can't use these methods to make tuples or strings suddenly mutable.

The following PyObject methods implement attribute manipulation and access. There is one significant restriction on the versions of these methods that take Java String as the argument. These methods require that the string passed must be *interned* because Jython uses Java's string interning facilities to speed up string lookup. In practical terms, this means that the arguments must either be string literals, or the result of a call such as *string*.intern().

__findattr__(PyString *name*), __findattr__(String *name*)
> The __findattr__ methods retrieve an object attribute value. They return null if the attribute does not exist. There are also analogous methods, called __getattr__ methods, which throw an exception if the attribute is absent. The returned value is a PyObject.

__setattr__(PyString *name*, PyObject *value*),
__setattr__(String *name*, PyObject *value*)
> Set the attribute *name* to the value given. These methods do not return a value.

__delattr__(PyString *name*), __delattr__(String *name*)
> Remove the attribute *name* from the object. Do not return a value.

Sequence and mapping access special methods are defined in PyObject to allow Java to use polymorphism to call these functions on any PyObject instance. However, unless specifically overridden by a subclass (such as PyList), they will just raise an AttributeError. Again, all the versions taking a Java String require an interned string.

```
public PyObject PyObject.__finditem__(PyString key)
public PyObject PyObject.__finditem__(String key)
public PyObject PyObject.__finditem__(int key)

public PyObject PyObject.__setitem__(PyString key, PyObject value)
public PyObject PyObject.__setitem__(String key, PyObject value)
public PyObject PyObject.__setitem__(int key, PyObject value)

public PyObject PyObject.__delitem__(PyString key)
public PyObject PyObject.__delitem__(String key)
public PyObject PyObject.__delitem__(int key)
```

The __finditem__ methods return null if no element indexed by key exists. Again, __getitem__ versions exist that raise an exception. All __opitem__(int *key*...) versions just convert the int argument to a PyInteger, then call the PyObject version. The following snippet shows how to iterate over a PyObject sequence in Java:

```
PyObject seq;
PyObject item;

for (int i = 0; (item = seq.__finditem__(i)) != null; i++) {
    ...
}
```

PyObject Subclasses

Most of the interesting Python data types are represented internally by subclasses of PyObject. This section gives a brief tour of the functionality of the subclasses:

PyDictionary

> Representation of a Python dictionary. Has a null constructor, which creates an empty dictionary. Another constructor takes a Java Hashtable, whose elements are assumed to be PyObject. A third constructor takes an array of PyObject instances. The elements of that array should alternate between keys and values. For example:
>
> ```
> new PyDictionary(new PyObject[] {new PyString("zero"), new PyInteger(0),
> new PyString("one"), new PyInteger(1) })
> ```
>
> corresponds to Python dictionary {'zero': 0, 'one': 1}.
>
> The PyDictionary class offers the Python methods of a dictionary (such as get) as Java methods. You can simply use the methods PyList PyDictionary.keys() or PyList PyDictionary.values() to iterate over the content of a PyDictionary.

PyInteger

> Internal representation of Python integers. Has one constructor, which takes a Java int. Does not have a constructor that takes a Java Integer class.

PyList

> Represents a Python list. Has three constructors. The null constructor, PyList(), creates an empty list. One constructor takes an array of PyObject instances, the other takes a Java Vector, whose elements are assumed to all be PyObjects. The Python list methods are defined in PyList as Java methods.

PyString

> Internal representation of Jython strings. Has two constructors, one that takes a Java String and one that takes a Java char.

PyStringMap

> An alternative implementation of PyDictionary with the same interface, but optimized for and accepting only string keys. PyStringMap is used internally to implement Python module, class, and instance namespaces.

PyTuple

> Represents an immutable tuple. Constructors are similar to PyList, but without the Vector constructor.

The Python object None is represented by the singleton Py.None. Jython internals also offer two useful predefined objects: Py.EmptyObjects (which is a zero-length PyObject[]) and Py.NoKeywords (which is a zero-length String[]).

The following example shows the use of some of the Py constructors and special methods:

```
import org.python.core.*;
import org.python.util.*;

public class PyObjectTest {
    public static void main(String[] argv) {
        PySystemState.initialize();
        PythonInterpreter interp = new PythonInterpreter();
        PyDictionary dict = new PyDictionary();
        dict.__setitem__(new PyString("zero"), new PyInteger(0));
        dict.__setitem__(new PyString("one"), new PyInteger(1));
        interp.set("dict", dict);
        interp.exec("print dict");
        interp.exec("print dict['zero'] + dict['one']");
    }
}

{'one': 1, 'zero': 0}
1
```

The setup in PyObjectTest is similar to the other examples in this chapter. This time, however, we create and populate the dictionary object directly in Java.

The conversions from Java to Python (described in "Java-to-Python Types: Automatic Conversion" in Chapter 6) can be explicitly performed using the following static function of the Java utility class Py:

```
public static PyObject Py.java2py(Object o)
```

A Python value can be coerced to a Java type according to the rules illustrated in "Automatic Type Conversion" in Chapter 6, using any of the following methods:

```
public static boolean Py.py2boolean(PyObject o)
public static byte Py.py2byte(PyObject o)
public static char Py.py2char(PyObject o)
public static double Py.py2double(PyObject o)
public static float Py.py2float(PyObject o)
public static int Py.py2int(PyObject o)
public static long Py.py2long(PyObject o)
public static short Py.py2short(PyObject o)
```

The method Py.py2boolean uses a looser standard than that stated in Chapter 6—it returns the truth value of any PyObject based on Python rules; it does not require the object to be an integer. The most generic conversion capability, which can be used to coerce a Python object to a generic Java class or interface, is offered directly by the PyObject class:

```
public Object PyObject.__tojava__(Class c)
```

The various subclasses of PyObject override this method to implement the rules in "Automatic Type Conversion" in Chapter 6. If the conversion cannot be performed, the singleton Py.NoConversion is returned. This Java code snippet converts a Python long to a Java java.math.BigInteger, an acceptable conversion:

```
interp.exec("x = 10L");
PyObject pyLong = interp.get("x");
java.math.BigInteger big = (java.math.BigInteger)pyLong.__tojava__(java.
math.BigInteger.class);
```

Finally, PyObject offers several versions of the __call__ special method, which invokes callable Python objects. Callable objects are Python functions, bound and unbound methods, and Python classes. Calling a Python class returns a newly constructed instance. The different versions of the __call__ method are:

```
public PyObject __call__(PyObject args[], String keywords[])
public PyObject __call__(PyObject arg1, PyObject args[], String keywords[])
public PyObject __call__(PyObject args[])
public PyObject __call__()
public PyObject __call__(PyObject arg0)
public PyObject __call__(PyObject arg0, PyObject arg1)
public PyObject __call__(PyObject arg0, PyObject arg1, PyObject arg2)
public PyObject __call__(PyObject arg0, PyObject arg1, PyObject arg2,
PyObject arg3)
```

All the overloaded methods call just the (PyObject args[], String keywords[]) version with the appropriate set of values. The call to the Python function is defined using the args array and the keywords array. Working from the end of both arrays, the last string in the keywords array is matched with the last value in the args array. Then the next-to-last items are matched, and so on, until there are no more keywords. The remaining elements in the args array are treated as normal arguments. So, if the args array had the integers [1, 2, 3, 4] and the keyword array had the strings ['a', 'b'], the resulting call would be equivalent to (1, 2, a=3, b=4).

Catching Exceptions

The code executed in a `PythonInterpreter` instance can throw either Java or Python exceptions. On the Java side, Jython wraps exceptions inside instances of `PyException`, a subclass of `java.lang.RuntimeException`, which means it need not be declared in throw clauses. If you are interested in catching these exceptions you should use the Java try statement, like this:

```
try {
    // interpreter invocation
} catch(PyException pye) {
    // ...
}
```

The actual exception object is accessible as *pye*.value, and it is sometimes lazily constructed as needed. The attribute *pye*.value is just a `PyObject` corresponding to the Python-side exception instance, and you can access its attributes using `__findattr__`. An exception can be tested against all Python exception types using the singleton objects *ExceptionType* in the `Py` class, such as `Py.SyntaxError`, `Py.IndexError`, and `Py.NameError`. You can both force the construction of the exception type object and check for a particular exception type through the static method `Py.matchException`(*pye*, `Py.`*ExceptionType*). A complete list of Jython exception types can be found in Appendix C.

You can test for a Java exception using the following idiom:

```
Object candExc = pye.value.__tojava__(Throwable.class)
if (candExc != Py.NoConversion) {
 // pye wrapped a Java exception
    Throwable exc = (Throwable)candExc;
    ...
}
```

Embedding Examples

The Jython distribution contains a nice example of the capabilities of embedding in the context of an add-on. The `PyServlet` class is a Java servlet, which is used to redirect requests to Jython servlets implemented through plain Jython *.py* files (for more on how this works from the servlet perspective, see "Servlets and PyServlet" in Chapter 10). The most interesting snippet of this file (from an embedding perspective) is presented here, where the Jython servlet is loaded into the system. The code in this sample is only part of the process of loading the Jython servlet, and some variables have already been set by the time this code is executed. For example, `path` is the path of the *.py* file being called, `name` is the actual name of the servlet (the filename without the extension), and `interp` is the active interpreter.

```
try {
    interp.execfile(path);
    PyObject cls = interp.get(name);
    if (cls == null)
        throw new ServletException("No callable (class or function) "+
                                   "named " + name + " in " + path);

    PyObject pyServlet = cls.__call__();
    Object o = pyServlet.__tojava__(HttpServlet.class);
    if (o == Py.NoConversion)
        throw new ServletException("The value from " + name +
                                   "must extend HttpServlet");
    servlet = (HttpServlet)o;
    servlet.init(getServletConfig());

} catch (PyException e) {
    throw new ServletException("Could not create "+
                               "Jython servlet" + e.toString());
}
CacheEntry entry = new CacheEntry(servlet, file.lastModified());
cache.put(path, entry);
return servlet;
```

The servlet code starts by executing the Python file containing the servlet. In most cases the Python file is just a module that defines a subclass of HttpServlet in Jython. After the servlet file is executed, PyServlet performs a get on the namespace to retrieve the PyObject with the name of the servlet. The result of that retrieval must be a callable object that returns a Jython subclass of HttpServlet. PyServlet then calls that object and converts the Jython servlet to a Java HttpServlet using the __tojava__ special method. Finally, PyServlet initializes the servlet, populates a cache, and returns the servlet.

It is a common idiom to use the embedded interpreter to manage the interface between the part of the code written in Jython and that written in Java, possibly using Java classes or interfaces that are subclassed by the Jython code. The net result of the approach is that the behavior defined in Jython is seen and used through a Java face. An orthogonal approach is to define at least one "application" Java object that is put in the interpreter namespace and can be used by Jython code to access and interact with the Java application state.

Example 12-1 demonstrates embedding Jython as a macro or command language. It is a really quick-and-dirty draw program that uses Jython as a command language. Figure 12-1 shows a sample window from the draw program. Note that the program does not redraw if the window is covered—to do that, you have to add a history of commands run, or draw to a memory buffer.

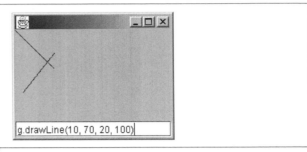

Figure 12-1. Embedded draw program

Example 12-1. A draw program

```java
import java.awt.*;
import java.awt.event.*;
import javax.swing.*;
import org.python.core.*;
import org.python.util.*;

public class PyEmbed extends JFrame {

    PythonInterpreter interp;
    JPanel easel;
    String startFile;
    JTextField textField;

    public PyEmbed(String startup) {
        this.startFile = startup;
        this.addWindowListener(new WindowAdapter() {
            public void windowClosing(WindowEvent evt) {
                System.exit(0);
            }});
        this.getContentPane().setLayout(new BorderLayout());
        this.easel = new JPanel();
        this.easel.setPreferredSize(new Dimension(200, 200));
        this.getContentPane().add(this.easel, BorderLayout.CENTER);
        this.textField = new JTextField();
        this.textField.setPreferredSize(new Dimension(200, 20));
        this.getContentPane().add(this.textField, BorderLayout.SOUTH);
        this.textField.addActionListener(new ActionListener() {
            public void actionPerformed(ActionEvent evt) {
                PyEmbed.this.interp.exec(PyEmbed.this.textField.getText());
                PyEmbed.this.textField.setText("");
            }});
        this.pack();
    }

    public void initInterp() {
        PySystemState.initialize();
        this.interp = new PythonInterpreter();
        this.interp.set("w", this);
```

Example 12-1. A draw program (continued)

```
        this.interp.set("e", this.easel);
        this.interp.set("g", this.easel.getGraphics());
    }

    public void show() {
        super.show();
        this.initInterp();
        this.interp.execfile(this.startFile);
    }

    public static void main(String[] argv) {
        PyEmbed embed = new PyEmbed("embed.py");
        embed.show();
    }

}
```

In Example 12-1, the interpreter is set up to initialize from a file, and then take commands from a command line and execute them. Before you get the command line, the program puts a few interesting values in the interpreter namespace so that they can be used from the Jython code. The main drawing graphics object is designated g, for example. The actual command line is sent to the interpreter in the inner class that is called when an action is performed on the text field. The relevant line of code is PyEmbed.this.interp. exec(PyEmbed.this.textField.getText());.

CHAPTER 13

Compiling Jython

All the uses of Jython that we have explored so far have required the use of the Jython interpreter, either directly through the interactive prompt, by launching the interpreter on a Jython script file, or by embedding the interpreter in a Java program. This approach makes perfect sense for standalone programs, but sometimes you need to run Jython code in a context where plain *.class* files are required and the standalone interpreter is not available. This requirement is true for many Java technologies, such as applets. To allow for this, Jython provides the *jythonc* static compilation tool, which compiles your Jython code to standalone Java-compiled *.class* files that can be distributed and used just as if they were originally written in Java.

Compiling Jython code allows you to use your Jython program as an applet class, bean class, and so on. You can also package your Jython program as a standalone *.jar* archive for distribution. Your compiled Jython classes can also be used and subclassed by a separate Java program. This chapter will explore the uses of *jythonc* to expand the reach of your Jython code.

Why Compile?

One of the first questions to answer about using a static compilation tool for Jython is why it is necessary to do so at all. After all, the Jython interpreter clearly creates *.class* files (actually *$py.class* files) when a Jython module is loaded. Why can't these *.class* files be used for distribution?

The answer has to do with how the interpreter works internally. To achieve a reasonable speed, Jython compiles all code to Java bytecode. To avoid a time-consuming compilation step, and because of the dynamic semantics of Python, the Jython interpreter generates Java bytecode on the fly, which is dynamically loaded by the interpreter as needed.

The *$py.class* files cache the bytecode generated for *.py* files, however other bytecode, which depends on dynamic information known only at runtime, cannot be easily cached. Examples include the glue code in proxy classes for interoperating with Java, or code corresponding to Python exec statements. Therefore, the *$py.class* files do not contain all the bytecode needed to run the program. This dynamic creation of *.class* files and bytecode is a departure from typical Java behavior, which assumes that all classes are compiled before the program starts.

To be able to use these dynamically created classes, Jython defines custom subclasses of java.lang.ClassLoader to load the classes into the Java Virtual Machine (JVM). A custom class loader is needed because only custom class loaders allow for Java class unloading and in-memory dynamic loading. Class unloading is required to allow for reload or exec without memory leaks. However, using a custom class loader can cause problems with the Java API (which is why Jython defines a custom subclass of java.io. ObjectInputStream to support serialization).

In general, a custom class loader can create all sorts of possibilities for malicious mischief (you could redirect class loading to malicious code, for example), so in a sandbox or other secure Java environment, permission to use a custom class loader is not granted. The inability to use the class loader prevents the direct use of the Jython interpreter in an applet or other secure environment.

Compilation with *jythonc* avoids this problem. The *jythonc* compiler performs in two steps. First, it compiles your Jython module to Java source code. To do this, it makes a series of static assumptions based on the Python code about what glue code and proxy code are needed, and produces source code for them as well. Then it uses an ordinary Java compiler to compile the source code to a *.class* file. As a result, the compiled Jython modules behave exactly like native Java classes, and can be used anywhere that *.class* files are accepted, as long as the Jython runtime (*jython.jar*) is available.

There are some pitfalls to using *jythonc*. For example, *jythonc* is unable to properly deal with structural aspects of the program, such as a base class list being dynamically set at runtime. The following Jython code shows a case where the base class is dynamically set based on runtime information:

```
import java
import configuration

if configuration.isGui:
  base = java.awt.Component
else:
  base = java.lang.Object

class C(base): pass
```

In this example, *jythonc* cannot detect what class C inherits from and therefore cannot produce a proper static proxy. It is simply unable to detect that C even needs a proxy. Code that uses dynamic execution (eval, exec, ...) and is compiled with *jythonc* may still need custom class loaders to work and, therefore, cannot work in a sandbox (such as a vanilla applet context). Java classes produced by *jythonc* cannot be imported effectively by the Jython interpreter. This may improve in the future, however.

The Compiler in Action

Let's take a closer look at what the *jythonc* compiler actually does. Example 13-1 should look familiar. It's the welcome application from Chapter 1, slightly reworked so that the code is in a class that inherits from javax.swing.JFrame.

Example 13-1. WelcomeFrame.py

```
import javax.swing as swing
import java.awt as awt
import java.lang as lang

def exit(event):
        lang.System.exit(0)

class WelcomeFrame(swing.JFrame):
    names = ["Groucho", "Chico", "Harpo"]
    quotes = {"Groucho": "Say the secret word",
            "Chico": "Viaduct?", "Harpo": "HONK!"}

    def __init__(self, title="Welcome to Jython", size=(200, 200)):
        swing.JFrame.__init__(self, title, size=size, windowClosing=exit)
        self.contentPane.layout = awt.FlowLayout()
        self.field = swing.JTextField(preferredSize=(200,20))
        self.contentPane.add(self.field)
        buttons = [self.createButton(each) for each in self.names]
        for eachButton in buttons:
            self.contentPane.add(eachButton)
        self.pack()

    def buttonPressed(self, event):
        self.field.text = self.quotes[event.source.text]

    def createButton(self, name):
        return swing.JButton(name, preferredSize=(100,20),
                actionPerformed=self.buttonPressed)

if __name__ == '__main__':
    WelcomeFrame().show()
```

Running Example 13-1 in Jython produces the exact same window as was produced in the interpreter example in "Welcome to Jython" in Chapter 1. (This is also shown later in Figure 13-1). The only change was to put most of the code inside the WelcomeFrame class.

To run Jython on this file, type the following command at a command prompt: **jythonc WelcomeFrame.py**. Obviously, you might have to include the directory names for both jythonc and WelcomeFrame depending on the shell you are using. The compiler processes for a while, then produces the output shown here. To work, *jythonc* needs to invoke a Java compiler that should be on the system path. The *javac* compiler, which comes with the Sun JDK, is often used.

```
% jythonc WelcomeFrame.py
processing WelcomeFrame
Required packages:
   javax.swing
   java.lang
   java.awt
Creating adapters:
   java.awt.event.WindowListener used in WelcomeFrame
   java.awt.event.ActionListener used in WelcomeFrame
Creating .java files:
   WelcomeFrame module
      WelcomeFrame extends javax.swing.JFrame
Compiling .java to .class...
Compiling with args: ['C:\\jdk1.3\\bin\\javac', '-classpath', 'C:\\jython-2.
1a3\\jython.jar; C:\\java\\jakarta-regexp-1.2\\jakarta-regexp-1.2.jar;, '.\\
jpywork\\WelcomeFrame.java']
0  Note: Some input files use or override a deprecated API.
Note: Recompile with -deprecation for details.
```

The output walks through the activities of *jythonc* as it compiles the file. First it processes the Python file to determine what packages are imported, and it creates adapters corresponding to the listeners used in the original code. The most important line in the output is WelcomeFrame extends javax. swing.JFrame as the .*java* source files are created. This indicates that *jythonc* has recognized that WelcomeFrame is a subclass of a Java class. For *jythonc* to make that determination, the class must be defined at the top level of a module. If the inheritance relationship cannot be statically recognized, no message appears—you don't get a message that Jython tried and failed to determine a relationship.

Java Source

The Java source file is saved by default in a subdirectory called *jpywork*. After creating the .*java* source file, *jythonc* compiles it and sends the current Java classpath and the *WelcomeFrame.java* file to the compiler. You can control where the files are placed, the location of the compiler, and other compiler options. For more details on command-line options to *jythonc*, see Appendix B.

The compiled source file *WelcomeFrame.java* is too long to list here in its entirety. A couple of snippets will suffice to give the general idea of what *jythonc* does:

```
public class WelcomeFrame extends javax.swing.JFrame implements org.python.
core.PyProxy, org.python.core.ClassDictInit {

    public static class _PyInner extends PyFunctionTable implements
PyRunnable {
```

This snippet shows the class declaration that *jythonc* creates for *WelcomeFrame.java*. The class WelcomeFrame is created, and it does extend JFrame. It also implements two internal Jython interfaces. The most important is PyProxy, which is for proxies of Java classes. In general, if there is a top-level class in the module that inherits from a Java class (as WelcomeFrame inherits from JFrame) and the class has the same name as the original Python module, the Java class for the module will also be a proxy class for the class and can be used as a normal Java class inheriting from the involved base class. Other top-level classes inheriting from Java, but not conforming to this naming convention, will have their Jython proxies defined as inner classes of the module Java class. Therefore, for a hypothetical Jython class Helper defined as a top-level class in the WelcomeFrame.py module and inheriting from java. lang.Object, *jythonc* would produce a Java proxy class WelcomeFrame.Helper.

Most of the work is actually done within the inner class _PyInner, which contains the defined Python functions as static methods. It also defines methods for other elements of the code. One instance of these methods is shown here. It is the Java translation of the list comprehension [self. createButton(each) for each in self.names].

```
private static PyObject __listcomprehension$1(PyFrame frame) {
    // Temporary Variables
    int t$0$int;
    PyObject t$0$PyObject, t$1$PyObject, t$2$PyObject, t$3$PyObject;

    t$0$PyObject = new PyList(new PyObject[] {});
    t$1$PyObject = t$0$PyObject.__getattr__("append");
    t$0$int = 0;
    t$3$PyObject = frame.getlocal(0).__getattr__("names");
    while ((t$2$PyObject = t$3$PyObject.__finditem__(t$0$int++)) != null) {
        frame.setlocal(5, t$2$PyObject);
        t$1$PyObject.__call__(frame.getlocal(0).invoke("createButton",
                                               frame.getlocal(5)));
    }
    return t$0$PyObject;
}
```

The __listcomprehension$1 method implements the list comprehension, putting the self.names list in the variable t3PyObject by using the internal __getattr__ method. The code then traverses the list, invoking the createButton method on each element and then appending it to the result list. The result list is t0PyObject, and the append method itself is stored in t1PyObject, which is what gets called. The logic in this method isn't that hard to follow, as long as you can decipher the machine-created variable names.

Top-Level Java

The following example shows the top-level code of the WelcomeFrame module, as translated to Java:

```
private static PyObject main$7(PyFrame frame) {
    frame.setglobal("__file__", s$12);

    frame.setlocal("swing",
        org.python.core.imp.importOneAs("javax.swing", frame));
    frame.setlocal("awt",
        org.python.core.imp.importOneAs("java.awt", frame));
    frame.setlocal("lang",
        org.python.core.imp.importOneAs("java.lang", frame));
    frame.setlocal("exit",
        new PyFunction(frame.f_globals, new PyObject[] {}, c$0_exit));
    frame.setlocal("WelcomeFrame",
        Py.makeClass("WelcomeFrame", new PyObject[]
            {frame.getname("swing").__getattr__("JFrame")},
            c$4_WelcomeFrame, null, WelcomeFrame.class));
    if (frame.getname("__name__").__eq(s$11).__nonzero__()) {
        frame.getname("WelcomeFrame").__call__().invoke("show");
    }
    return Py.None;
}
```

The top-level code of the module is placed in a static main$*num* method of the inner class. (The PyFrame argument, by the way, implements a Python scope.) The top-level module starts by defining the three module imports. Then it uses the utility function Py.makeClass to create the actual WelcomeFrame class. Finally, it executes the if __name__ == 'main' as an actual Java if statement, and if the statement's condition is true, it creates a WelcomeFrame instance by calling the class object, then invokes the show method. Finally, it returns None.

Finally, this example shows the main method of the WelcomeFrame class, as seen by Java:

```
public static void main(String[] args) {
    String[] newargs = new String[args.length+1];
    newargs[0] = "WelcomeFrame";
```

```
        System.arraycopy(args, 0, newargs, 1, args.length);
        Py.runMain(WelcomeFrame._PyInner.class, newargs, jpy$packages,
                jpy$properties, null, new String[] {"WelcomeFrame"});
    }
```

All that the main method does is set up the arguments list to include the WelcomeFrame, then call a utility method that triggers the main method of the inner class. The main methods of the Java classes generated by *jythonc* for each module trigger the execution of the module top-level statements.

At the end of the *jythonc* process, there is a *WelcomeFrame.class* file suitable for use with an ordinary Java runtime (the java command assumes that the current directory is the one that includes *WelcomeFrame.class*):

```
java -classpath .;C:\\jython-2.1a3\\jython.jar WelcomeFrame
```

under Windows or:

```
java -classpath .:/usr/local/jython-2.1a3/jython.jar WelcomeFrame
```

for Unix flavors.

The window will show up as expected.

Packaging in Java Archives

The ability to compile a single Jython file to Java is useful, but limited. To really use your Jython files, you need the ability to compile several files and bundle them together in a *.jar* archive. Several command-line options to *jythonc* allow you to do just that.

The --jar option allows you to specify the name of a *.jar* file in which to store the compilation results. Of course, you also need a way to specify the set of files that you want included in the archive. You can simply list all the files you want compiled one by one in the command line. The files can be listed either as paths or as module names (without the *.py* extension). If they are listed as modules, they must be in sys.path.

Listing the files individually can get a bit tedious, so *jythonc* has a number of options for automatically including a group of files. The most basic is the --deep option, which automatically includes all Python dependencies of the modules listed. Using the --deep option ensures that all the Python files you might need are bundled in the *.jar*. To include Java dependencies, you can use the --addpackages option, which causes dependencies from third-party Java libraries to be added to the archive. The list of included packages always includes the libraries org.python.modules and org.apache.oro.text.regex, which define the Java-implemented modules in the Jython standard library.

In some contexts, most notably running an applet under certain browsers, everything you need must be included in one *.jar*—in this case, including the Jython core packages. There are two options for including that information. The --core includes all the Java classes in the *org.python.core* package. The --all option includes the entire *org.jython* package tree—core, parser, dynamic compiler, and all—enabling dynamic execution when appropriate permissions for creating class loaders are granted. Both of these options automatically trigger the --deep option as well so that the produced *.jar* is completely self contained.

When the *.jar* is created, Jython will add a manifest file, which includes a Main-Class declaration for the class corresponding to the first Python module on the *jythonc* command line. The inclusion of that manifest file will cause the main method of that class to be executed when the *.jar* is run. As we saw in the previous section, running that main method will be equivalent to executing the top-level code of that first module.

Here is a very simple *welcome.py* snippet that runs the WelcomeFrame example used previously in this chapter:

```
import WelcomeFrame
WelcomeFrame.WelcomeFrame().show()
```

We then can call *jythonc* with the command jythonc-core-jar welcome.jar welcome.py. This call to *jythonc* results in the cration of a new file, *welcome.jar*, which includes the compiled Java classes for *welcome.py* and *WelcomeFrame.py*. The compiled WelcomeFrame is included because it is a dependency of *welcome.py*. The *.jar* can then be executed with the command java -jar welcome.jar. This causes *welcome.py* code to be executed and loads the same welcome window already seen at the end of the last section. It is important to remember that the java -jar command ignores the system classpath, so it is important for the *.jar* to be self contained.

Using Jython in Java

The static proxies produced by *jythonc* as *.class* files are ready to be used and subclassed by Java code. Just like the dynamic proxies created by the *jython* interpreter, they properly deal with overriding of Java methods by Python methods. But *jythonc* also offers an option for adding new Java-visible methods directly to the proxies, a feature not supported by the interpreter. This feature is triggered simply using special comments in your Jython code.

Example 13-2 shows how to use our Jython example from Java. We'd like to be able to get an instance of our WelcomeFrame class, add a new button and quote, and have the window display.

Example 13-2. Using WelcomeFrame from Java

```
import WelcomeFrame;
import javax.swing.JButton;

public class FrameUser {
    public static void main(String[] argv) {
        WelcomeFrame f = new WelcomeFrame("From Java");
        JButton newButton = f.createButton("Zeppo");
        f.addQuote("Zeppo", "Hello");
        f.getContentPane().add(newButton);
        f.pack();
        f.show();
    }
}
```

If you try to compile this program, however, assuming that WelcomeFrame is properly in your classpath, you get an error recognizing addQuote and an error recognizing createButton. The addQuote error makes sense—there is no method addQuote in the WelcomeFrame class. But there is a method createButton, which is not visible to the Java compiler. For the previous example to work, we need to make the createButton method visible to the Java complier, and add an addQuote method that is also visible.

To prepare the *WelcomeFrame.py* module for use by Java programs, we need to make a few changes, as highlighted in Example 13-3.

Example 13-3. Changes to WelcomeFrame.py

```
import javax.swing as swing
import java.awt as awt
import java.lang as lang

def exit(event):
        lang.System.exit(0)

class WelcomeFrame(swing.JFrame):
    names = ["Groucho", "Chico", "Harpo"]
    quotes = {"Groucho": "Say the secret word",
            "Chico": "Viaduct?", "Harpo": "HONK!"}

    def __init__(self, title="Welcome to Jython", size=(200, 200)):
        "@sig public WelcomeFrame(String title, java.awt.Dimension size)"
        self.title = title
        self.windowClosing = exit
        self.contentPane.layout = awt.FlowLayout()
        self.field = swing.JTextField(preferredSize=(200,20))
        self.contentPane.add(self.field)
        buttons = [self.createButton(each) for each in self.names]
        for eachButton in buttons:
            self.contentPane.add(eachButton)
        self.pack()
```

Example 13-3. Changes to WelcomeFrame.py (continued)

```
    def buttonPressed(self, event):
        self.field.text = self.quotes[event.source.text]

    def createButton(self, name):
        "@sig public javax.swing.JButton createButton(String name)"
        return swing.JButton(name, preferredSize=(100,20),
                actionPerformed=self.buttonPressed)

    def addQuote(self, marxBrother, quote):
        "@sig public void addQuote(String marxBrother, String quote)"
        self.quotes[marxBrother] = quote

if __name__ == '__main__':
    WelcomeFrame().show()
```

There are changes of note in Example 13-3 as compared to the original listing in Example 13-1. The _init_, createButton, and addQuote methods now have a docstring, which begins with @sig and then contains a Java method signature. This is a special directive to *jythonc* to create a method in the proxy (outer) Java class so that it is visible to other Java code. The outer class method copies the signature and forwards a call to the inner class method that is created as part of the normal compilation process. Following is the outer class method for createButton:

```
public javax.swing.JButton createButton(java.lang.String name) {
    PyObject inst = Py.jgetattr(this, "createButton");
    return (javax.swing.JButton)Py.tojava(inst._jcall(new Object[] {name}),
            javax.swing.JButton);
}
```

This outer class method manages the transition between Java data and Jython data. The first line of the method returns the Jython callable object corresponding to the createButton method. The second line actually calls that method with the name argument, and coerces the return value back to a javax.swing.JButton.

There are a couple of things to notice about the @sig directives. As you can see from the createButton Java method, references to Java classes in the directive must be fully qualified. The reference must be javax.swing. JButton, not merely JButton or swing.JButton, even though the latter would be valid inside the Jython program. You need to be careful when specifying the classes because *jythonc* does no type checking to ensure that the classes specified in your @sig directive are actually valid to pass to or return from the given method. Occasionally, such a problem will be detected by the Java compilation step within *jythonc*. More frequently, the problem won't manifest itself until you try to compile or run the Java class that is using the Jython class.

Those methods in the Jython class that override parent class methods automatically get versions placed in the outer class with the same signature as the parent—the @sig directive is unnecessary. These versions simply implement the vanilla proxy behavior. However, if specified, the @sig directive can add new non-overriding, Java-visible signatures calling the appropriate Jython method. If the Java method has multiple signatures, the Jython method must be able to deal with all the signatures that are called.

The @sig directive also applies to constructors, as you can see from the addition of the directive to the __init__ method in Example 13-3. In this case, the signature needs to apply to the constructor method of the Java class to be created (rather than to a public __init__ method). In Example 13-3, because the arguments have defaults, *jythonc* actually creates two versions of the constructor from this @sig directive. One constructor is created that takes a *title* and a *size* argument, and one is created that takes only a *size* argument.

The @sig directive behaves slightly differently if the Python method has arguments with a default value. Versions of the method are created in the proxy both with and without the optional arguments. If there is more than one optional argument, a version is created for each legal set of arguments. The following method signature:

```
def meth(a, b=0):
    "@sig public void meth(int a,int b)"
```

will extend the proxy with both a meth(int a) and a meth(int a,int b) signature.

You may have also noticed that we changed the __init__ method in Example 13-3 by removing the call to the parent JFrame class constructor. We made this change to work around a limitation of *jythonc*. When an external Java class calls the constructor of a *jythonc*-created proxy class, and the Jython class calls its parent class constructor, a runtime error is raised because the proxy has already been created on the Java side.

If no @sig directive is defined, constructors work like overridden superclass methods. A constructor is created for each parent class constructor. These constructors call the superclass version of the code with the received parameters and then pass those to the __init__ Jython method. With a @sig directive, constructors with the specified signatures are created that try to call the zero-argument constructor of the parent class and then call __init__ with the received arguments.

There are other limitations on *jythonc*-constructed Java code. You cannot create a Java static method from Jython—top-level function definitions in the module cannot be called directly from Java. If you attempt to @sig a top level method, the directive will be ignored. Attributes defined in the Jython class are also inaccessible directly from Java. In Example 13-3, you cannot access the attribute self.field directly from other Java code—you first need to create an explicit access method and give it an @sig directive.

After making all these changes to WindowFrame, the FrameUser class from Example 13-2 compiles and runs, producing the display in Figure 13-1.

Figure 13-1. Welcome screen from FrameUser

Finally, you can make your Jython code a little easier to locate from other Java code by using the *jythonc* command-line option—package *package*. This option places all the newly created Java classes in the given package and sub-packages respecting the Python package's structure. When the *.class* or *.jar* files are created, package rules will be obeyed and directories will be created as needed to place the package at the correct spot in the filesystem.

A Simple Applet

To use a Java applet, you need to compile it using *jythonc* due to the class loader and sandbox issues mentioned at the beginning of this chapter. Using *jythonc* for applets is straightforward. Here is the Java code for a very simple applet:

```
from java.applet import Applet

class Hello(Applet):
    def paint(self, g):
        g.drawString("Hello from Jython Essentials!")
```

And here is a minimal HTML page that includes it:

```
<html>
<body>
<center>
<applet code="Hello" archive="hello.jar"
    width = 500
    height = 100>
</applet>
</center>
</body>
</html>
```

These are the *jythonc* invocations necessary for producing a self-contained *hello.jar* for the applet, both for Windows and Unix.

```
$# Unix
$setenv CLASSPATH /pub/java/JDK/1.1/lib/classes.zip:/home/pedroni/jython21/
jython.jar
$/pub/java/JDK/1.1/bin/java org.python.util.jython ~/jython21/Tools/jythonc/
jythonc.py --jar hello.jar --core Hello.py

>rem Windows
>set classpath=\jdk11\lib\classes.zip;\jython21\jython.jar
>\usr\jdk11\bin\java org.python.util.jython \jython21\Tools\jythonc\jythonc.
py --jar hello.jar --core Hello.py
```

Notice that we use `--core` to include Jython runtime with the *.jar*. The extended classpath and directory information occur because we normally assume that Jython is installed with a Java 2 environment. But for an applet to work within a browser without the Java plug-in, *jythonc* needs to be invoked in a Java 1.1 environment. The example shows how to call *jythonc* under Java 1.1 exploiting the preexisting Jython installation. Alternately, of course, the HTML could search for the Java 2 plug-in. The class org.python. util.jython is the main class for the interpreter inside *jython.jar*.

Installing Jython

Before you can run Jython, you need to download it and install it. Jython information is available on the Web at: *http://www.jython.org*. The home page contains the most up-to-date information about versions. The specific download page is *http://www.jython.org/download.html*. Typically, the latest stable version and the latest development version are both available. As of this writing, the latest version is Jython 2.1, and development versions for Jython 2.2. Jython version numbering is intended to correspond to the CPython version whose features are being matched. The Jython version typically comes out three to six months after the CPython version.

To run Jython, you also need a Java Virtual Machine (JVM)—preferably JDK 1.2 or higher. However, not all JVMs will work for Jython. If the JVM is not 100% compatible, it's likely that Jython will flush the problems out. On most platforms, the recommended JVM is the JDK/JSK from Sun, Version 1.3 or higher, available at *http://java.sun.com/j2se/1.3/*. Version 1.4, in beta as of this writing, speeds up class reflection in such a way as to promise a significant performance enhancement for Jython. The Linux Blackdown JVM and IBM's JVM have also both been tested. More complete information on platform and JVM options is available at *http://www.jython.org/platform.html*.

Jython is distributed as a self-extracting Java *.class* file. Once you download it, you need to run the file through your Java runtime. The exact command depends on which JVM you are using, but it will likely be something like the following:

```
java jython-20
jre jython-20
```

You should not include the *.class* extension on the Jython filename. You may also need to set your classpath to include the current directory when you call the Java runtime. In order to help the installer to select the right

Java runtime it may be necessary to invoke the Java runtime by specifying its full path. Depending on your platform and JVM version, the full command might look something like the following:

```
env CLASSPATH=.; /usr/local/java/bin/java jython-20
\jdk\bin\java -cp . jython-20
java -classpath . jython-20
```

The Jython installer pops up a GUI, prompts for a destination directory, and drops all its files into that directory. The top level of the directory includes a *README* file and the files needed to invoke Jython, including the Jython runtime *jython.jar*, and the shell scripts for launching Jython and the *jythonc* tool are created by the installer. Lower-level directories of interest include:

Com
> Contains the *zxJDBC*'s Java source code

Demo
> Contains simple applet, Swing, and Java integration examples

Doc
> Contains Jython documentation

Lib
> Contains the Jython standard libraries

org
> Top level for Jython's Java source code

Tools
> Contains code for the Jython compilation tool, *jythonc*

The installer will ask you to choose whether you want to also install Jython's Java source code, the various demos, and all the standard library modules. The only reason not to install the full library would be if you plan to use modules from a parallel CPython installation on the same machine.

You can also use the installer without a GUI in batch mode:

```
java jython-20 -o install-dir [demo] [lib] [source]
```

You can specify the installation and the optional components you want.

There are two mailing lists for Jython. The *jython-user* list is for programmers who are using Jython and is a good place to ask Jython usage questions. The *jython-dev* list is for programmers actually maintaining and developing Jython itself and for focused discussions about its future evolution. You can subscribe to them by following the link "Mailing Lists" at *http://www.jython.org*. Archives at this location go back to October 2000, which is when Jython moved to SourceForge.

If you have questions about the Python language, its official site is at *http://www.python.org*. Even if you don't plan on using CPython, it's nice to have a CPython distribution around when programming in Jython because it will frequently have newer or more library modules, many of which will work as is in Jython. General questions about Python can also go to the USENET newsgroup *comp.lang.python*, which is also mirrored to an email mailing list.

Jython Options and Registry

This appendix covers the options you can use when invoking *jython* or *jythonc* from the command line. In addition, it covers the Jython registry, which is where Jython looks for system-specific values such as the path for Python modules.

Jython Options

The actual *jython* file on your system is a very short batch or shell script. All it does is start your Java Virtual Machine (JVM), set the Java python.home property, and call the main( ) function of the org.python.util.jython main interpreter class.

The basic structure of a call to *jython* is zero or more flags, followed by an optional source argument. If there is a source argument, any number of optional program arguments can follow it. Any program arguments are passed to the source in the sys.argv array (as is typical among command-line arguments, the first element in the array sys.argv[0] is the path of the source itself).

```
jython [options] [source] [args]
```

The command-line options are as follows:

-D*prop*=*value*
> Sets a Jython property value *prop* to *value*. Overrides any registry value for that property.

-i
> Runs the source script, then invokes the interpreter to allow inspection of the state after the script runs.

-E *codec*
> Sets *codec* for reading characters from the console.

-S

By default, Jython imports a module named *site.py* on startup if it exists. Using this flag suppresses that default.

--help

Prints a help message and exits.

--version

Prints a version message and exits.

The source options are as follows. If no source is specified, Jython brings up the interactive prompt.

filename

Runs Jython on the file specified.

-

Reads the program from the standard in stream. Useful on Unix systems to allow other programs to pipe their output directly into Jython.

-c *command*

Invokes the Jython interpreter on the string passed in as the *command*. No other option can appear after this flag.

-jar *jarfile*

Runs Jython on the specified *.jar* file. Jython looks for a file in the *.jar* named *__run__.py* to start the execution.

Jython Compiler Options

The *jythonc* compilation tool is a Jython shell script that calls a script in the */Tools/jythonc* directory of your Jython installation. A call to *jythonc* consists of zero or more option flags followed by zero or more module names. When called, *jythonc* generates Java source code, which is then compiled to Java *.class* files and optionally archived in a *.jar* file.

Each Jython option can be invoked using a single dash short form or a double dash long form. (The long form can also be invoked with a single dash, but that usage is deprecated and may be deleted from a future version.) The option flags are presented as --*longForm* (-*shortForm*). Note that several of the options include files in an eventual *.jar* archive, and therefore make sense only if you are creating an archive.

--addpackages *packages* (-A *packages*)

A comma-delimited list of external packages whose classes should be included in the created *.jar* file if one of the classes being compiled depends on them. By default, includes org.python.modules and org. apache.oro.text.regex.

--all (-a)
>   Includes all the Jython core classes in the eventual *.jar*. Automatically implies the --deep option.

--bean *jarfile* (-b *jarfile*)
>   Compiles the listed module or modules into a *.jar* file named *jarfile*, and includes a bean manifest to allow the file to be used as a pre-packaged JavaBean component.

--compiler *path* (-C *path*)
>   Specifies the use of a compiler other than the default Java compiler on your path. The *path* should be whatever you would enter to invoke the compiler from the command line, including directory information if needed. If the path is NONE, compilation stops after the generation of Java source files.

--compileropts *options* (-J *options*)
>   Specifies options to be passed directly to the Java compiler used, including debug or deprecation options.

--core (-c)
>   Includes the core Jython classes (the *org.python.core* package) in the *.jar*. Needed for applets to run in browsers that do not support multiple archive files. Automatically implies the --deep option.

--deep (-d)
>   Compiles all Python dependencies of the listed modules (everything that is imported by the modules).

--falsenames *nameList* (-f *nameList*)
>   The *nameList* is a comma-delimited list of names that should always be evaluated false. This can be used as a mini C preprocessor to denote, for example, code that should be compiled only for the debug version of a program.

--help (-h)
>   Prints the standard help message describing the options and exits.

--jar *jarfile* (-j *jarfile*)
>   Packages all the compiled modules into the named *.jar* file. Automatically implies --deep.

--package *packageName* (-p *packageName*)
>   When creating the Java source code, place it inside the named package (start each file with a package *packageName.pyPackage* statement).

--skip *modules* (-s *modules*)
>   A comma-separated list of modules that should not be compiled.

--workdir *directory* (-w *directory*)
>   Specifies the directory where the temporary Java source files should be placed. The default is ./jpywork.

The list of modules that comes after the options is a space-delimited list of module names. The names can be valid modules on the Python path, in which case they should appear exactly as they would in an import statement. The names can also be paths to *.py* files, in which case they should be relative or absolute paths to the actual file.

The Jython Registry

Because Jython is based on Java, it does not have a cross-platform method of accessing system variables similar to the Windows registry or Unix environment variables. Jython maintains its own registry of useful system values. The values in the registry can be specified in a few different places. The registry includes Java system values, although they can be overridden by registry values from a Jython source.

The primary Jython source for registry values is the Jython *registry* file, which is in the Jython root directory. The Jython root directory is specified by a Java property called python.home if it exists (the jython batch script will usually set this property when run). If it does not exist, Jython looks for a property called install.root. If neither of these is found, Jython searches the Java classpath for the *jython.jar* file, and the directory containing it is assumed to be the Jython root directory. The registry file is assumed to be *jythonRoot/registry*.

A registry file in the user's directory *userHome/.jython* will override corresponding values to the Jython root registry if it exists. Finally, options passed to Jython at the command line using the -D option will override any other source.

The registry file is a standard Java properties file that contains the following values. The registry file itself contains a description of many of these values and a few others.

python.cachedir
>   Specifies the directory used internally by Jython for cached information about Java packages in *.jar* files. The user must have write permission on the directory. If the directory is relative, it is interpreted relative to the Jython root.

`python.console`

Allows you to specify an alternative Java class to run the interpreter console. The class must be a subclass of `org.python.util`. `InteractiveConsole`. For example, `org.python.util.ReadlineConsole` can enable GNU `readline` support, if the necessary Java libraries are available.

`python.console.poll`

Setting this to true causes the console to poll the system standard input stream. This might improve performance on an operating system without system threads.

`python.console.encoding`

Specifies the encoding used for reading commands from the console. Does not affect the encoding used to import modules from the filesystem.

`python.jythonc.classpath`

Extensions to the classpath that are specifically used when running *jythonc*.

`python.jythonc.compiler`

Specifies a default Java compiler for *jythonc*, similar to the `--compiler` option for that tool.

`python.jythonc.compileropts`

Specifies options to be sent to the compiler from *jythonc*, similar to that tool's `--compileropts` option.

`python.modules.builtin`

Allows you to override, add, or remove built-in modules if, for example, you had an alternate version with more functionality. The list is comma delimited, and entries have the form *pythonName:javaName*, where *pythonName* is the name by which the module is referred to when imported by Jython modules, and *javaName* is the class name of the actual code. If *javaName* is not specified, the class name is assumed to be `org.python.modules.`*pythonName*. If *javaName* is `null`, *pythonName* is removed from the list of modules.

`python.options.caseok`

On Windows systems, setting this to true will make Jython's search for module files case insensitive. Setting this option to true will also optimize imports on Unix platforms by skipping the test for filename case.

`python.packages.paths`, `python.packages.directories`

Properties used when Jython scans and maintains its package cache. You will probably not need to touch these.

`python.path`

Equivalent to CPython's `PYTHONPATH` environment variable. Specifies additional directories beyond the Jython library to look for Jython modules.

python.prepath

Prepended to sys.path before the default *jythonRoot*/Lib entry. Defaults to . .

python.security.respectJavaAccessibility

If this is false and you are running against a JDK of 1.2 or higher, you will be able to access protected and private members of a Java class.

python.verbose

Sets the level of internal report messages that Jython will return to you. Valid levels, from quietest to loudest, are error, warning, message, comment, and debug.

APPENDIX C

Jython Exceptions

The following is a list of Python language exceptions raised by Jython, along with a discussion of their potential Java equivalents. Deprecated exceptions are not included.

ArithmeticError
> Abstract base class of all the mathematical exceptions (such as ZeroDivisionError).

AssertionError
> Raised by Python's assert statement, which has the form assert *expression, message*. If the expression evaluates to false, the exception is raised, with the optional message as additional data. In Java 1.4, an assert statement and an AssertionError have been added to the language.

AttributeError
> Raised when an attempt to reference or call an object attribute fails because the object does not have the attribute. The attribute name is the value of the exception. Java generally catches these in compilation, but if you are using reflection, it can either be a NoSuchFieldException or a NoSuchMethodException. If you try to call an attribute of a None value, you'll get this exception as well, so NullPointerException is also related.

EnvironmentError
> Abstract base class for exceptions raised outside Jython (such as OSError and IOError). Usually created with two arguments. The first is placed in an attribute called errno, and the second is in the attribute strerror and is usually the external error message. There is an optional third attribute, filename.

EOFError
> Raised when a built-in read function hits the end of a file and hasn't read any data. Similar to java.io.EOFException.

Exception

Abstract root class of the exception hierarchy; never raised directly. User-defined exceptions should be derived from this class (or one of its children). Unless redefined by the derived class, converting the exception to a string returns the value of all arguments passed to the exception constructor. The arguments are stored in the args attribute.

FloatingPointError

Raised when a floating-point operation fails.

IOError

Raised when an I/O operation goes wrong, similar to Java's IOException. In Jython, IOError instances generated by the system have filename, errno, and strerror set to None.

ImportError

Raised when an import or from statement cannot find the expected module or Java class. Also fails if the from statement cannot find the specific name it is looking for. The Java equivalent is java.lang. ClassNotFoundException.

IndexError

Raised when a list index is out of bounds; analogous to Java's ArrayIndexOutOfBoundsException.

KeyError

Raised when a dictionary reference is made to a key that is not in the dictionary. Java does not have a similar exception. Java map instances return null in this case.

KeyboardInterrupt

Raised if the user hits the interrupt key (usually Ctrl-C) under CPython. Jython defines it for compatibility with CPython but is unable to detect the interrupt key because of Java limitations.

LookupError

Abstract base class of all errors caused by a faulty lookup (IndexError and KeyError).

MemoryError

Raised in the event that the system does not have memory to allocate an object, but hasn't yet crashed. Jython throws it when it manages to catch a Java OutOfMemoryError.

NameError

Raised if a local or global name is not found. Java usually would catch these errors in compilation. If the name is part of an object reference, AttributeError is raised instead.

NotImplementedError

A method should raise this error if its implementation is left to a subclass, the equivalent of the Java keyword abstract when applied to methods.

OSError

Raised primarily by the os module to indicate an error in an operating system call. Under the os, generated OSError instances have meaningful filename and strerror attributes but errno is set to 0.

OverflowError

Raised when an arithmetic result is outside the range of acceptable values for its data type. In Jython, that usually means int values.

RuntimeError

Rarely used exception for an error that doesn't fit in any of the other categories. In Jython, mostly used for unexpected internal conditions.

StandardError

Abstract child of Exception; base class of all exceptions other than SystemExit.

SyntaxError

Generally raised when modules are interpreted; indicates a syntax error in the Python code. A SyntaxError instance exposes filename, lineno, and offset (column), text, and msg of the error as attributes. Most of these items are caught at compile time in Java.

SystemError

Raised to indicate some kind of non-panic internal error condition.

SystemExit

Raised by the function sys.exit( ). If it is not handled, causes Jython to exit.

TypeError

Raised when attempting to call a function on an invalid type—for example, trying to add a string to an integer. Some of these kinds of errors are caught at compile time in Java; others would indicate a ClassCastException.

UnboundLocalError

Subclass of NameError; specifically raised if a local name is used before it is created.

UnicodeError

Indicates that an exceptional condition has occurred during encoding or decoding Unicode characters.

ValueError

Generic error for other problems with arguments to functions not already covered by TypeError or AttributeError. In practice, the distinctions between those three errors are not always clear-cut. The closest Java relation is IllegalArgumentException.

ZeroDivisionError

Raised when the program attempts to divide by zero. Java would throw java.lang.ArithmeticException.

APPENDIX D
Jython and CPython Differences

Jython is an alternative implementation of the Python language. Although in most cases Jython behavior is identical to CPython, there are still cases where the two implementations differ. If you are already a CPython programmer, or are hoping to use CPython code under Jython, you need to be aware of these differences. This Appendix attempts to categorize known differences between CPython and Jython.

There are several reasons why Jython and CPython differ. Some of the design decisions made to take advantage of Java functionality have led Jython farther away from CPython. And the limitations of the Java platform lead to other differences. Some of these differences will be resolved in the near future, as development continues on both tracks—CPython 2.2 is already scheduled to start to resolve some of the differences about classes and types. Recent design discussions on new CPython features suggest that the Python language is unlikely to make future changes that would be incompatible with Jython. However, there is still a time lag between a new CPython release and the corresponding Jython one. The following list is based on Jython 2.1a3 and CPython 2.1.1.

Jython Extensions

Exceptions
> Subclasses of java.lang.Exception can be raised from Jython code using the same syntax and semantics as Jython exceptions. Java exceptions raised from Java code called by Jython can be caught and handled just like Jython exceptions.

False values

> In Jython, the following values of Java objects evaluate to Python Boolean false: java.lang.Boolean.FALSE and boolean false, empty instances of the classes Vector, Hashtable, and HashMap, or any empty instance of any class implementing the Dictionary, List, Map, or Collection interfaces.

Import of Java classes

> Java classes on either the Java classpath or in sys.path can be imported into Jython using the import or from statements. Only the top-level package need be specified—for example, import java allows access to the entire standard Java library. Normal Python naming rules for modules apply—after the import statement, classes must be referred to using fully qualified names—for example, java.util.HashMap. Once imported, instances of these classes can be created using normal Python syntax—for example, x = java.lang.String( ).

Java arrays

> The jarray module can be used to create Java arrays from within Jython.

Sequences

> Any Java object of type Vector, Enumeration, Iterator, or List can be used as the sequence argument of a Jython for statement.

Subclassing Java classes

> A Jython object can inherit from, at most, one Java class and a set of Java interfaces, in addition to an arbitrary number of Python classes.

Major Design Differences

Debug and optimization

> Jython does not currently recognize the CPython command-line switch -0, which removes assert statements and other debug information. In Jython, the __debug__ global value, which controls this behavior, is always set to 1 and is not writable.

Garbage collection

> CPython uses a reference-counting–based scheme for garbage collection, while Jython uses the Java garbage collection algorithm. The main implication is that in Jython you cannot predict when an object will actually be deleted. Also, circular object references are collected normally in Jython, which was not the case for CPython versions before 2.0.

Import of nested packages

> In Jython, importing a package allows access to subpackages without explicitly importing them. CPython does not support this feature.

Integer arguments

In CPython, built-in functions that are intended to take integer arguments, such as range, will also accept floating-point numbers and convert them to integers. In Jython, attempting to pass a floating-point number to a built-in function expecting an integer will raise an exception.

Namespace dictionaries

In Jython, the dictionaries used by module and object namespaces are optimized for string keys, and will raise an error if a non-string object is used as a key. In CPython, although the language semantics imply that module namespaces have string keys, this is not enforced, so you can manually place a non-string object as a key.

Type/class distinction

In versions of CPython through 2.1, there is an implementation difference between built-in types and user-defined classes. Built-in types do not have __class__ attributes, and cannot be subclassed. In Jython, there is no such distinction. {}.__class__ is a valid Jython statement. Built-in types can also be subclassed, although the exact behavior is unspecified. CPython 2.2 begins a series of changes to address this issue.

Slice notation

In Jython, a slice expression can take a third element, which is the step increment between indexes. For example, [1, 2, 3, 4, 5][0:5:2] returns [1, 3, 5]. The statement would be an error in CPython.

Minor Design Differences

AttributeError versus TypeError

The distinction between an AttributeError and a TypeError is not the same between CPython and Jython. Code that raises an error in one implementation may raise the other error in the other implementation.

Continuation in try clauses

In Jython, it is legal to include a continue statement inside a try clause. If encountered, the continue causes control to go to the end of the try block. This is not legal in CPython.

Function object attributes

A couple of the attributes of function objects (notably, func_code) that are writable in CPython are not writable in Jython.

Restricted mode

Jython does not support CPython's restricted mode execution. Use of the Java security model is the recommended alternative.

Differences Due to Java Details

Binary file flag

The b file flag for Jython file objects will also control how Unicode characters are saved to the file—essentially it will suppress the high byte of the Unicode character.

Code objects

Jython represents compiled code as Java bytecodes. As a result, several of the attributes supported by CPython code objects are not needed or supported in Jython.

I/O errors

Jython arguments passed to an IOError are different from the ones used by CPython because of differences in the Java io library.

Keywords as identifiers

Because some Python keywords are commonly used as method names (such as print), Jython allows Python keywords to be used as an identifiers in cases where the meaning is not ambiguous (after a ., for example). This is a SyntaxError in CPython.

Numeric types

In Jython, the numeric types map directly to the underlying Java fixed-range numeric types. For example, Jython integer values are wrappers around Java int values and floats around double values. In CPython, the underlying range of numeric types is system-dependent.

Unicode strings

CPython has separate data types for strings and Unicode strings. Because all Java strings are Unicode, Jython does not make this distinction. In addition, all modifiers that turn Unicode behavior on or off in CPython, such as the u"" string expression syntax, have no effect in Jython. CPython uses the Unicode 3.0 standard—the standard used in Java is JVM dependent, and there may be slight differences in character properties. Similarly, the char() function can, in Jython, be used over the full Unicode range of characters 0 through 65535. Currently the \U escape always raises an error in Jython.

Differences Due to Java Limitations

File type limitations

File objects in Jython are missing some functionality with respect to their CPython counterparts. This functionality, such as the istty() method, does not exist in Java.

Keyboard interrupts

Jython cannot catch keyboard interrupts such as Ctrl-c.

Modules missing functionality

The os module in Jython is missing its process functionality as compared to its CPython counterpart. In addition, several functions are not implemented due to inability to get information from Java. See Chapter 11 for details. The socket module is missing some functionality. The sys module is missing some attributes, such as executable, which are not valid within Java. Some of the deprecated aliases in the thread module are not supported in Jython. The time module may give slightly different values for some functions.

Standard modules missing

Several standard modules that are implemented in C for CPython have not yet been ported to Jython. Some, such as the Tkinter interface toolkit, are unlikely to be ported.

Minor Issues

Floating-point number syntax

Jython allows leading zeros in a floating number, such as 0002.5. CPython does not.

Floating-point output syntax

When printing a floating-point number in exponential notation, Jython uses a capital E, while CPython uses a lowercase e. Jython also switches to exponential notation for lower numbers than CPython does. There are slight differences between the less significant digits of floating-point numbers. For example, 1.0/3 returns 0.33333333333333331 in CPython, but 0.3333333333333333 in Jython.

Introspection differences

In general, introspection on CPython and Jython objects using special methods and attributes does not always return the same result. For example, some built-in modules return different __name__ attributes in CPython and Jython. For example, sys does not have a __name__ attribute in Jython, but it is 'sys' in CPython.

Open parentheses in the interactive interpreter

In CPython, the interactive interpreter recognizes open parentheses as a valid mechanism to continue a line after a carriage return. The Jython interactive interpreter does not, and will return an error. Jython behaves correctly when running from a file script.

Java Objects Versus Python Objects

Jython allows you to use instances of Java classes in almost the same way that you can use instances of Python classes. There are a few exceptions:

Access control
> You cannot access attributes of a Java class that are protected or private unless the Jython registry attribute python.security. respectJavaAccessibility is set to true.

Adding attributes
> You cannot add attributes to a Java instance at runtime with an assignment statement. To gain this ability, you can create a Jython subclass of the Java object. You will then be able to add attributes to the instance of the subclass.

Initialization
> In a Jython subclass of a Java object, a no-argument constructor of the parent class is automatically called before the first attribute access in the __init__ method or at the end of the __init__ method if the constructor has not already been called.

Overloaded methods
> If there is an overloaded Java method with versions for both a basic type and its wrapper type, the wrapper version will be accessible only via Java reflection.

Pickling
> Java objects cannot be serialized using the pickle or cPickle modules. This is also true for Jython subclasses of Java objects.

Special attributes
> Java objects do not store attribute values in the special attribute __dict__. The __class__ and __bases__ attributes are read-only.

APPENDIX E
Java-to-Python Quick Reference

This is a quick reference guide to the syntactic differences between Java and Python. It is not intended to provide full information on semantic differences between the two languages.

Basic Data Types

Python has a more limited set of numerical types than Java, but otherwise the two languages are similar. Python does not perform automatic conversions between types, however each basic type has a built-in function of the same name that attempts to convert the argument to that type.

Java	Python	Comment
boolean		Python has no specific Boolean type. False is represented by 0, and by any empty string, sequence, or mapping.
char	string	A character is just a string of length 1.
byte, short, int	int	
long	long	A Python long has unbounded length.
float, double	float	Python floats have the same width as Java doubles.

Advanced Data Types

Python's more advanced built-in types have more functionality and flexibility built into them than their Java equivalents.

Java	Python	Comment
java.lang.String	string	
java.util.List	list	

Java	Python	Comment
java.util.HashMap	dictionary	
java.io.File	file	Python files contain much of the functionality of Java I/O streams.

Logical Operators

Python tends to use English words for its logical operators rather than symbols. Python has no equivalent to the Java operators ^ (binary XOR) and ?: (ternary conditional operator).

Java	Python	Comment
&&	and	Python operator always short circuits.
||	or	Python operator always short circuits.
!	not	
==	is	Test for identical object identity.
equals()	==	Test for same value.
obj instanceof *class*	isinstance(*obj*, *class*)	
x < y && y < z	x < y < z	In Python, chained comparisons are legal.

Arithmetic Operators

Most operators are the same between the two languages. Python has no equivalent to the ++, and -- increment and decrement operators. Python also has no equivalent to the <<< and >>> sign extension shift operators. However, Python does use the ** operator for raising a number to a power.

Python also has a string formatting operator, %, which can be used in place of string concatenation. More details can be found in "Strings" in Chapter 2.

Control Statements

In Python, blocks are delimited by indentation. A block starts when a line ends with a colon. All lines inside that block must be indented the same amount from the line that started the block. The block ends when a line starts at the same position as the line that started the block.

Java	Python	Comment
;	newline	Python statements end with a newline, unless there is an open delimiter or if the line ends with a backslash.
`for(int i; i < x; i++) {` `}`	`for i in range(x):`	Looping through numbers.

`for(Iterator it; it.hasNext();)`
`{`
`    it.next();`
`}`
	`for i in it:`	Walking through sequence.

`if (cond) {`
`} else if (cond) {`
`} else {`
`}`
	`if cond:`
	`elif cond:`
	`else:`	

`while (cond) {` `}`	`while cond:`	
`throw exception`	`raise exception`	

`try {`
`} catch (exception) {`
`} finally {`
`}`
	`try:`
	`finally:`
	
	`try:`
	`except:`
	`else:`
		Python has two distinct forms of this statement.

Python has no equivalent to the Java synchronized, switch, or do statements.

Many constructs in which a new sequence is created by applying a function to an existing sequence can be performed in Python without using a for statement by using either the built-in map and filter functions (see Chapter 2), or by using list comprehensions (see Chapter 3).

Definition Statements

The following table compares the Java and Python statements for the definition of classes, methods, instances, and packages:

Java	Python	Comment

`accessType returnType`
`methodName(args) {`
`}`
	`def methodname(args):`	Method or function definition.

`class Class extends Parent {` `}`	`class Class(Parent):`	Class definition.
`Class obj = new Class()`	`obj = Class()`	Instance creation.
`import package;`	`import package` `from package import *`	Python import statements are runtime binding statements, not compile-time declarations.

Python allows for more complex argument passing in method invocation, including keyword arguments, default arguments, and automatically exploding lists when passing.

Python allows functions and statements to be outside class definitions.

Python is dynamically typed. Method dispatch in Python is managed completely at runtime, and you do not need to cast an instance down the hierarchy just to call a specific method.

String Methods

The following are Python equivalents to the methods defined in java.lang. String. There are no direct equivalents to the methods equalsIgnoreCase, intern, regionMatches, or toCharArray. For a full listing of methods that Python strings support, see "Strings" in Chapter 2.

Java	Python	Comment
String.valueOf(*nonString*)	str(*nonString*)	
s.charAt(*integer*)	s[*integer*]	
s.compareTo(*string*)	cmp(s, *string*)	
s.concat(*string*)	s + *string*	
s.endsWith(*string*)	s[-len(*string*):] == *string*	
s.getChars(*int, int, char[], int*)	x = s[*int:int*]	Python uses an index slice.
s.indexOf( )	s.index( ) s.find( )	find returns –1 on failure, index raises an exception.
s.lastIndexOf( )	s.rindex( ) s.rfind( )	Return values as for index and find.
s.length( )	len(s)	
s.replace(*char, char*)	s.replace(*str, str, [max]*)	Python allows arguments to be of arbitrary length.
s.startsWith(*string*)	s[:len(*string*)] == *string*	
s.substring(*int, int*)	s[*int:int*]	Python uses an index slice.
s.toLowerCase( )	s.lower( )	
s.toUpperCase	s.upper( )	
s.trim( )	s.strip( )	

List Methods

The following table has the Python equivalents to the methods defined by the java.util.List interface. In Python, lists are basic types and are accessed using bracket notation the way that Java arrays are. However, their functionality is more like Java lists. Python has no direct analog of the List methods containsAll, removeAll, or retainAll, but they would not be hard to build. Python does not need the iterator( ) or listIterator( ) methods to walk through lists—for statements can do that automatically. Python also has no need for the toArray( ) function. For full details on lists and their additional functionality, see "Sequences: Lists and Tuples" in Chapter 2.

Java	Python	Comment
s.add(obj)	s.append(obj)	
s.add(obj)	s.insert(index, object)	The second version is a slice assignment.
	s[index:index] = object	
s.addAll(list)	s.extend(list)	
s.addAll(index, list)	s[index:index] = list	
s.clear( )	del s[:]	
s.contains(obj)	obj in s	
s.get(index)	s[index]	
s.indexOf(obj)	s.index(obj)	
s.isEmpty( )	len(s) > 0 or not s	
s.lastIndexOf(obj)	s.reverse( ) s.index(obj) s.reverse( )	There are, of course, other ways of doing this in Python.
s.remove(obj)	s.remove(obj)	Python version raises an error if the object isn't in the list.
s.remove(index)	del s[index]	
s.set(index, obj)	s[index] = obj	
s.size( )	len(s)	
s.subList(start, end)	s[start:end]	The Python slice has richer functionality.

Dictionary Functions

Python dictionaries are the analog of Java's java.util.Map interface implementations. The following table lists the equivalent Python code for methods of the Map interface. There is no direct equivalent of the method putAll, but one could easily be built. Additional Python methods can be found in "Mappings and Dictionaries" in Chapter 2.

Java	Python	Comment
d.clear( )	*d*.clear( )	
d.containsKey(*obj*)	*d*.has_key(*obj*) *obj* in *d*	The in version works in Python 2.2 or higher.
d.containsValue(*obj*)	*obj* in *d*.values( )	
d.entrySet( )	*d*.items( )	Python version returns a sequence of (*key*, *value*) tuples.
d.get(*key*)	*d*[*key*]	
d.isEmpty( )	len(*d*) > 0 or not *d*	
d.keySet( )	*d*.keys( )	
d.put(*key*, *value*)	*d*[*key*] = *value*	
d.remove(*key*)	del *d*[*key*]	
d.size( )	len(*d*)	
d.values( )	*d*.values( )	

Index

We'd like to hear your suggestions for improving our indexes. Send email to *index@oreilly.com*.

source files, compiling, 221
special characters
  filename pattern matching, 187
  regular expressions, 191
  strings, 33
special methods
  binary arithmetic operators, 102
  general instance, 99
  overview, 98
  sequences and mappings, 101
  typecast and radix changing
    functions, 103
  unary arithmetic operators, 102
split( ) function, 39, 186, 188
splitlines( ) function, 39
splittext( ) function, 186
SQL statements, formatting styles, 162
standalone files, 6
standalone window source code, 6
startDocument event, XML parsing, 174
startElement function, XML
    parsing, 174
startswith( ) function, 39
starttag method (HTML source browser
    source code), 157
starttag method (HTMLsource browser
    source code), 157
stat( ) function, 184
statements
  assignment, 47
    augmented, 49
    unpacking, 48
  break, 56
    for loops, 57
  class, 83
    proxy classes and, 121
  continuation in code, 46
  continue, 56
    for loops, 57
  control flow, 46
  def, 85
  del, lists and, 27
  do, 56
  else
    for loops, 57
    try blocks and, 62
    while loops, 56
  except, 62
  exec, 64
  for, compared to Java Iterators, 5
  from, 79

importing Java classes, 104
__future__, 73
future, 73
if elif else, 54
if, list comprehension, 60
import, 67, 78–80
indenting in code blocks, 53
list comprehension, 59
name-binding, 67
overview, 46
pass, code blocks, 54
placing two on a line of code, 47
raise, 63
return, functions and, 69
switch, 55
try, 61
while, 56
yield, generator functions, 69
static methods, 90
static variables, 89
stderr, sys module, 181
stdin, sys module, 181
stdout, sys module, 181
str( ) function, 35
str( ) method, 99
__str__ method, 99
strings
  array conversion, 112
  concatenation, 34
  creating, 33
  data type category, 20
  float data types, converting to, 23
  formatting, 35
    dictionaries and, 43
    Web templating tools, 168
    web templating tools, 168
  functions, 36–40
  integers
    converting from, 36
    converting to, 23
  jarray functions, as type
    parameter, 113
  membership operator (in), 35
  objects, converting, 35
  overview, 33
  parsing HTML source code, 158
  paths and, 77
  raw, 34
  relationship to lists, 35
  triple-quote, as documentation, 47
  Unicode, 34

About the Authors

Samuele Pedroni is one of the main Jython developers. He holds a CS-flavored diploma in mathematics from the ETH Zurich (Swiss Institute of Technology in Zurich). He came to Jython with an interest in improving it with respect to Java importing and reloading. He has developed several important patches related to Java integration, classloaders, and the reworking of Java/Python importing rules and design.

Noel Rappin has a Ph.D. in computer science from the Georgia Institute of Technology, where his research included methods for teaching object-oriented programming and design. He has extensive production experience in both Java and Python. Noel also contributed an introductory chapter to the book *Squeak: Open Personal Computing and Multimedia* (Prentice Hall).

Colophon

Our look is the result of reader comments, our own experimentation, and feedback from distribution channels. Distinctive covers complement our distinctive approach to technical topics, breathing personality and life into potentially dry subjects.

The animal on the cover of *Jython Essentials* is a bank vole. Voles are small rodents related to lemmings. Different species can be found all over the world, though the bank vole is specific to Europe and Asia.

Voles range in length from 3.5 to 7 inches. They have rounded bodies with gray or brown fur and beige undersides. Bank voles have blunt muzzles, small eyes and ears, and short tails. They feed on buds, leaves, fruit, and some insects. Most bank voles live in the woods, making their nests under logs, in tree roots, or underground. Other vole species burrow underground in extensive tunneling systems, rarely coming above ground.

Voles live up to 18 months, though this time is often cut short, as other animals frequently prey upon them.

Linley Dolby was the production editor and proofreader, and Audrey Doyle was the copyeditor, for *Jython Essentials*. Sarah Sherman, Darren Kelly, and Claire Cloutier provided quality control. Tom Dinse wrote the index.

Emma Colby designed the cover of this book, based on a series design by Edie Freedman. The cover image is a 19th-century engraving from the Dover Pictorial Archive. Emma Colby produced the cover layout with Quark-XPress 4.1 using Adobe's ITC Garamond font.

Melanie Wang designed the interior layout, based on a series design by David Futato. Mihaela Maier converted the files from Microsoft Word to FrameMaker 5.5.6 using tools created by Mike Sierra. The text font is Linotype Birka; the heading font is Adobe Myriad Condensed; and the code font is LucasFont's TheSans Mono Condensed. The illustrations that appear in the book were produced by Robert Romano and Jessamyn Read using Macromedia FreeHand 9 and Adobe Photoshop 6. The tip and warning icons were drawn by Christopher Bing. This colophon was written by Linley Dolby.

12407061R00172

Made in the USA
Lexington, KY
08 December 2011